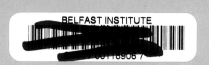

key moments in cinema

Ci

Geoffrey Macnab

hamlyn

key moments in

nema

contents

Horse in Motion
1878

*Muybridge &
Motion*

When a horse hits full stride, how many of its hooves are off the ground? That was the question gnawing away at wealthy, San Francisco-based businessman Leland Stanford. He was sure that, at certain moments, when a horse was in full flight, all four of its feet were off the ground. He was reportedly prepared to put up money (as much as $25,000) to back his opinion against that of rival millionaire, Fred McCrellish. There was a problem, though. Who could judge such a matter? The human eye was not quick enough, nor were the cameras that existed at the time.

Stanford owned trotting horses, the best in the country, and in 1870 he hired a photographer, Eadweard Muybridge, to attempt to capture one, Occident, in motion. Given the nature of the equipment available to him, this was a formidable task. Muybridge set to work at Sacramento racecourse, fashioning his own shutters from slats of wood and building a bank of cameras that would be triggered by strings and rubber bands as the horse trotted by. The underexposed images that Muybridge produced (and that later

appeared in the *San Francisco Alta*) were hardly a model of clarity. 'Little better than silhouettes', was the opinion of the sceptics, but what mattered were Occident's feet – at certain points, all four were indeed off the ground.

In 1877–1878, Muybridge again went to work on behalf of his wealthy benefactor, using 24 cameras to photograph another of Stanford's horses, Abe Edgington. His later work became ever more elaborate, and he was not restricted to horses as subjects, trotting or galloping. Inspired by French inventor Etienne-Jules Marey's experiments in analysing the successive phases of animal locomotion, he began to train his eye on dogs, deer, oxen and birds in flight. In the process, he proved that scientists and artists had been getting it wrong for years – very few paintings or drawings accurately depicted animals in motion. 'The conventional galloping horse of the painter must, we imagine, be discarded after this,' lamented one journalist after hearing Muybridge lecture in 1882.

Did Muybridge invent cinema? To put it bluntly, he did not, and to his detractors he was a charlatan who made his fortune by exploiting devices dreamed up by others. Engineer John D. Isaacs helped him set up the equipment to photograph Stanford's horses, and there had been other projectors before the 'zoopraxiscope' that Muybridge invented to accompany his lectures. Marey had a better claim to be the 'inventor of cinema' with his photographic 'gun', produced in 1882, that could take 12 pictures a second. This had a major advantage over Muybridge's banks of cameras: all Marey's pictures were taken from the same point of view, as if observed by the human eye. Despite such developments, Muybridge has caught historians' imaginations in a way that rival inventors, scientists and photographers have not. Perhaps this is as much to do with his colourful biography as with his achievements.

MUYBRIDGE'S SHADY PAST

There is a seven-year gap between Muybridge's first set of pictures of horses in 1870 and the much more sophisticated photographs he took for Leland Stanford in 1877. Why the delay? In 1874, Muybridge had shot dead a certain Harry Larkyns, a charming, old-style Western rogue who had seduced his wife. He was arrested and charged with murder. He admitted killing the man, but claimed he was mentally unstable as a result of an 1860 accident when he had been thrown from a stagecoach and had landed on his head. This was hardly a convincing defence for what was a cold-blooded, premeditated killing. Nevertheless, he was acquitted – mainly, it seemed, because the all-male jury felt that adultery was worse than murder. Keen to escape the media glare and not to antagonize Larkyns' friends and relatives further, Muybridge fled the US, heading south to Panama, where he continued to take remarkable photographs. By the time he returned north, the scandal had died down. He was able to resume his work for Stanford and, through his lecture tours, to transform himself into a full-blown international celebrity.

below Eadweard Muybridge (1830–1904). 'Athlete Running. Photographed synchronously from two points of view. Time intervals: '042 second.' The disadvantage was that his photographs of movement were not taken from the same point of view, as if really observed by the human eye.

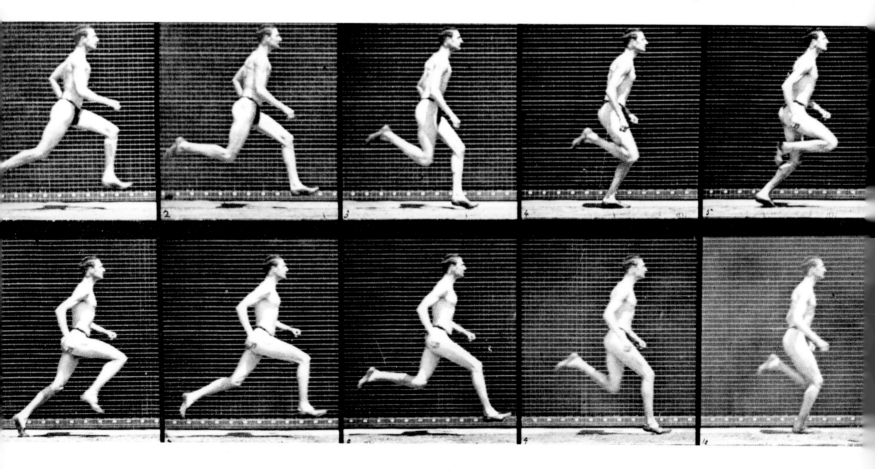

MUYBRIDGE'S LEGACY

Muybridge was born in Kingston-upon-Thames in England in 1830 and emigrated to the US 22 years later, but never became an American citizen. Christened plain Edward, his vain nature led him to change his name to the much grander-sounding Eadweard in imitation of Anglo-Saxon kings. His most famous early pictures – of Yosemite Valley and cityscapes of San Francisco – revealed the extent of his artistry; he always seemed to know where to place the camera. His output includes synchronously photographed series of images of naked women that anticipate the kind of erotic movies shown in peepshows, and vaguely sinister studies of disabled children, emaciated old women, and other assorted human grotesques. But it is for his awesomely beautiful photographs of animals that he will be remembered; the painter Francis Bacon, the sculptor Frederic Remington and the composer Philip Glass are among the artists who have been inspired by them.

Muybridge's main legacy to the filmmakers who followed him a generation later was his obsessive interest in capturing and projecting moving images. He was hardly unique in this. The history of optical toys and tricks stretches back thousands of years. Records of shadow shows can be traced to 11th-century China, and the ever-inquisitive Leonardo da Vinci experimented with trompe l'oeil effects in the mid-15th century. Less than 200 years later, in Rome in 1640, Athanasius Kircher patented a form of magic lantern. The science is not especially baffling: light passes through a transparent image and projects that image, in an enlarged form, onto a screen. Kircher's aim was to demystify a process that had previously been associated with sorcery.

In the 19th century, scientists, artists, manufacturers and fairground hustlers all had a vested interest in developing the new photographic technology, and provided the key staging points in the journey towards cinema. In the 1830s, French painter and inventor Daguerre patented a photographic process whereby images could be caught on a silvered copper plate. In the early 1880s, Joseph Plateau, a Belgian anatomy professor, came up with a device called a Fanatoscope which made images appear to move. In 1885, George Eastman developed a new kind of paper roll film, and four years later, he started selling celluloid roll film. Marey experimented with using these film strips to record series of photographs. At around the same time, Thomas Edison patented the Kinetoscope, a machine through which one person at a time could peer at moving images. The first Kinetoscope parlor was opened in the US in 1894.

THE LUMIERES UNVEIL THE CINEMATOGRAPHE

Auguste and Louis Lumière are regarded as the 'founding fathers' of cinema. Inventors in Germany (Max Skladanowsky), the US (Edison and Major Woodville 'Loop' Latham) and Britain (R.W. Paul and William Friese-Greene) all came up with their own projecting machines or film cameras, but the Lumières were first. Their Cinématographe, a device that combined camera, projector and printer, was patented in February 1895, tested privately in the spring, and demonstrated in public six months later at the Grand Café on the boulevard des Capucines in Paris. The brothers used the Cinématographe to record everyday life. Their films might show a train roaring into a station – an

above Louis and August Lumière. The Lumière brothers were as much businessmen as artists. Despite the worldwide success of the Cinematographe, they gradually withdrew from filmmaking to concentrate on exploiting their inventions commercially.

image that caused spectators to cower in terror – or workers leaving the Lumière factory, where they manufactured photographic supplies. The camera they used was much less bulky than Edison's, and whereas Edison's movies had to be shot in a claustrophobic studio called the 'Black Maria', the Lumières were able to go out into the streets and to demonstrate, as one critic put it, 'the beauty of movement in the mundane'.

THE GREAT TRAIN ROBBERY

Edwin S. Porter (1869–1941) is credited as both 'father of the story film' and 'the inventor of editing'. He worked in different genres, making comedies as well as dramas. The two most exhaustively analysed of the many films he made were *The Life of an American Fireman* (1902) and *The Great Train Robbery* (1903). The former used editing to stoke up tension, and the latter was one of the first Westerns and also one of the earliest scripted films.

Scripts did not appeal to Porter's boss, Edison, who believed that film was best suited for recording live events and that its primary purpose was to inform as much as to entertain. He was discomfited by Porter's editing of *American Fireman* and accused him of 'cutting people in half' by showing them in close-up. He believed that the camera ought always 'to show the entire body, including the feet'. *The Great Train Robbery*, a 12-minute epic which features a heist, gunfights, chases on horseback, and even a future star,

Gilbert M. Anderson (who later became known as Broncho Billy), had enormous influence. 'In time,' observed scriptwriter Budd Schulberg (whose father worked with Porter), 'that amazing little film inspired every one of the original handful of pioneers from Griffith to Lasky and Goldwyn.' Despite this, Porter was eventually left behind. For all his experiments in storytelling, he never quite shook off the documentary influence. Most of his films were on well-known subjects and were 'dependent', in Charles Musser's words, 'on an audience's prior knowledge of the plot'. After leaving Edison in 1909, he set up his own production companies, but lost much of his fortune in the 1929 Wall Street Crash.

D.W. GRIFFITH

Even if he had not made *The Great Train Robbery*, Porter would have been assured of at least a footnote in film history simply because he gave D.W. Griffith, then a struggling young actor, a part in one of his films, *The Eagle's Nest*. David Wark Griffith, Kentucky-born, had the airs and graces of a Southern gentleman. He was brought up in genteel poverty in Louisville; his father, who trained as a doctor, had fought for the Confederates in the Civil War, and had been impoverished in its aftermath. At first it seemed unlikely that his son would revive the family fortune. After a stint as a reporter on a local paper in Kentucky, he spent several years eking out a precarious living on stage, playing supporting roles, travelling round the country with various repertory companies. By the time he arrived in New York in 1907, he had decided to try to break into the film industry – not as an actor but as a writer.

Although Porter turned down his first story idea, and gave him an acting job instead, the following year, 1908, Griffith began writing and directing films for Biograph. Working at a ferocious rate, shooting several movies a week, (he made over 400 in six years), he experimented with editing, close-ups, fade-outs and every other device he could think of to tell stories in images. Like Porter before him, he confounded his bosses and cinema-goers alike with some of his new-fangled techniques. Even his cameraman was sceptical. 'He claimed that you couldn't take pictures of people's faces and leave their bodies out,' Griffith later told a reporter. 'My answer was a trip to the art gallery. I saw plenty of paintings without bodies attached, and I won the argument.'

Griffith brought together a group of young actors for his films, and although Biograph steadfastly refused to allow their names to be credited, such talents as Blanche Sweet, Mae Marsh, Mary Pickford and the Gish sisters went on to become huge stars. He was, as Martin Scorsese has put it, 'the first master storyteller of the American screen'. Generally his inspirations were 19th-century novelists and poets – Dickens, Tolstoy and Whitman – but he was versatile. Along with the melodramas for which he is best known, he made gangster movies (*The Musketeers of Pig Alley*), comedies, Westerns and historical epics. He even made a film based on Darwin's theory of evolution (*A Man's Genesis*).

GRIFFITH: THE FATHER OF AUDIENCE RESEARCH

In his book, *Adventures with D.W. Griffith*, Karl Brown, who worked with Griffith for many years, observes that he benefited from having been such 'an exceedingly bad actor'. In his time on the road, he had performed in

above The Kentucky-born D.W. Griffith liked to cultivate an image as an archetypal Southern gentleman. Shown here on set, wielding an enormous megaphone, he strikes a typically dapper pose.

opposite Edwin S. Porter's *The Great Train Robbery* (1903) was not only groundbreaking in its dramatic use of editing, but was one of the first westerns – even if it was shot on the East Coast.

THE BIRTH OF A NATION

Griffith left Biograph in 1913, supposedly because the company would not allow him to make longer, feature-length movies. In 1915, he directed his notorious Civil War epic, *The Birth of a Nation* and it made a fortune at the box-office. But the following year, the even more ambitious *Intolerance* flopped and he was saddled with debts – he had invested much of his own money making the film – that he spent the rest of his career trying to pay off. 'When I work for someone else,' he once reflected, 'I always make money for them. When I back my own ideas, I am bound to lose.'

Griffith was a paradox. In profiles, journalists portray him as 'the Poet-Philosopher of the Photoplay', a dreamy, self-effacing man. 'He creates artistic poems in celluloid far above the prose pictures of other producers, because, adding to his innate ability, he produces not for money, nor for fame... but for the love of the doing,' enthused one hack. Griffith's movies never shied away from sentimentality. *Broken Blossoms* (1919), the story of a friendship between beautiful young waif Lillian Gish and gentle, sad-eyed Chinese man Richard Barthelmess, features some scenes so mawkish that they make the description of Little Nell's death in Dickens' *The Old Curiosity Shop* seem cold-hearted. In *Intolerance*, he railed against prejudice wherever it was found – whether in ancient Babylon or revolutionary France. Yet this same director made the overtly racist *The Birth of a Nation*, in which the Ku Klux Klan are treated as heroes. One of Griffith's assistants, Karl Brown, described the book on which it was based (*The Klansman* by the Reverend Thomas Dixon Jr) as 'a hymn of hate'. Griffith was from the South, and probably attracted to such source material because it reflected the faded Dixieland world of gallant gentlemen and Scarlett O'Hara-like belles to which his father had belonged, and which the Civil War had helped to destroy. He somehow seemed oblivious to the spite and self-pity in the novel.

above D.W. Griffith's *The Birth of a Nation* (1915) remains one of the most contentious movies ever made. Its epic sweep and evocative reconstruction of the American Civil War still impress, but contemporary audiences find its racism (and, in particular, its championing of the Ku Klux Klan) hard to stomach.

every two-bit theatre in America, appearing in 'turkeys of the rankest raw melodrama' in front of 'the cheapest of audiences'. He knew exactly what those audiences craved; he understood their psychology. They wanted broad-hued melodramas in which villains were villains, and the heroines (often played by the Gish sisters) were purity and innocence incarnate. Although Griffith is frequently labelled as arrogant and self-obsessed, few other directors made so much effort to please their audiences. Brown reveals that Griffith would hold preview after preview and that he would delete any scene that his audience did not like. 'He depended absolutely, even slavishly, upon audience reactions. Whatever audiences responded to was right, no matter how wrong it might seem from other considerations, and anything audiences did not respond to was wrong, regardless of how finely enacted or how beautifully photographed,' Brown wrote.

EDISON AND THE TRUST

It is impossible to chronicle the key moments in early cinema without focusing on individuals. The major technical innovations and the most important refinements to storytelling technique would not have happened without the efforts of the determined, often eccentric visionaries whose achievements are sketched above. Nevertheless, film was an industry. Griffith might have remained an out-of-work actor without the backing of the Biograph Company. The real puppetmasters were not Porter or Griffith, but the owners of the studios, laboratories and cinemas without which the business would never have flourished. In the US, most early films were made by three rival concerns: Biograph, Vitagraph and Edison. In France, the dominant company, with outlets all over the world, was Pathé. Films were often shown in makeshift cinemas, usually converted theatres. In the US, these were called nickelodeons, and it is estimated that there were more than 10,000 in existence by 1910. They charged five cents for admission, stayed open from early morning till midnight, and combined songs, magic lantern slides, illustrated talks and movies in a show that lasted for around an hour. Their audiences were predominantly working-class, even if their owners (craving respectability) yearned to reach more affluent, up-market cinema-goers. The nickelodeons were soon superseded as new, more lavish cinemas were built.

As the film-going habit caught on, the fight for control of the industry intensified. Each company stole from its rivals and tried to sue when it, in turn, was targeted. In 1908, Edison and various partners pooled resources to form the Motion Picture Patents Company (MPPC), or, as it was nicknamed by the independent producers whose efforts it tried to stymie, 'the Trust'. Anyone who wanted to use their equipment or hire their films had to pay the Trust for the privilege. This organization was involved at every level of the filmmaking process and issued licences to independent producers, distributors or exhibitors. It had agents and detectives to enforce its rules; anybody who broke an MPPC contract could be sued or driven out of business. In 1910, the MPPC formed The General Film Company to handle distribution of its members' films, thus strengthening further its stranglehold on the industry.

BATTLE LINES ARE DRAWN

Right from the outset, the American film industry divided into two hostile camps. On the one hand, there was the Trust. On the other, there were the 'independents', making their movies by stealth, using unlicensed equipment. Like most cartels, the Trust was inflexible, and treated film in much the same way as it might have done string. Movies were made at a standard length and sold at a standard price. Bigger cinemas paid more than smaller cinemas for the right to show films, but such matters as stars, budget and genre were not taken into consideration.

The independents were adaptable and adventurous. Entrepreneurs like William Fox (founder of the Fox Film Corporation), Carl Laemmle (later to build up Universal Studios) and Adolph Zukor (the mogul behind Paramount) realized that audiences might enjoy longer, feature-length films rather than the shorts the Trust provided, and that they might appreciate knowing the names of the actors who starred in the movies they had paid to see. After years in which the independents were taken to court again and again, Fox launched a counter-suit against the Trust, accusing it of operating in 'restraint of trade'. The case was first heard in 1913 and more than two years later a ruling was passed down that the MPPC had gone 'far beyond what was necessary to protect the use of the patents or the monopoly which went with them' (quoted in *The American Film Industry*, ed: Thomas Guback, page 127). By the end of World War I, the MPPC had collapsed. Forty years before, Muybridge's photographic experiments had provoked equally bitter disputes over who, exactly, owned and had invented what. The history of early cinema is littered with such claims and counter-claims. No steps, not even those of Muybridge's galloping horses, went uncontested.

below top Thomas Edison's famous but claustrophobic 'Black Maria' studio built in 1893 on the grounds of the Edison Laboratory in West Orange, New Jersey. The Black Maria may have been short-lived as a viable film studio, but it later turned up in the 1954 Universal comedy, *Abbott And Costello Meet The Keystone Cops*.

below bottom Thomas Alva Edison (1847–1931), the Wizard of Menlo Park. Edison was behind the invention and refinement of such artefacts as the incandescent light bulb, the mimeograph machine, the stock ticker and the kinetoscope. He was also the most powerful figure in the Motion Picture Patents Company, the cartel of movie producers formed in 1909 to prevent independent filmmakers from breaking into the industry.

2

Florence Lawrence
1886–1938

The Star System

In 1938, a bit-part actress called Florence Lawrence committed suicide by swallowing ant paste. It was a seedy and pathetic ending, but not an unusual one: many other actors in Hollywood had faded away in equally squalid circumstances. Lawrence was 52 years old, a forgotten figure struggling to make a living at MGM, and would not be remembered today at all if it were not for one thing – she was the very first film star.

The star system evolved comparatively late. Although the leading companies in the US and Europe were beginning to put lead players under contract as early as 1909, they avoided publicizing the actors' names because they were terrified (with good reason, as it turned out) that filmmaking costs would spiral: once they were known to the public, actors could demand vastly increased fees.

Around 1910, producer Carl Laemmle, a maverick entrepreneur who later built up Universal Studios, was caught in a vicious trade war with the Trust (the Motion Picture Patents Company, the Edison-led cartel that sought to control film production and distribution). It was a David and Goliath struggle. He was an independent producer pitted against a group of companies who had a virtual stranglehold on the industry. What could be more daring, he wondered, than to sign up one of the most popular actresses then working for Edison?

The actress was nicknamed 'the Biograph Girl' after the Edison-affiliated company she worked for; everybody recognized her from such films as *Richard III* and *Salome*, but few cinema-goers knew her name.

Laemmle was an old-fashioned showman with a love of double bluff. He placed a story in the newspapers stating that 'the Biograph Girl' (whose identity – Florence Lawrence – he finally revealed) had died in an accident. Once readers had had time to absorb the sad piece of news, he followed it up with a new story stating that Lawrence was not dead at all. In fact, she had recently signed up with his company IMP (Independent Motion Picture Company of America), and was to appear in the very next IMP movie. The rumours about her death, he stated with magnificent duplicity, had been put about by her jealous former employers at Biograph. Laemmle's stunt ensured that the public realized that their favourite actress was now working for him. It also ensured that, henceforth, stars would be known by name.

The Florence Lawrence story does not altogether stand up to scrutiny. There is evidence, in the form of posters and advertisements, that Edison's companies were promoting star names a year or more before Lawrence's 'accident'. Laemmle, ironically, spent much of the rest of his career grumbling that stars were the bane of the industry. In later years, he refused to pay the salaries that top-name actors felt able to demand, and boasted about being 'the first producer to buck the star system – the ruinous practice that has been responsible for high-priced but low-grade features'. He was loath to invest in expensive, first-run theatres in which to show his movies. As a result of his caution, Universal remained a B-studio with second-string actors while more ambitious rivals soared ahead.

STARS BECOME BIG BUSINESS

By the end of World War I, movies had become 'an essential part of modern living', according to a 1927 prospectus aimed at potential investors in the 'motion picture industry'. Stars were the lodestones around which this new industry was organized. In the star, 'the producer gets not only a production value in the making of his picture, but a trademark value and an insurance value, which are very real and very potent in guaranteeing the sale of this product to the cash customers at a profit', said the prospectus. As one fan magazine put it, 'they are the heroes, the heroines, the rascals or the comics of a shadow world into which millions of us are happy to escape'.

What made a star? Producers could trot out the usual blandishments – personality, acting ability, looks etc. – but nobody really knew. It quickly became apparent that cinema was not quite like any other industry. Each new product was a prototype: there was never any guarantee of box-office success. Great names from the stage were wheeled in front of the camera, but almost invariably failed to capture audiences' affections. The best that filmmakers could do was to organize their business in as efficient and systematic a way as possible. From 1910 onwards, fearsome bidding wars broke out for the

Mary Pickford

above Mary Pickford (1893–1979), or 'Little Mary' as she was nicknamed, seemed like the most demure star of all on screen, but behind the scenes had a reputation as one of the most hard-headed businesswomen in Hollywood. 'It took longer to make one of Mary's contracts than it did to make one of Mary's pictures,' Sam Goldwyn once joked of her.

left Charlie Chaplin (sitting), minus moustache and bowler-hat, puts pen to paper to confirm the creation of United Artists, the independent company set up by some of Hollywood's biggest stars in 1919.

opposite Joan Crawford and Wallace Beery, two of the stars who lit up MGM's 1932 classic, *Grand Hotel*.

services of the most popular actors. The price of making movies shot up – not because the technology was any more advanced but because star salaries were so high. As one wag noted, 'acting, historically one of the most precarious of all professions, suddenly found itself among the best paid on earth'.

THE LUNATICS TAKE OVER THE ASYLUM

Mary Pickford, arguably the biggest star of the era, the 'girl with the long curls' who had some indefinable quality that entranced cinema-goers, began her screen career in 1909, earning a pittance with D.W. Griffith at Biograph. Over the next decade, she switched employers more regularly than the most sought-after sports stars. First, in 1910, she followed Florence Lawrence to IMP, Carl Laemmle's company. Then, in 1912, she returned to Biograph, but the money was not up to scratch. Pickford may have seemed all demure innocence in front of camera, but she was always a ferocious businesswoman. After a stint on stage with theatre impresario David Belasco (who had helped discover her in the first place), Pickford made the move to Adolph Zukor's Famous Players, where she was paid $1,000 a week. In 1916, she became an independent producer herself, giving her more control over her own projects, but she was still not satisfied. In 1918, First National offered her a deal worth millions to sign with them. Charlie Chaplin, who had been making films for Mutual, also signed for First National in 1918. His contract, worth more than a million dollars, required him to make eight two-reel films. It also, he believed, guaranteed him more independence.

First National was not as hospitable to Chaplin and Pickford as they had anticipated. Not long after they signed, the company began merger negotiations with fellow giant, Paramount. Rather than run the risk of having their careers controlled by a huge new organization, the stars decided to strike out on their own. Together with Douglas Fairbanks and D.W. Griffith, they set up the United Artists Corporation. 'The lunatics have taken over the asylum,' joked one Hollywood executive on learning that three actors and a director had formed their own company.

THE GOLDEN HONEYCOMB: *GRAND HOTEL*

Glamour was the watchword at MGM, which boasted it had 'more stars than were in the heavens'. In *Grand Hotel* (1932), the studio's enthusiasm for glossy, star-driven melodramas was taken to its extreme. The film unfolds against the backdrop of Berlin's most opulent hotel – re-created in extravagant fashion on the MGM lot by art director Cedric Gibbons. The guests include some of the biggest names on the studio books: Greta Garbo plays Grusinkaya, a fading beauty of a ballet dancer; John Barrymore, a dapper, Raffles-like jewel thief; Joan Crawford, the beautiful young stenographer, prepared to do anything to get ahead; Wallace Beery, a bellowing, larger-than-life braggart of a businessman; and Lionel Barrymore, a humble bookkeeper, suffering from a terminal illness, determined to live out his last days in pomp and style.

Despite the gilded settings, the guests are an unhappy, neurotic bunch. They behave in the same haughty, self-obsessed way as the Hollywood stars themselves often did off-screen. Audiences would have known that Garbo was as stubborn as a mule when it came to contract negotiations, that John Barrymore liked his alcohol, and that Crawford, like the go-getting secretary she plays, was a poor girl on the make. It is the movie in which Garbo sighs out her mournful one-liner, 'I want to be alone'. This was not exactly news to studio executives used to dealing with the famously reclusive Swedish star, who never allowed outsiders on set, refused to work a minute of overtime, and was inclined to shoot off back to Europe whenever the MGM bosses wouldn't give her what she wanted. If Garbo was highly strung, so were the rest of the cast. Given their continual jostling for status, it cannot have been comfortable for them to work alongside one another. As British critic Kenneth Tynan pointed out, the hotel is 'a towering honeycomb of cubicles that must have borne more than a passing resemblance to the Metro studios at the time'.

The film was made to put the studio's luxury goods, namely its best-known contract actors, in the shop window. They do not seem at all happy being there: Garbo's dancer comes close to suicide because, as she moans, following her most recent performance 'the applause did not come' – and everybody else has problems too. It is as if MGM wanted to tell audiences that although stars were rich and famous and lived pampered lives, that did not stop them from being as miserable as anybody else in America. Their unhappiness makes them easier to identify with and suggests that there really was trouble in paradise. It also, perversely, makes them that much more alluring. The fatalism and despair that seep into the story make it seem all the more exotic.

A-class star vehicles were expensive to produce but easy to sell. *Grand Hotel* cost $700,000. It not only won the Best Film Oscar, but went a long way to ensuring the studio made $8 million profit, when, thanks to the Depression and the cost of converting to sound, most of its rivals were posting losses.

THE LAST TYCOON

Irving Thalberg, born in Brooklyn in 1899, had been a sickly, bedridden child. His mother was ambitious on his behalf, but his health was so feeble that it looked as if he would never be able to hold down any sort of job, let alone run a studio and its stars. He trained in shorthand and typing and began his working career as a secretary, in which capacity he was hired by producer Carl Laemmle. Thalberg's rise and rise is one of the more astonishing stories in Hollywood history. He is the character who inspired F. Scott Fitzgerald's valedictory novel about Hollywood, *The Last Tycoon*. By the time he was 21, he was head of production at Universal.

STAR-BUILDING WITH IRVING THALBERG

By 1934, MGM had over 60 leading actors under contract. Production boss Thalberg was meticulous in the way he managed their careers. Everything revolved around the stars – and the cinema-goers who paid to see them. The studio monitored public reaction as thoroughly as it could. If someone seemed popular, Thalberg would make sure that the fledgling star appeared in as many movies as quickly as possible. 'The public make the stars,' he once told a journalist. 'I show actors to their best advantage and watch for the response.' He insisted that studio readers 'analyse all material on the basis of the players who are working for us', and set up a formidable publicity department to keep the stars in the public eye.

Members of the publicity department became accomplished forgers, capable of imitating the signatures of the actors they were looking after. They answered all the fan mail, sent out innumerable signed photographs, vetted telephone calls, responded to invitations, wrote speeches and provided clothes for 'the talent'. 'Escorts were provided, romances promoted or destroyed, elopements supervised and marriages arranged or rent asunder,' remembered studio script doctor Sam Marx. The ever-resourceful publicists and their colleagues in the wardrobe department even furnished actresses with fake breasts, 'naturally in pairs, with perfect aureoles and nipples, carrying the name of those for whom they were designed. They hid from their fans any hint that nature had left them underprivileged.' When there were rumours that an MGM male star was gay, the publicists immediately provided him with beautiful women to hang on his arm at premières and parties. They policed the contract actors so thoroughly that few stars were ever able to say anything indiscreet during an interview with the press – studio reps would sit in with them, monitoring their answers. The stars received enormous salaries but – at least during Thalberg's ascendancy – they had to do what they were told in return.

Thalberg's obstinacy and strength of character is illustrated by his repeated clashes with wastrel genius, actor-director Erich von Stroheim, who made a series of sophisticated, witty but wildly expensive melodramas for the studio in the early 1920s. *Foolish Wives* (1922), about an American woman

opposite The boy wonder Irving Thalberg (1889–1936) prepares to accept the 1935 Best Picture Oscar (*Mutiny On The Bounty*) from a beaming Frank Capra. A year later, Thalberg would be dead.

below Erich von Stroheim (1885–1957) was one of the most brilliant but also most extravagant directors of the silent era. Thalberg, then Universal production boss, clashed with him repeatedly, eventually firing him from the 1923 feature, *Merry-Go-Round*.

THE PRICE THEY PAY

There was an awkward moment during the Berlin Film Festival press conference for Joel Schumacher's film, *8mm* (1999). A journalist asked the star, Nicolas Cage, whether reports suggesting that he was paid in excess of $20 million per movie were true. Before Cage had a chance to answer, the journalist pointed out that several European movies could be made for that sum. It seemed an obscene amount of money.

'Whatever the market rate is... is the market rate,' Cage mumbled, looking embarrassed. He pointed out that he had appeared in several low-budget independent films and that he would never think of charging a young, independent director $20 million for his services. Schumacher, sitting alongside Cage, came to the actor's defence. 'Nobody in Hollywood is paying that kind of salary for nothing,' he said. 'If their relatives could do what we do, they [the studio executives] would hire them instead.'

neglected by her husband who begins an affair with a dashing Prussian officer type (played by von Stroheim), went over schedule and over budget. With a magnificent disdain for the practicalities of making and releasing a feature film, the actor-director shot over 50 hours of footage that he eventually, and reluctantly, winnowed down into a three-and-a-half-hour feature. Thalberg, dismissing von Stroheim's pet idea that it be shown in two parts, shortened it yet further. It did well at the box-office, but having already cost $1 million, an astronomical figure for the time, barely limped into profit. The problems recurred on von Stroheim's next film, *Merry-Go-Round* (1923). This time, though, Thalberg sacked him as soon as he stepped out of line.

Von Stroheim, the Silesian hatter's son who tried to pass himself off as a Prussian aristocrat, was the director as star. In his productions, everything was subservient to his own grand vision. His name and face appeared on the posters, and he invariably eclipsed the other actors. Thalberg's filmmaking philosophy was very different to his.

STARS v. DIRECTORS

Irving Thalberg believed that directors served a functional purpose – they were hired to put the story over as well as possible and to make sure that the actors were seen to best advantage. Their personalities and pet foibles were not supposed to intrude. 'I consider the director is on the set to communicate what I expect of my actors,' Thalberg used to tell filmmakers in his pep talks at MGM. 'It's my experience that many directors only realize 75 per cent of our scenarios, and while audiences never know how much they missed, I do. You

gentlemen have individualistic styles and I respect them. It's one of the principal reasons we want you here. But if you can't conform to my system, it would be wiser not to start your film at all.'

Although he sacked von Stroheim and curbed the extravagances of countless other directors, Thalberg was not opposed to spending when he felt it was warranted. Whether silent epics like *The Hunchback of Notre Dame*, which he produced at Universal with Lon Chaney in the leading role, or all-star extravaganzas like *Grand Hotel*, the projects with which he was associated were always on the grandest scale. He thought nothing of recutting or even recasting and reshooting films that failed to click with audiences at specially organized previews. He and his staff would provide stars with new wardrobes and new identities, and he even gave the public the chance to help create a star. After a nationwide contest which offered $500 to whomever dreamed up the best name, pretty young Texan waitress and ex-shopgirl Lucille Le Sueur was rechristened Joan Crawford by MGM. A bedridden woman in New York had come up with the name. It caught on very quickly. 'We've got ourselves another star,' Thalberg boasted to Mayer when he realized how popular Crawford had become.

POWERLESS PEACOCKS

The star system that Thalberg ran at MGM and which the other studios strove to copy was riven with contradictions. The actors were rich and pampered. With their expensive cars, gorgeously decorated houses and perfect clothes (all of which were displayed regularly in star profiles in fan magazines) they seemed to live the perfect lifestyle. They helped to sell not only the movies that they appeared in, but every kind of product, from soap to dresses. They were commonly talked about as gods and goddesses, 'embodiments of ideal ways of behaving', and yet, for all their lustre, they were relatively powerless. Their careers and personae were moulded by executives like Thalberg and Jack Warner. They had little say about what roles they would play, and they were tied to contracts; if they complained, they would be dropped. Their time in the spotlight – as Florence Lawrence's spectacular downfall illustrated – tended to be short-lived

From the days of Chaplin and Mary Pickford, top Hollywood stars have always been paid astronomical amounts. It is too simplistic to attribute their eye-popping salaries merely to market forces. Stars are what sell movies. Historically, the major studios wanted to ensure that smaller companies could not poach their top contract artists, and no small company could match the salaries that, say, MGM paid in its heyday. Besides, the golden myth of excess always made for good publicity. The fact that the stars were so well paid added to their aura.

After the break-up of the studio system, when films were packaged by producers and agents in one-off deals, stars were still the most important part of the equation. As one analyst put it, 'exhibitors book by stars, and stars who are popular find financing'. Stars began to demand percentage 'points' in the movies in which they appeared. Thus, Marlon Brando was able to make an astonishing $4 million for roughly ten minutes on screen as Jor-El, the father of Superman, in the 1978 blockbuster, *Superman – The Movie*.

above Nice work if you can get it. Marlon Brando appeared for less than quarter of an hour in *Superman* (1978), but still earned $4 million for his efforts.

opposite Nicolas Cage received $20 million for his role in Jerry Bruckheimer-produced action-spectacular, *The Rock* (1996).

Hollywood
Svengalis

3

The Song of Bernadette
1943

Film stars' careers were often driven by outsiders – pushy mothers, ambitious husbands or wives, archly manipulative producers and directors. George Du Maurier's potboiler novel, *Trilby*, adapted into a play by Paul M. Potter, describes a relationship all too common in Hollywood – that of the young *ingénue* and her sinister guru. In Du Maurier's story, a tone-deaf young model (Trilby) comes under the influence of the ambitious Svengali, who hypnotizes her and turns her into a world-famous singer. Svengali's real-life descendants in the film industry were legion.

SELZNICK AND JONES

It was 1941 when David O. Selznick first met Jennifer Jones. By then, it was already five years since he had launched the biggest talent-findng hunt in film history – for the perfect Scarlett O'Hara to star in *Gone with the Wind*. Phylis Isley, as Jones was then called, was a struggling young actress from Tulsa. She had first arrived in Hollywood with her then-husband Robert Walker in 1939 and had secured a couple of parts in B-movies without properly establishing herself. She auditioned for Selznick, who was immediately struck by 'the power of the girl's eyes'. He put her under contract, and in a little under a year, it is estimated, the producer spent more than $7,500 polishing up his new protégé. She was given

diction lessons; studied with Sanford Meisner, who was one of the most influential acting coaches of the day; took English literature courses at college; and was finally given a new name, a seven-year contract, and the lead part in the new Selznick weepie, *The Song of Bernadette* (1943). She won an Oscar, went on to star in countless other Selznick productions, and eventually married him.

'He told her that he would make her the greatest star of the world. His intentions were obvious, but she refused to have anything to do with him… it was the most outrageous courtship. He spent millions to put her on a throne of blood,' **wrote British director Michael Powell of Selznick.**

GARBO AND STILLER

In 1924, on a trip to Europe, MGM's cantankerous boss Louis B. Mayer signed up one of Scandinavia's best-known film directors, Mauritz Stiller. The Helsinki-born filmmaker, who had come to Sweden on a false passport to avoid being conscripted into the Tsar's army, had presided over the 'golden age' of Swedish silent cinema. He had already made over 40 films when he cast a young actress from The Royal Dramatic Theatre in Stockholm in his four-hour 1924 epic, *Gösta Berlings' Saga*. The actress, a former department store

left *Flesh and the Devil* (1936). John Gilbert and Greta Garbo were lovers both on screen and off.

opposite Marlene Dietrich as lovely Lola Lola in the movie that transformed her from a Berlin nightclub siren into an international star, Josef von Sternberg's *The Blue Angel* (1930).

assistant, was not exactly graceful. She had big galumphing feet, and she was on the plump side. Stiller, however, was mesmerized by her. He did everything he could to transform this labourer's daughter into an elegant and sophisticated movie star. It was Stiller who changed Greta Lovisa Gustafsson's name to Greta Garbo.

When Mayer offered Stiller a contract, the director refused to come to the US unless he could bring the actress with him. That is how Garbo arrived in Hollywood. Mayer was not optimistic about her prospects and commented with typical bluntness: 'In America, men don't like fat women.' The studio had no idea what to do with her, although they noticed how well she photographed as the Spanish peasant girl in the romance *The Torrent*, and that she received positive reviews for her performance as the vamp in her second Hollywood film, *The Temptress*. The top brass therefore gave her a more enticing role, opposite the immensely popular male lead John Gilbert, in the torrid melodrama *Flesh and the Devil* (1926). Garbo, still only 22, played a world-weary seductress who comes after Gilbert; she and Gilbert had a much-publicized love affair in real life too. Cinema-goers were entranced by the actress they nicknamed 'the Swedish sphinx'.

It is hard to explain Garbo's allure. An aloof, clumsy figure off camera, she was mesmerizing on screen, and projected a passion and depth that few who knew her suspected she possessed. Whether because of Stiller's assiduous coaching or through some innate talent of her own, she was a consummate screen actress. 'Garbo had something behind the eyes that you couldn't see until you photographed it in close-up,' director Clarence Brown, who made several movies with her, commented. 'You could see thought. If she had to look at one person with jealousy and another with love, she didn't have to change her expression. You could see it in her eyes as she looked from one to the other.'

Garbo had one other accomplice, almost as important as Stiller to the flowering of her career – the cameraman William Daniels, one of the best at MGM, who first worked with her on *Torrent* and photographed nearly all of her subsequent films. Not only did he light her exquisitely, he also made sure that there was no intrusion on set while she was working. For the famous recluse, filmmaking was almost a private activity – the fewer people involved the better.

Ironically, just as Garbo's career took off, Stiller's crumbled. He was too much the European maverick to accept the constraints put on him by studio bosses. He went back to Sweden in 1927 (having tried but failed to persuade Garbo to come with him) and died the following year.

DIETRICH AND VON STERNBERG

'If she had nothing more than her voice, she could break your heart with it. But she has that beautiful body and the timeless loveliness of her face. It makes no difference how she breaks your heart if she is there to mend it.'
(Ernest Hemingway)

The image that still lingers is of the Prussian aristocrat and his decadent muse. Josef von Sternberg was the most arrogant of Paramount's directors. He, along with Erich von Stroheim, helped create the stereotype of the monocle-wearing, megaphone-wielding tyrant in breeches and riding boots who would terrorize his actors and technicians. 'He pulled his intellectual superiority around him like the heavy overcoat he affected even in sunny California,' remembered Budd Schulberg, whose father B.P. Schulberg was von Sternberg's boss at Paramount. Yet von Sternberg was an Austrian Jew from a relatively humble background, not the European aristocrat that he pretended to be.

Born in Vienna in 1894, Jonas Sternberg arrived in the US, where his father had gone to seek work, in 1901. He spent his formative years there, entering the film business in New Jersey as a 'patcher', a job that involved stitching old

film reels back together. He received further film training while working for the Signal Corps during World War I. It was a practical but far from glamorous introduction to the industry. He then moved out west to Hollywood, where he was hired as an assistant director. Sternberg's bosses decided to add a 'von' to his name to make him seem more sophisticated, and he did not demur. Eventually, he was given a movie to direct: *The Salvation Hunters* (1925) was intended as a vehicle through which to launch British stage star George K. Arthur's career in America, but it was the young director, not his leading actor, who received the plaudits.

Von Sternberg had a ferocious work ethic. He was largely self-taught, and yet had read so widely and had spent so much of his time in art galleries that he could easily pass as an intellectual. By the time he arrived in Berlin in the late 1920s to cast *The Blue Angel* (1930), Germany's first all-talking picture, he was already acknowledged as a master. Emil Jannings was to star in the film as a pompous, strict schoolteacher who becomes slavishly devoted to the lovely cabaret singer Lola Lola, eventually losing his job and position in society and humiliating himself just to be close to her. Where to find an actress who could play such a character?

The characters Dietrich plays in Sternberg's films are all variations on Lola Lola, but he never moralizes at her expense. Whether as Empress of Russia (in *The Scarlet Empress*), a demure wife who turns into an outrageous cabaret star (*Blonde Venus*), or a nightclub entertainer (*Morocco*), she's still the same jaded, flirtatious, *femme fatale*. Sternberg's camera was as besotted with her as the men cast opposite her: the stiff-necked British matinée idols like Clive Brook or Herbert Marshall, blustering buffoons like Emil Jannings's teacher, and the strapping French foreign legionnaire Gary Cooper are all constantly tormented by sexual jealousy.

The films exist almost as an excuse for the beautifully lit close-ups of the star. Von Sternberg dresses her in ever more outlandish clothing: one moment

MARLENE DIETRICH

Dietrich was from a far more privileged background than von Sternberg. Born in 1901, her father, who died when she was seven, was precisely the kind of blue-blooded soldier that von Sternberg loved to imitate, and her stepfather was also a high-ranking military man. She had originally intended to become a violinist, but thought about acting instead when she suffered a wrist injury that would have made a musical career impossible. Dietrich was hardly an *ingénue* when she auditioned for von Sternberg in Berlin in 1929. She had already been an actress and nightclub performer for almost a decade, and, having made several movies, publicists had already begun to talk about her as a German 'Garbo'. She had lived through the turbulent post-war years in Berlin, been married, had a child, and indulged in countless affairs – with men and women. Everybody knew her. 'Not that whore!' Erich Pommer, one of the head producers at UFA, the production company behind *The Blue Angel*, is reported to have complained when he learned that von Sternberg was planning to cast her.

she is in top hat and tails, the next covered in ostrich feathers and sequins. There is plenty of self-parody in the star image that von Sternberg created for Dietrich. Although the films teeter on the verge of kitsch, they transcend their own absurdities. The director's obsession with his actress is so all-consuming that Dietrich is transformed into a full-blown tragic heroine. He was helped in this by the studio spending a fortune publicizing her. Paramount, jealous of the success MGM had enjoyed with Garbo, wanted to prove that it had an equally alluring, equally exotic star of its own.

GINGER AND LELA ROGERS

Lela Rogers was as pushy and ambitious as mothers get. Even her husband was awed by her, and he had deserted her by the time their daughter, Virginia, was born in Independence, Missouri, in 1911. He turned up again briefly – to kidnap Virginia – and then disappeared again. Lela tracked him down, reclaimed her daughter, and set about stage-managing her career.

Ginger (as she became known) originally wanted to be a teacher. She grew up the typical all-American girl in Fort Worth, Texas. When she won a Charleston dancing contest at the age of 14, her mother decided that show business might be the best option for her. Lela, despite having a demanding full-time job as a journalist, devised routines for Ginger and even recruited a team of performers, the Red Heads, to act as her back-up. Ginger and her troupe performed five shows a day. Mother and daughter travelled all over the country, Lela acting as manager and hustler – a real-life version of Rose, the stage 'mom' in the Broadway hit, *Gypsy*.

It was Lela who decided to take Ginger to Hollywood. While also working as a screenwriter, she lobbied furiously on her daughter's behalf and soon Ginger began to get some bit parts. The one thing Lela was not responsible for was the colour of her daughter's hair. When a studio hairdresser dyed it blonde (she was a natural brunette), Lela was initially furious and wanted to sue the studio. Ginger protested that she liked the new colour. 'Frankly, baby, I'm beginning to like it myself,' Lela replied.

Of course, Lela could not do Ginger's dancing for her, and the experts were not bowled over by her natural ability. It was always hard work, but then that was what her mother had brought her up to believe in. Just as Lela held down a dozen jobs at once and still found time to oversee Ginger's career, the young actress/dancer rehearsed incessantly. She appeared in nine films in 1933 alone.

Rogers was attractive and flirtatious, and at the beginning of her career critics compared her to the man-eating Mae West. Like the Lana Turners and Liz Taylors, she swapped husbands with seemingly reckless abandon, marrying five times. She was hardly a puritan, but it was always apparent that her work mattered to her more than anything else. After being pressed so hard by her mother, she was tough enough to withstand the punishing rehearsal routines that Fred Astaire demanded.

As Rogers began to take control of her own career, Lela, who had become a leading executive in a film studio, decided she needed a new challenge. Somehow, it is not surprising that she became one of J. Edgar Hoover's most trusted Hollywood acolytes. During the period of the Hollywood blacklists, she threw herself into hunting down communists with the same enthusiasm that she had once shown for masterminding little Ginger's career.

opposite Rudolph Valentino (1895–1926), Hollywood's favourite 'Latin Lover' and the biggest matinée idol of them all, made audiences swoon with his sensuous tango routines.

below If you want to get ahead in Hollywood, it helps if you have a battleaxe of a mother. No mums came fiercer than the formidable Lela Rogers, pictured here on the backlot of RKO Studios with her daughter Ginger in 1936.

VALENTINO AND RAMBOVA

Winnifred Hudnut was an art director and aspiring actress at the Metro Pictures Corporation. She may have been born in Utah, but that did not stop her from behaving like an Eastern European mystic. Under the name Natacha Rambova she began to fashion the career of a young, Italian-born actor with whom she had worked on the melodrama, *Camille*, in 1921 – she had designed the rococo sets through which he and his co-star Alla Nazimova had pranced. Rudolph Valentino became a star thanks to his role as Julio in *Four Horsemen of the Apocalypse*, also in 1921. In May the following year he married Rambova.

Film historians paint Rambova as manipulative and eccentric, and she is often accused of sabotaging Valentino's career. She dressed him in exotic, effeminate clothes, treated him as if he were a lapdog and gave him what her detractors considered to be disastrous advice. A famous article written in the *Chicago Tribune* shortly before his untimely death from peritonitis in 1926 called him a 'painted pansy' and bemoaned the imitators ('effeminate youths, pomaded, powdered, bejewelled and bedizened') whom he supposedly inspired. When he was dead, Rambova held seances to contact him.

There is a strong whiff of racism and homophobia in the way that Valentino is written about. He was the exotic outsider, at first consigned to playing villains (Hollywood casting agents did not believe that anyone so Italian-looking could make a plausible hero) and then, after his breakthrough in *The Four Horsemen of the Apocalypse*, as the 'Latin lover'. Whether he played Arabs (as in *The Sheik*) or Indians (as in *The Young Rajah*), it made no difference. His brand of masculinity – androgynous, sensual – made studio bosses and critics alike uncomfortable. He brought out their fear of miscegenation and their distrust of men who did not behave like the craggy, all-American outdoor hero.

Rambova recognized that the reason so many female fans were captivated by Valentino was because of his exoticism. She played it up just as had June Mathis, chief of the script department at Metro, who insisted on him being cast as the tango-dancing gaucho in *The Four Horsemen*. They were doing nothing different from what von Sternberg did with Dietrich or Stiller with Garbo, but received little of the credit.

Hollywood just could not take Valentino seriously. Everybody knew about his background as a professional dancer and gigolo, and they suspected that he was bisexual. Despite earning first Metro and then Famous Players-Lasky a fortune, he was treated atrociously. His salary was a fraction of that paid to many far less popular stars, and Famous Players-Lasky even refused to give him a comfortably furnished dressing-room. The studio bosses failed to back him when his first wife, little-known actress Jean Acker (who had abandoned him on their wedding night), turned up out of the blue and accused him of marrying Rambova bigamously. Rambova encouraged him to stand up for his rights and he took the studio to court in an attempt to get out of his contract. As a result, he was blackballed by the studios and his career went into decline. The studios still wanted him, but would only offer him roles on the condition that Rambova was not involved. It was little surprise that their marriage came to an end. By the mid-1920s, his career was beginning to pick up again, and his last film, *The Son of the Sheik* (1925), was one of his biggest hits.

MISTER LOVER MAN

The son of an ex-cavalry captain, Valentino, born Rodolfo Guglielmi, grew up in a middle-class Italian household. He came to America in 1913 when he was 18, not as an impoverished immigrant, but as an adventurer in search of his fortune. As shown by his protracted lawsuit against former employers Famous Players-Lasky, he was more resourceful than his reputation as a sybaritic Latin lover suggests. Valentino's funeral was mobbed by thousands of weeping women. There were allegations that he had been poisoned. Mysterious *femmes fatales* were spotted leaving wreaths on his grave. John Dos Passos wrote a memorable account of Valentino's funeral in his book, *U.S.A.* 'In the muggy rain the cops lost control... the funeral chapel was gutted, men and women fought over a flower, a piece of wallpaper, a piece of the broken plate-glass window. Show windows were burst in. Parked cars were overturned and smashed. When finally the mounted police after repeated charges beat the crowd off Broadway, where traffic was tied up for two hours, they picked up twenty-eight separate shoes, a truckload of umbrellas, papers, hats, torn-off sleeves.' Not even the most ingenious publicists – or indeed Natacha Rambova – could have dreamed up a stunt quite as extravagant as this.

Science Fiction

Georges Méliès
1902

A rocket hits the moon's right eye, like a meringue finger landing on a squashy mass of cream and jelly. The moon, which has a human face, grimaces. This is the key moment in Georges Méliès' 1902 picture *Trip to the Moon* (*La Voyage dans la Lune*), one of the first science-fiction films in cinema history. Méliès himself featured in the lead role, Professor Barbenfoullis, President of the Astronomers' Club. Acrobats from the Folies-Bergère played the Selenites, the strange army the explorers encounter during their lunar jaunt.

While the Lumières were pragmatic, level-headed entrepreneurs, Méliès (1861–1938), approached filmmaking from a very different perspective. He was the cinema's original special effects wizard, the spiritual father of such prestidigitators as George Pal, Ed Wood, Ray Harryhausen, Douglas Trumbull and even Stanley Kubrick. His trickery began at a young age, and even as a boy he used to stage puppet shows. He hoped to become an artist but was forced by his father into the family business – shoemaking. Working in a factory did have its compensations, and it was here that he learned about mechanics, but his real interest, was in pantomime and music hall. Above all, he loved magic and conjuring tricks. When his father died in 1888, he sold his share in the family business to his brothers and used the money to buy a theatre from the widow

of actor Emile Robert-Houdin. Here, he set up in business, presiding over extravagant magic shows.

In December 1895, Méliès was invited to the first public showing of the Lumières' Cinématographe. He was delighted by what he saw: he already used magic lanterns in his stage show and thought this new device could improve his act still further – if he could get his hands on it. Clearly the Lumières would not be willing to share their invention with a potential rival, so Méliès bought a projector from R.W. Paul in London. After a few months tinkering with this, and studying various other machines, he managed to come up with a camera-projector of his own, the Kinetograph, which he nicknamed his 'machine gun'.

Méliès worked at a prolific rate. During 1896 alone, he made more than 70 films. He learned that the camera could perform conjuring tricks of its own. It could make people vanish – all he needed to do was stop the camera, allow the performer to walk out of frame, and then start shooting again. He was not interested in shooting in real locations where he would not be able to control what was happening in front of camera, and so built his own studio in his back garden. At first, Méliès' film shows at the Robert-Houdin took their place alongside live performances. Soon, however, he decided to show nothing but films. To heighten spectators' enjoyment, he provided musical accompaniment, inventive sound effects and a spoken commentary.

Although he made documentaries in his back garden, Méliès much preferred coming up with his own ideas rather than being restricted by events in the world at large. Not that he paid much attention to storytelling. He was far more interested in tricks and spectacle than in the niceties of plot. 'I was appealing to the spectator's eye alone, trying to charm and intrigue him,' Méliès confessed. 'Hence the scenario was of no importance.' He viewed cinema as the best tool yet invented for the benefit of the professional conjuror. Apart from anything else, the camera allowed him to hone each new trick until it was perfectly realized. It also enabled him to take spectators all the way to the moon. He could do as many takes as necessary (or as he could afford) without having to worry about letting down the audience.

CINEMA'S FIRST MAGICIAN

Between 1897 and 1904, Méliès made hundreds of films, only a small proportion of which have survived. Just as Muybridge often appeared in his own photographic experiments, the magician/director liked to take leading roles in his movies. He played – appropriately enough – wizards or devils. His films often took similar subject-matter to those of the Jules Verne science-fiction stories that he and the French public devoured so avidly, but whereas Verne treated his material in earnest, pseudo-scientific fashion, Méliès opted for fantasy. Some critics dismiss his work as clumsy and unadventurous: however ingenious the tricks he dreamed up, the camerawork was leaden, the perspective offered cinema-goers was always the same – that of an audience member sitting in the front row of the stalls – and each film was like a potted pantomime.

Méliès was cinema's first magician, more concerned with special effects than with fluid visuals or subtle characterization. He was a contradictory figure, part Merlin, part drone: somebody with a hugely inventive imagination who took an all too rigid approach to his craft; a bohemian who behaved like a small businessman. 'M. Méliès and I are in the same business. We lend enchantment to vulgar material,' the poet Apollinaire wrote of him. His work also hinted at his religious and sexual preoccupations. In *The Temptation of St Anthony* (1898), the transformations include a skull that takes human shape and a Christ on the crucifix who turns into a beautiful woman. Paul Hammond, Méliès' biographer, notes how often his movies showed damsels emerging, Venus-like, out of sea shells: 'The shell is a sign of femininity, its shape and colouring often mimics the form of the vulva.'

Méliès' downfall anticipates that of countless other individualists stymied by an industry that was run increasingly along big-business lines. His company, Star Films, began to unravel as soon as he struck a deal with the most predatory of the early French film tycoons, Charles Pathé, in late 1911. Under the terms of their contract, Pathé was to finance and distribute Méliès' movies. In practice, Pathé was emasculating a rival and Méliès' much-coveted independence was lost. He was now dependent on a businessman who proved far from sympathetic to his goals. Under the terms of the pact with Pathé, Méliès had to put up his own property as collateral. He was beginning to fall out of fashion, and other events conspired to destroy his filmmaking career: war was imminent, and his brother, who represented him overseas,

squandered his money. Méliès retired from the business, and destroyed many of his own films. After World War I, he ended up running a shop belonging to his wife (a former actress in his films), which sold confectionery and toys at the Gare Montparnasse. He was rediscovered by a new generation of historians and filmmakers just before his death from cancer in 1938. His career as a director had finished more than 20 years before, but his place in film history was assured. And he had been first into space.

A SINISTER VISION OF THE FUTURE – FRITZ LANG'S *METROPOLIS*

Fritz Lang's conception of the futuristic city in *Metropolis* (1926) was inspired by his first sight of New York by night with its skyscrapers and glittering lights. He was aboard a ship, about to arrive in America, and was immediately entranced. The city he and his designers contrived does full justice to the architectural splendour and incandescence of the New York that so enraptured him. It boasts pleasure gardens, skyscrapers and walkways suspended high above the ground. Aircraft flutter around the buildings. It seems to be a modernist Utopia. The city's underbelly, though, is where most of the film is set. While a privileged few enjoy a carefree life, a mass of workers move like automatons through the lower city, operating the machinery which makes their industrialist boss rich beyond the dreams of Croesus. 'Quite the silliest film,' opined English science-fiction writer H.G. Wells, but Lang deals with the struggle between bosses and lumpenproletariat in a more striking and courageous way than Wells ever did in his fiction.

RAY HARRYHAUSEN AND STOP-FRAME ANIMATION

Picture a gawky, distracted teenager in the back garage, making models of prehistoric animals. He is surrounded by odds and ends – his materials are the joints from the rear-view mirrors of ancient motor cars, discarded old flexible lamps, rubber, wood, corrugated iron, and anything else that springs to mind. Out of all the bric-a-brac, he fashions creaky, home-made dinosaurs. This is the image filmmaker Ray Harryhausen draws of himself as a youngster growing up in California during the 1930s. A venerable figure now, with a deeply lined face, and a slow, deliberate drawl of a voice, he has an air of such Prospero-like sagacity that it takes quite some effort to imagine him as ever having been an adolescent. But all sorcerers must serve their apprenticeships somewhere. Harryhausen admired Méliès but his immediate inspiration was Willis O'Brien, the special effects wizard behind *King Kong*, which Harryhausen saw on its opening night in 1933 at Grauman's Chinese in Los Angeles, then probably the most famous cinema in the world.

Out in the foyer, there was a big bust of Kong that had been used in the picture. The head was about eight or nine feet high and it was operated mechanically using compressed air. Below it there were trees and jungle foliage, with pink flamingos strutting round. A great array of stills was on display. Before the film, there was one of Sid Grauman's stage productions, with people in native costumes performing on trapeze. Then, when *King Kong* finally started, with Max Steiner's score, it transported Harryhausen into never-never land. It took him from the Depression days, the real world, and led him into the most outrageous fantasy that has ever been put on the screen.

above The mad scientist surveys his handiwork: Rudolf Klein-Rogge as Rotwang in Fritz Lang's *Metropolis* (1926).

opposite The German poster for *Metropolis*. As the skyscrapers looming over the robot's head hint, Lang's vision of the futuristic city was inspired by the modernist skyscrapers of 1920s New York.

above *King Kong* (1933) boasted bravura special effects, courtesy of stop motion-magician and former Edison employee, Willis O'Brien.

HARRYHAUSEN LEARNS TO DESTROY THE WORLD

Coming out of the theatre, young Harryhausen was as puzzled as he was astounded. He knew King Kong was not a man in a gorilla suit, but that was all he did know. His curiosity whetted, he decided to experiment with a camera and models himself. But animating dead matter is no easy process. Before he mastered his craft, he had to teach himself many different skills: how to draw, how to cast, how to sculpt, how to paint the backgrounds, how to photograph them properly. He eventually got a job with Willis O'Brien on *Mighty Joe Young* (1949), a belated, camp follow-up to *King Kong*. Then, in the 1950s, as he emerged as a formidable talent in his own right, Harryhausen went on a wrecking spree. He spent much of the decade making low-budget sci-fi pictures which allowed various monsters to rampage across the USA, destroying cities. He laid waste Washington, the Golden Gate Bridge, and even New York, in such films as *The Beast from 20,000 Fathoms* and *It Came from Beneath the Sea*.

When he tired of knocking down buildings, Harryhausen moved into the realm of myth instead. Under his guidance, Sinbad, Jason, Perseus and, in *One Million Years B.C.*, Raquel Welch in an animal-skin bikini, tussled with an impressive array of Gorgons, pterodactyls, dinosaurs and sword-wielding skeletons. It is hard to imagine a more lonely, painstaking business than stop-frame animation. Harryhausen was still busy with *Clash of the Titans* a year and a half after everybody else had gone home. It took him five months to match the animation with the live action in a famous sequence from *The Valley of Gwangi* which sees cowboys lasso a dinosaur, and getting a pterodactyl to fly off with Raquel Welch was no easy matter. However laborious the process, the results are frequently astonishing.

PLAN 9 FROM OUTER SPACE – THE WORST SCI-FI FILM EVER MADE?

In Ed Wood's films, you can always spot the joins: continuity editing is slack, sets are cobbled together with papier-mâchée, shower curtains and anything else that comes to hand. However, through some bizarre alchemical process, his work transcends its own limitations. Although his movies are lousy by any formal criteria, they shine with his Méliès-like sense of wonder in the magic of the medium. Wood's was, quite literally, a poor cinema. Not much of an entrepreneur, he was nonetheless prepared to cajole funds out of everybody from his actors to Baptist missionaries. (*Plan 9 from Outer Space* was originally to be called *Grave Diggers from Outer Space*, but its religious financiers insisted the title be changed.) His career proves that it is quite possible to become a director without money, obvious talent or even an audience. 'The sky to which she once looked was only a covering for her dead body,' the sonorous narrator of *Plan 9* tells us after a little old woman is buried. This same narrator then goes on to announce, apropos of nothing, that 'we are all interested in the future because that is where we are going to spend the rest of our lives'. Unwieldy metaphors and clunking dialogue are Wood's trademarks. It is as if he is trying to compensate for shabby sets with grandiose language. The effect is at once risible and irresistible.

DESTINATION MOON

'The moon... impossible!' proclaim the US scientists in Irving Pichel's 1950 Technicolor fantasy, *Destination Moon*. They are being overly pessimistic. This is the beginning of the Cold War after all, and it has become a matter of national pride for some of Uncle Sam's boys to be lunar-bound before those darned Russkies. Four upright Americans defy the government to head off into space at 32,000 feet per second. Their secret weapon – or at least what won the film its Oscar – was the special effects contrived by model-maker extraordinaire, George Pal. Like Méliès, the Hungarian-born Pal (1908–1980) was a devoted enthusiast of Jules Verne and H.G. Wells. After moving to America in 1939, he won six Academy Awards. Among his other films were *The Time Machine* (1960), *Tom Thumb* (1957) and *War Of The Worlds* (1952).

above Willis O'Brien's groundbreaking work on *King Kong* and *Mighty Joe Young* inspired another young special effects artist, Ray Harryhausen. This still of bikini-clad cavewomen fleeing from what seems to be a giant tortoise comes from one of Harryhausen's most celebrated efforts, *One Million Years BC*.

below *Destination Moon* (1950) showcased the talents of the great Hungarian-born animator/special effects artist, George Pal, who won six Academy Awards in the course of his career.

HELLO HAL

Months before shooting began on *2001: A Space Odyssey*, director Stanley Kubrick set a small army of technicians to work designing the sets and props and dreaming up the special effects. As his biographer Vincent LoBrutto notes, there were boat builders, architecture students, fine artists, sculptors, lithographers, metalworkers and ivory carvers. They had to research their subject so extensively that building and launching a NASA spaceship would have seemed child's play by comparison. For many audiences, the most startling creation of all in the film was HAL 9000, the remorselessly logical, chess-playing computer with the prissy voice (provided by actor Douglas Rain). With his vast mainframe, HAL may seem archaic to modern-day audiences who know how small and compact computers have become. That does not make him any less sinister.

STOMACH PAINS – JOHN HURT GIVES BIRTH TO AN ALIEN

Director Ridley Scott did not tell the actors what was about to happen to Kane, played by John Hurt, halfway through *Alien* (1979). The cameras were rolling for what they thought was a low-key scene aboard the spaceship *Nostromo*, when suddenly Hurt's stomach seemed to explode. Blood and guts flew everywhere and out from his innards appeared the alien. This ranks among the most painful birth scenes in cinema. Hurt had been rigged up with a false chest, underneath which was a plentiful supply of offal. At the key moment, the special effects crew detonated the chest and out popped the succubus-like beast. 'We had to make it totally repulsive and yet as scary as hell,' Ridley Scott later noted. 'I looked at sketches of blobs and octopuses and dinosaurs. They were all awful.' Eventually, he stumbled on *Necronomicon*, a book by H.R. Giger, a Swedish Surrealist. 'I found a painting of a demon with a jutting face and long, extended, phallic-shaped head. It was the most frightening thing I'd ever seen. I knew immediately that here was our creature.'

SCI-FI WITH AN ECO-TWIST

Silent Running (1972) begins with a huge close-up of a snail crawling across a leaf – an image that looks as if it comes from some entomological documentary. It is probably the gentlest, most idiosyncratic sci-fi film ever made. Twenty-nine-year-old Douglas Trumbull was hired to devise an

right Stanley Kubrick assembled a small army of technicians (including the supremely gifted Douglas Trumbull) to work on *2001: A Space Odyssey*. Shot in wide screen, the movie won the Oscar for Best Special Effects in 1968.

intergalactic equivalent to *Easy Rider*. 'We were allowed to make the film with absolutely no controls, and with no intervention on the part of the studio. It was a fantastic opportunity,' he remembered. Money was tight: he had a little over $1 million – a fraction of the budget that Kubrick had had for *2001* (on which Trumbull worked as a special effects supervisor).

Trumbull pays lip service to genre conventions: there are plenty of explosions, the spaceship is full of gizmos and fighting breaks out between the astronauts. One, Lowell (Bruce Dern) ends up stuck on his own, miles away from any human help. This, though, is more an eco-fable than a sci-fi thriller. Lowell is part Robinson Crusoe, part eco-warrior. His plan is to refoliate the earth.

In one extraordinary scene, the three lovable robots ('Drones' as they are called) carry out an operation on Lowell's badly wounded leg. With minute precision, they cut away the cloth of his trousers and apply the bandage over the bloody gash. Lowell's relationship with Huey, Duey and Louie is like that of a shepherd with his dogs. He plays poker with them; talks to them incessantly. In conceiving them, Trumbull claims to have been inspired by one of the circus performers in Tod Browning's *Freaks* (1932), a bilateral amputee who walks everywhere on his arms – and the robots in *Silent Running* are actually played by amputees. Trumbull explained why he had made the robots so adorable: 'I've been involved with machines and special effects for a long time, and it bothers me that technology is considered inhumane and worthless... [With *Silent Running*] I wanted to show that, really, machines do things for people – they are what you want them to be.'

above Steven Spielberg helped usher in the era of the blockbuster with films like *Close Encounters Of The Third Kind* (1977), above, and *Jaws* (1975).

left The phallus-like succubus explodes from John Hurt's stomach in probably the most memorable moment in Ridley Scott's sci-fi classic, *Alien* (1979).

5

Nosferatu
1922

Horror Films

F.W. Murnau's *Nosferatu*, released in 1922, was the first (albeit unofficial) screen adaptation of Bram Stoker's 1897 novel, *Dracula*. The filmmakers had not secured the rights to the book, and so, to avoid legal problems, they were obliged to change the title, the characters' names, and to switch the action from Transylvania to Bremen, but the origins of the story are not in doubt.

Nearly 80 years on, *Nosferatu* remains among the most potent and disturbing horror films ever made. The sight of Max Schreck's sunken-cheeked, bald, emaciated vampire rising slowly and awkwardly from his coffin still sends a shiver through cinema-goers. 'It was as if a chilly draught from doomsday had passed through *Nosferatu*,' wrote the Hungarian critic Béla Balázs in 1924. Nor has the film dated: Murnau's fascination with the links between sex and disease are more topical than ever in the AIDS era. The director and his screenwriter Henrik Gaalen adhere closely to Stoker's original, but whereas most subsequent screen vampires are sleek, elegant and aristocratic, wear voluminous capes and have their hair swept back as if they're matinée idols, Nosferatu is verminous and evil, rats and flies following in his wake. Bat-eared, with his hands hanging like talons from his sides, he is the kind of figure that inhabits a child's nightmare. The film's full title, *Nosferatu, eine Symphonie des Grauens* (*Nosferatu, a Symphony of Horror*),

reveals something of Murnau's intentions. It differs from Robert Wiene's stylized *The Cabinet of Dr Caligari* (1919) or Lubitsch's films of the period in that it was not shot entirely in the studio. Murnau went out on location in his native Westphalia, where he was able to contrast the miasmatic, night-time world of Nosferatu with pastoral imagery of hills, clouds, trees and mountains. When hoodlums in film noir are seen hugging doorways or creeping up tenement staircases, the more they skulk, the more they evoke the image of Schreck's diabolic Nosferatu, bathed in shadow, sidling his way towards a new victim. Heavy chiaroscuro, oblique camera angles and jarring close-ups – the devices that crank up the tension in Val Lewton horror movies, and eerie, urban thrillers like *Double Indemnity* (1944) and *The Postman Always Rings Twice* (1946) – were all anticipated by Murnau's masterpiece.

CONNIE VEIDT GOES SLEEPWALKING

Whereas *Nosferatu* was shot on location, the other great German Expressionist horror film of the era, *The Cabinet of Dr Caligari* (1919), was entirely studio-based. It unfolds in a dreamlike world where all perspectives are distorted, every door is lopsided, and even the most commonplace objects assume a sinister significance. Just like the vampire in *Nosferatu*, the

above Conrad Veidt as the sleepwalker in the 1919 German Expressionist classic, *The Cabinet of Dr Caligari*.

opposite The brilliant Peter Lorre (1904–1964) brought both pathos and menace to his role as the child murderer in Fritz Lang's *M* (1931).

somnambulist Cesare (Conrad Veidt), is first seen emerging from a coffin. Pale-skinned, dressed in black, he is a carnival freak who can only be jolted out of his eternal sleep by the command of his master, the florid-faced, eminently sinister Dr Caligari (Werner Kraus).

Whereas Max Schreck's Nosferatu was malevolence incarnate, Veidt's Cesare is a more ambiguous figure. He looks like a tortured romantic artist, and his jerky, sleepwalking movements resemble those of Boris Karloff's monster in Universal's later Frankenstein films. In one key scene, when he is about to stab the heroine, he is so taken with her beauty that even in his Caligari-controlled trance, he stops himself. Such delicacy of feeling would never have got in the way of Nosferatu. The ending of *Caligari* is ambiguous. Carl Mayer's original screenplay portrayed the doctor as a symbol of corrupt, authoritarian post-World War I Germany. In the film that reached the screen, the unsatisfying coda implied that Caligari's skullduggery was all in the fervid imagination of Francis (Friedrich Feher), an inmate in a lunatic asylum. Caligari is the director of the asylum. 'At last I understand the nature of his madness. He thinks I am that mystic Caligari. Now I see how he can be brought back to sanity again,' the doctor remarks after Francis tries to assault him. But who should the audience trust – the authority figure or the madman? Depending on your point of view, Caligari is either a symbol of tyranny and dictatorship or an innocent doctor trying to look after a paranoid patient. Unsurprisingly, the Nazi regime later labelled the film 'degenerate' and banned it.

THE HUNTER HUNTED – PETER LORRE IN *M*

In Fritz Lang's *M* (1931), Peter Lorre plays a paedophile, Beckert, who preys on little girls in Berlin and murders them. He has assumed a near-mythical status and children even sing about him in their rhymes. There are posters offering a reward for his capture on every street corner. Lang makes the same heavy use of chiaroscuro as Murnau had in *Nosferatu*, and when Beckert approaches a young victim, we see her staring ingenuously up at him as his shadow falls over her. Both the police and the criminals are equally keen to flush the monster out – the former because their jobs depend on it, the latter because they know the authorities will not stop pestering them until he is behind bars. They hunt him down as if he is vermin, and a lynch mob mentality eventually takes hold. When an old man is seen talking to a child he is mistaken for the killer and the crowd sets upon him. A father walking his child to school is also attacked by the mob. The persecution of the innocent is a constant theme in Lang's work; it does not take very much, he implies, for decent, law-abiding citizens to turn into avenging furies.

When Lang finally reveals Beckert to us, he turns out to be a chubby-faced, doe-eyed man in a coat and felt hat. His voice is soft and he looks very, very frightened. After his capture, cowering in front of a kangaroo court, he seems more pathetic than evil. 'I can't help myself! I haven't any control over this evil thing that's inside me – the fire, the voices, the torment!' he whimpers. In *Nosferatu*, the vampire is evil and repugnant, while here Beckert, the child killer, is sick. The film exposes the hypocrisy of the vagrants and petty thieves who sit in judgement over him. His crimes may be heinous, but the real reason they want him gone is that he is bad for business.

THE BEASTS IN UNIVERSAL'S STABLE

Throughout the 1920s, the enterprising Universal boss Carl Laemmle went on talent-scouting trips to Europe. Among the luminaries he signed up were two key figures in German Expressionist cinema, Conrad Veidt and director Paul Leni. The former arrived in Hollywood in the mid-1920s, and the latter in 1927 to direct one of the first of the 'haunted house' horror films, *The Cat and the Canary*. Like Veidt, Leni was already a well-known figure in his native Germany, where he had worked as a painter and set designer on experimental theatre productions before creating such horror classics as *Backstairs* (1921) and *Wax Works* (1924).

In 1928, Leni cast Veidt in *The Man Who Laughs*, a Hollywood horror-pic with a distinctly European sheen, which anticipated all the Dracula, Wolfman and Frankenstein films that Universal would make a few years later. Adapted from a story by Victor Hugo, the film's protagonist is Gwynplaine, a man whose mouth is frozen into a permanent rictus of a smile thanks to the horrifying injuries he suffered as a child. Rarely has a smile seemed so grotesque. It is as much a stigma as the burns which scarred the antihero (Lon Chaney) in Universal's earlier *The Phantom of the Opera* (1925). Gwynplaine is a close cousin to Veidt's Cesare in Caligari – a kindly, sensitive soul who looks like a freak. As so often in the later Universal horror films, there is a maudlin undertow to the story. Gwynplaine falls in love with a pretty, demure blind girl (Mary Philbin), the only one not disgusted by the hero's rabidly grinning face.

BELA LUGOSI

Leni died in 1929 of blood poisoning, and was followed only a year later by Lon Chaney, who had been due to star in Universal's new film version of *Dracula*. Chaney's death from bronchial cancer paved the way for Bela Lugosi, who had played the vampire on Broadway, to make the transition to the big screen.

At first, the Universal executives were very wary about filming *Dracula*, feeling that such subject-matter was too 'European' and too 'morbid'. However, the studio had done well with its Paul Leni films, and the success of *Dracula* on stage suggested that there was an appetite for this kind of fare. In Tod Browning's movie version, Lugosi plays Dracula as unctuous and urbane, and he speaks in such a weirdly exotic accent that we know immediately he is not to be trusted. Unfortunately, time has diminished the film's impact, and after so many other screen Draculas, Lugosi's bloodsucker seems camp and slightly comic. Karl Freund's sweeping camerawork, the imaginative sound editing (constant creaks and scrapes) and the vast sets help stoke up the tension, but as soon as the peasants start crossing themselves and Van Helsing (Edward Van Sloan) blunders onto the scene, the sense of menace disappears. The studio itself realized how close Lugosi came to self-parody and in later years paired him with its most successful double-act of the 1940s, Abbott and Costello. In the drug-raddled twilight of his career he also worked with Ed Wood – something no actor who took his craft seriously would ever have done. Nevertheless, *Dracula* was a success for Lugosi, and after that Universal started cranking out horror pictures at an alarming rate.

THE BRIDE OF FRANKENSTEIN

Karloff may have been one of the most distinctive monsters in film history, but he is upstaged by his mate in James Whale's 1935 sequel to *Frankenstein*. 'Elsa Lanchester in her white shroud and Nefertiti hairdo is a truly fantastic apparition... a delicate suggestion of both the wedding bed and the grave,' wrote one reviewer after seeing her in *The Bride of Frankenstein*. English actress Lanchester (Charles Laughton's wife) was an inspired choice for the part: she is only on screen for a matter of minutes, but her impact is extraordinary. She looks like something that might have been dreamed up by British punk fashion designer Vivienne Westwood. Her shock of hair, which was held in place by a wired, horsehair cage, seems to grow straight upward, and there are bandages draped around her arms. Lanchester, who also plays a demure Mary Shelley in the film's prologue, claimed that her hissing, twitching and screaming were inspired by her memories of the swans in Regent's Park: 'They're really very nasty creatures!' Her eccentricity is matched by that of celebrated character actor Ernest Thesiger as the gin-quaffing mad scientist, Dr Septimus Pretorius, who exhorts Frankenstein to build his monster a mate.

SOME LESSER MONSTERS

If Dracula and Frankenstein movies were the behemoths in Universal's horror zoo, there were also various lesser beasts and ghouls in the studio pens. Predominant among these was The Mummy, the 3700-year-old bandage-swathed Egyptian corpse first played by Karloff in 1932, The Invisible Man, Claude Rains also wrapped up in bandages in a memorable H.G. Wells

opposite James Whale's *The Bride of Frankenstein* (1935),ranks as one of the best sequels in Hollywood history. Whale (right) is pictured here with Boris Karloff.

opposite bottom Lon Chaney Jr preys on Evelyn Ankers in George Waggner's *The Wolf Man* (1941). Make-up artist Jack P. Pierce used yak hair and a rubber snout to give Chaney his distinctive look.

below He may have had a voice like that of a Hungarian waiter, but for many Bela Lugosi (pictured here) remains the quintessential Dracula.

NUTS AND BOLTS AND KARLOFF

A strange transformation is wrought on the hero of Mary Shelley's 1818 novel, *Frankenstein*, in Universal's 1931 screen adaptation. The driven, arrogant scientist Victor is turned into a rather neurotic English ex-public schoolboy by the name of Henry (Colin Clive), who seems to have wandered out of the pages of P.G. Wodehouse. His enthusiasm for inventing is dismissed as an adolescent obsession. 'Why does he go messing around in an old, ruined windmill when he has a house, a bath, good food and drink, and a darned pretty girl to come back to?' blusters his tweedy old father when Henry disappears into his home-made laboratory. Nuts, bolts, brains and stolen corpses are the ingredients as Henry fashions his monster (Boris Karloff). English director James Whale steers a sure course between comedy and horror. The monster is at once a pathetic figure, craving friendship and warmth, and a malignant presence that must be destroyed at all costs.

adaptation of 1933, and The Wolfman, Lon Chaney Jr as the hale and hearty college boy who periodically turns into a hairy beast in the rip-roaring 1941 film.

THE LEWTON/TOURNEUR TOUCH

In Universal's horror films of the 1930s, the ghouls are always seen, and so how they looked was crucial. Boris Karloff used to have to endure four hours of torture at the hands of Universal's make-up wizard, Jack Pierce, before he was ready to go on camera as Frankenstein's monster, and to pad himself out he wore a double-quilted suit beneath his costume. Rival outfit RKO was much more circumspect. In the low-budget horror movies that Val Lewton produced at the studio during the 1940s, the emphasis was always on the psychological rather than the physical. Lewton was lucky to have Jacques Tourneur, a supremely talented director, working for him. Tourneur's filmmaking philosophy was the opposite of that espoused at Universal. 'The less you see, the more you believe,' he claimed.

The first Tourneur/Lewton collaboration, *Cat People* (1942), set the template for their movies together. The heroine, Irene (Simone Simon), has been put under an ancient Balkan curse. She believes that if she makes love to her architect husband, she will turn into a panther and kill him. To the psychiatrist, this seems like a straightforward neurosis: she is terrified of her own sexuality. She is also intensely jealous and begins to prey on the woman, Alice (Jane Randolph), she believes her husband is meeting behind her back. We never see the creature, but we are always aware of its presence. In one terrifying sequence, we see Alice walking alone at night down an empty street.

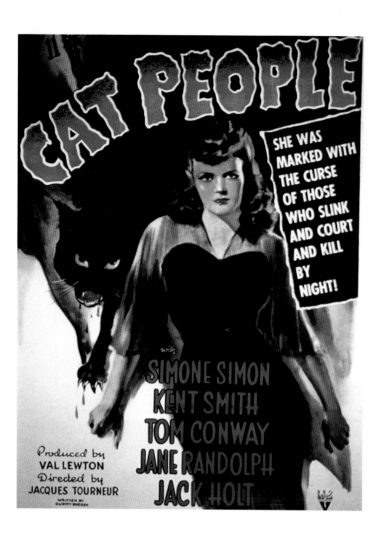

She is convinced that Irene is following her and keeps looking back. The trees billow. There are shadows on the walls beside her. When a bus eventually stops, the sound of its doors opening is like a cat's hiss. Even more effective is the sequence in which Alice is alone in a swimming pool. She sees a cat and then a shape on the stairs. Terrified, she dives into the pool. There are echoes. The walls are alive with rippling shadows. Her shrieks reverberate around the hall. Just as she expects to see the phantom, Irene turns up. We think that Alice has been hallucinating, but after clambering out of the pool she finds that her robe has been torn to shreds, apparently by a big cat's claws. Tourneur had both pragmatic and aesthetic reasons for not showing the monster. His budget did not extend to elaborate special effects. It was far wiser, he decided, to put audiences in the same position as Alice herself. She knows she is being stalked, but is not sure by what. A fear which cannot quite be described or defined is far more intense than one that can be explained away in the cold light of reason.

THE EUROPEAN/HOLLYWOOD NEXUS

The richness of Universal's horror films lies in their jarring collisions of influences. These were movies shot at Universal City, but often set in the backwaters of Eastern Europe. The mumbling, superstitious peasants with their garlic and crucifixes were played by the army of California extras who appeared in any roles going in Westerns and crime thrillers too; but many of the key protagonists, both behind and in front of the cameras, were Europeans. There were German writers and directors, notably Edgar Ulmer and Curt Siodmak, plenty of English – for instance, Lanchester, Whale, Karloff and Rains – and one or two Hungarians and Russians, among them Bela Lugosi and Maria Ouspenskaya.

The European influence was obvious in the nods towards Freud, the expressionistic sets, and the often almost impenetrable accents of the lead players, but these were, nevertheless, movies made along factory lines. Swathing the backlot in Transylvanian mist was a well-known way of saving money: if you could only see a quarter of the set through the gloom, that meant that the studio only needed to build a quarter of the set. Arguably, the greatest of the Universal horror pictures was one in which vampires, werewolves and monsters played no part – Edgar Ulmer's chilling 1934 film, *The Black Cat*, which brought Karloff and Lugosi together. Both are lost and gloomy souls, and we are made aware that there is bad blood between them – betrayals, murders, broken love affairs. Lugosi plays Dr Vitus Werdegast, an academic returning to his homeland in Carpathia after many years as a war prisoner, while Karloff is Poelzig, an architect with satanic leanings. As if to confound genre expectations, Poelzig lives not in a chilly, cavernous castle, but in a modernist, Art Deco palace which looks as if it was designed by Frank Lloyd Wright and furnished by Charles Rennie Mackintosh. For once, the kitsch, self-parodic humour that runs through so many other Universal horror films is kept at bay. This is one of the most creepy and unsettling movies made at the studio.

LEATHERFACE

'There isn't really that much blood in the film... probably about two ounces,' writer-director Tobe Hooper claimed of *The Texas Chainsaw Massacre* (1974), the low-budget horror classic which unleashed one of the most repulsive bogeymen since Schreck's Nosferatu. Whereas the vampire was emaciated, Leatherface (Gunnar Hansen) is big and well-built. He treats human beings in the same way butchers treat animals – they're there to be cut, chopped up, and hammered to death; frozen and then eaten.

Hooper was inspired to make *Texas Chainsaw* by the grisly yarns his Wisconsin relatives used to tell him about a killer who made human-skin lampshades and upholstery. It was only after the film was completed that he discovered that the killer these relatives were referring to was Ed Gein, the mother-fixated handyman whose pet hobby was digging up corpses. Gein has inspired countless other horror movies and is the link between films as different as *Psycho*, *Silence of the Lambs* and *Three on a Meat Hook*. He has been imagined in countless different ways, but Hooper was the first to arm him with a chainsaw. 'It's a film about meat,' Hooper claimed, 'about people who are now gone beyond dealing with animal meat and rats and dogs and cats. Crazy, retarded people going beyond the line between animal and human.' At times, it is quite repulsive – for example a grotesque sequence in which we see Leatherface, the grandfather, the 'naff-haired' hitch-hiker and the gas-station psycho sit down at table to eat their sausages in grotesque parody of an all-American family meal. Throughout, Hooper mixes the most lurid, Grand Guignol imagery with moments of great subtlety. Whether it is an armadillo upside down on the road, or a murky shot of cattle's heads, he makes the most incongruous scenes seem threatening. The film underlines the truth of Fritz Lang's assertion that what most scares modern-day audiences is the fear of physical pain caused by violence. Hooper is relatively restrained in the amount of bloodshed he shows, but what he implies is truly terrifying. Critic Alexander Walker called *The Texas Chainsaw Massacre* 'the purest of all horror films'. Ironically, that is what many had said of *Nosferatu* all those years before.

opposite Producer/director team Val Lewton and Jacques Tourneur fashioned the superb 1942 horror film *Cat People* from slender means. They relied on suspense and suggestion rather than blood-curdling make-up or special effects.

below left In William Friedkin's terrifying *The Exorcist* (1973), a perfectly normal, happy, healthy young girl (Linda Blair) is possessed by the devil.

below Leatherface brandishes his saw in Tobe Hooper's low-budget horror classic, *The Texas Chainsaw Massacre* (1974).

The Odessa Steps

Battleship Potemkin
1925

It all started as a history lesson. In 1925, the Soviet authorities decided to celebrate the 20th anniversary of the failed 1905 Revolution, one of the key staging posts in the march to overthrow the Tsar. They assigned the task of making a film about the Revolution to a certain Sergei Mikhailovich Eisenstein, an architect's son from Riga. Eisenstein was the coming man of Russian cinema. He had trained as an engineer and served in the Soviet army before embarking on a new career in the arts. He had already directed one feature, *Strike*, and, as a designer, had been responsible for some of the most adventurous stage sets in early Soviet theatre.

The tyro director and his co-screenwriter Nina Ferdinandovna Agadzhanova-Shutko set to work on the script. In its early drafts, it was a massive affair, encompassing everything from the Russo-Japanese War to the massacre of innocent bystanders by the Tsar's troops. The writers dealt with the mutiny of the sailors aboard the *Battleship Potemkin* only in passing. Given Eisenstein's genius for editing, it is fitting that he began to cut away at the project before it reached the cameras. He realized that the original idea was just too ambitious and his first attempts at shooting had been hampered by the weather and a clumsy, truculent cameraman. In the end, he decided to focus on just one episode – the *Potemkin* mutiny in Odessa. There were to be many

startling images in the film – the city at dawn shrouded by mist, the maggots in the meat, the stand-off between the sailors and their officers – but *Battleship Potemkin* is remembered above all for the massacre on the Odessa steps, probably the most famous sequence in film history. The sequence starts with the townsfolk, who are supporting the mutineers, fleeing the troops by running in panic down the Odessa steps. Many stumble. The white-jacketed troops open fire. A child is killed. Her mother gathers him up in her arms and marches back up the steps to confront the troops with the horror of what they have done. She too is shot. There are corpses littered all over the steps. The soldiers have no pity. They continue their remorseless march down the steps, opening fire as they go. Another mother, a beautiful young woman, is shot. She clutches her stomach and, as she does, the pram that she has been holding slowly teeters forward. As the wheels edge over one step, it gathers momentum and careers down the entire length of the staircase with the baby sitting bemused. These bloody events are dealt with in an extraordinarily poetic and subtle way. Eisenstein intercuts wide shots – in which it seems as if there are thousands fleeing the rifles – with close-ups detailing the particular anguish of individuals caught up in the maelstrom. The steps seem to go on forever. The shots of the pram careering out of control sum up the helplessness of the victims. They also

above A shot of a mother with a dead child from the famous Odessa Steps sequence in Sergei Eisenstein's *Battleship Potemkin* (1925).

right It has been the misfortune of Sergei Eisenstein (1898–1948) to be labelled a propagandist for the Soviet regime. Artist, filmmaker, prankster, designer, he was a far more complex and flamboyant figure than official histories suggest.

underline the brutality of the assailants – not even babies are safe. This is not continuity editing as understood by Hollywood, where telling the story is always paramount. The cutting has more to do with mood, emotion and symbolism than with narrative. 'This is Eisenstein's continuity,' noted Jean-Luc Godard, 'contrasting one form with another and in the same operation binding them indissolubly together. So the passage from medium shot to close-up becomes the passage from major to minor in music, for instance, or vice versa. Eisenstein is dance because, like it, he seeks within the heart of people and things the immobility within movement.'

THE JESTER

In photographs, Eisenstein, a shock-haired, chubby-cheeked little man in tweed jackets and bow ties, seems very different from the average Bolshevik *apparatchik*. One of his mentors was the flamboyant Futurist poet, painter and filmmaker, Vladimir Mayakovsky, who wrote verse with titles like *A Slap in the Face of Public Taste* before embracing the Revolution with an idiosyncratic fervour which surprised even Lenin. Eisenstein's autobiography is playful and anecdotal, full of entertaining yarns about his encounters with Cocteau in Paris, and Disney and Chaplin in Hollywood. He used to tease Chaplin about his lack of a sense of humour. He loved limericks and dirty jokes, and had a nice line in obscene drawings. When he was on location in Mexico shooting the one film he made outside Russia, *Que Viva Mexico*, the American customs authorities were scandalized by one of his cartoons he had sent in a trunk from Mexico to Hollywood (which they confiscated). It showed Jesus hanging from the Cross with his penis elongated into a hose. One of the two thieves, crucified beside him, has the end of the hose in his mouth. Such frivolity did not endear him any more to the Soviet authorities than to their American counterparts. Under Stalin, even Eisenstein had to learn to conform. He was forced to grovel to the regime after the suppression of his 1936 film, *Brezhin Meadow*, just to ensure that he could keep on working. 'My error is rooted in a deeply intellectual, individualist illusion,' he confessed, 'In recent years I have become self-absorbed.' He describes the film as catastrophic and politically bankrupt. This was self-laceration taken to extremes. Equally debasing were his later, fawning remarks about Stalin. 'Thanks to the wisdom and foresight of the Soviet government and Comrade Stalin,' he crows in 1941, 'our Union is the only place in the world where the artist can create in peace, where the builder can build in peace, and the inventor can solve his problems in peace.' Under Stalin, the cultural doctrine of Socialist Realism had been introduced, affecting all branches of the arts. Poets like Mayakovsky were encouraged to write verse about heroic tractor drivers, and any flight of fancy or experimentalism was regarded with grave misgivings. The flowering of art and filmmaking during the first years of the Soviet Union was quickly forgotten.

THE IMPORTANCE OF THE KETTLE

Many commentators have been puzzled as to the precise origins of Eisenstein's theory of montage. A kettle, he argued in his 1942 essay, 'Dickens, Griffith and Ourselves', is the answer to the riddle: keep your eye on it long enough and the connections between Charles Dickens, melodrama, the films of D.W. Griffith and Eisenstein's editing techniques will become apparent through the steam. The kettle he is referring to is to be found in the opening line of Dickens's story, *The Cricket on the Hearth*, and the reason he is getting so heated up about it is that he regards it as the literary equivalent of a close-up. 'Once you see this kettle as a typical close-up, you exclaim: why didn't I spot that before? It's just like Griffith! I've seen close-ups like that at the start of so many episodes and scenes in his work.'

Even as a child, Eisenstein thought in cinematic terms. His first memory, he states in his autobiography *Beyond the Stars*, was a close-up 'of a branch of cherry or lilac coming in through the window of the nursery'. He saw the close-up as the equivalent of synecdoche in poetry: concentrate on the specific detail, and you can bring the big picture into focus. If Dickens influenced Griffith, Griffith influenced all the early Soviet filmmakers (and not just Eisenstein) in equal measure. They pored over every frame of *Intolerance*, and were soon galvanized into developing their own theories of editing. They were far more playful and experimental than their image as austere Soviet artists might lead us to believe.

THE KULESHOV EFFECT

In 1923, Eisenstein had attended a film workshop held by Lev Kuleshov, the most innovative teacher of the era. Like Eisenstein, Kuleshov was a disciple of Griffith. One of the reasons he and his students put so much emphasis on editing was that they had precious little film stock. The country was still impoverished, and there were blockades. Rather than making 'new' films, Kuleshov therefore undertook experiments with the few movies that he had access to: he and his students used to play around with these films, rearranging them to see what kind of different meanings could be given to them. They drew up editing schemes on paper for films they hoped they would one day be able to make. The most famous of Kuleshov's many experiments featured the actor, Ivan Mozhukhin. Kuleshov alternated the same master shot of the actor staring blankly into camera with various other images: a bowl of soup, a dead woman in a coffin and a child playing. Audiences read different emotions in Mozhukhin's face depending on what was juxtaposed with it. The soup led them to think that he was hungry, the coffin that he was sad, and the child that he was happy. The audiences also claimed to be highly impressed by Mozhukhin's acting and his ability to project all these different emotions. Kuleshov and one of his best students Vsevolod Pudovkin went on to work together on a bizarre comedy, *The Extraordinary Adventures of Mr West in the Land of the Bolsheviks* (1924). In it, American businessman Mr West (dressed up to look like a cross between a carpetbagger and a cowboy) roams around the Soviet Union. At first, he is censorious about what he sees, but once he meets the locals (and is subjected to a few of Kuleshov's trademark editing tricks), he begins to warm to the country. The real surprise about the film is how light-hearted it is – like a Mack Sennett Keystone comedy, done Soviet-style.

PUDOVKIN'S *MOTHER* – THE ICE FLOE

Like *Battleship Potemkin*, Pudovkin's *Mother* (1926) is set in 1905. Adapted from Maxim Gorky's story about a family split apart during a strike, it combines melodrama with revolutionary politics. The son is thrown into prison for joining

below Eisenstein made *October/Ten Days That Shook The World* (1927) to mark the 10th anniversary of the Russian Revolution.

the strike. His father is a blackleg, bribed by the bosses. His mother, a simple, working-class woman, slowly becomes politicized as she sees what is happening around her.

Throughout the film, Pudovkin puts Kuleshov's teachings into practice. This is not a film where the actors have to contort their faces to signify grief or joy. The editing does this for them. Pudovkin uses images from the natural world to delineate emotion. When the son is happy, Pudovkin cuts to images of bubbling brooks and of radiant sunlight. During the spectacular finale, he keeps on showing the ice on the river flowing forwards. The symbolism may be obvious but it is effective: the workers' march on the prison is as inexorable as the flow of the river. In scenes reminiscent of D.W. Griffith's *Way Down East*, we see the son, escaped from prison, trying to run to safety across the ice. He is reunited briefly with his mother, who has joined the workers, but although he dies in front of her, the tide of revolution cannot be turned. *Mother* uses every trick imaginable: oppressive guards are filmed from below to make them seem intimidating, while prisoners are filmed from above. Pudovkin is as keen on close-ups as Eisenstein. He continually frames the bosses and their lackeys from oblique, unflattering angles to reveal their vanity and stupidity.

HITCHCOCK AND THE RUSSIANS

It is difficult to assess just how influential Soviet theories of montage were on filmmakers in the West. In Hollywood, cinema remained a narrative medium. Editing was used primarily to help storytelling, not as an expressive tool in its own right. After the introduction of talkies, Soviet ideas about editing no longer seemed so relevant. Nevertheless, Pudovkin, Eisenstein, Kuleshov and others did have a direct influence on certain filmmakers. The pram sequence from *Battleship Potemkin* has been imitated or referenced many times, for instance in Brian De Palma's *The Untouchables*, Terry Gilliam's *Brazil* and Woody Allen's *Bananas*. Screen acting gradually became more and more understated, but whether this is directly attributable to the example set by Pudovkin and Kuleshov is a moot point.

Certain European and American filmmakers did acknowledge their debt to the Russians, most notably Alfred Hitchcock. During the 1920s, Pudovkin's and Eisenstein's films were shown privately at the Film Society in London (the censors would not allow them to go on public exhibition). Hitchcock was among the most enthusiastic members of the Society, which had been founded in 1925 to showcase experimental and foreign-language films, and he was especially taken with Pudovkin's work. As historian Philip Kemp has noted, many of his later pronouncements on cinema sound very similar to those made by the Russian.

'The screen ought to speak its own language, freshly coined, and it can't do that unless it treats an acted scene as a piece of raw material which must be broken up, taken to bits...' **(Hitchcock)**

'Film art does not begin when the artists act and the various scenes are shot... film art begins from the moment when the director begins to combine and join the various pieces of film.' **(Pudovkin)**

opposite Nikolai Cherkassov (1903–1966), one of the great actors of Soviet cinema, looking like the big, bad wolf in the title role of Eisenstein's *Ivan The Terrible Part II* (1946).

below James Stewart in Alfred Hitchcock's *Rear Window* (1954). Hitchcock, who had seen the work of Eisenstein and Pudovkin in the 1920s, freely admitted that their ideas about montage were a big influence on him.

Take any well-known Hitchcock film (not including *Rope*) and you are likely to find scenes edited in accordance with Soviet principles. The montage sequence showing Cary Grant fleeing from the crop-dusting plane in *North By Northwest* or the one in *Rear Window*, in which James Stewart stares helpless at a killer across the street, are perfect examples.

EISENSTEIN AND THE BIG BAD WOLF

Eisenstein loved to draw. He had been to Hollywood and had met Disney. In his final film, *Ivan the Terrible* (1944–1946), occasional hints of the debt to Disney shine through. With its score by Prokofiev, stylized performances, and emphasis on the rituals of court in 16th-century Russia, the film unfolds in operatic fashion. For once, the editing between images is less important than the baroque images themselves. Ivan, 'the man who united Russia in the 16th century', as he is described, is an ambivalent figure, at once heroic and terrifying. Celebrated actor Nikolai Cherkassov plays him in febrile fashion, hinting at his weaknesses and fears as well as showing his iron will. In the film's most distinctive image, he is shown during his exile standing in profile in an icy mountain cave. Beneath him is a vast column of his supporters. They have come to beg him to return to court. Dressed in fur, with his gaunt, thin face and long straggly beard, he looks like a very close relative of one of the Disney characters Eisenstein must have encountered during his trip to Hollywood – the big, bad wolf.

Sound

'Who the hell wants to hear actors talk!' (**Harry Warner, not long before the release of** *The Jazz Singer* **in 1927**.)

A FALSE START

Although there was a drive to equip American cinemas with state-of-the-art sound systems in the mid-1920s, it was all about bringing music – and not talk – to the masses. Nobody at this stage cared about dialogue, but Warner Bros wanted to compete with the MGMs and Paramounts of Hollywood and believed that sound might enable them to do so. They were lagging behind the bigger studios, which owned luxurious picture palaces where real-life orchestras could play; most of the Warner theatres, on the other hand, were smaller and more modest in scale.

The technology for sound was hardly new: Thomas Edison was trying to marry sound and image as early as the 1890s and Iowa-born inventor Lee de Forest (1873–1961) had been experimenting with talking films for years. De Forest had made several short talkies in the early 1920s, but Phonofilm, his pet system, suffered from diabolical audio quality. The sound was so muffled that his most important patron, producer William Fox, lost faith in him and had the sound equipment taken out of his theatres.

In 1926, Warner Bros formed a subsidiary, Vitaphone, with Western Electric, to take advantage of a new sound-on-disc system developed for the cinema. The technology was inherently faulty: the sound was recorded onto a disc, not onto the film itself, and there was always the chance that sound and image might fall out of sync. Warner Bros' original intention was to use the new system to record music and sound effects, not dialogue. 'Do you realize what this means? From now on we can give every small town in America, and every movie house, its own 110-piece orchestra,' Harry Warner enthused.

The first Vitaphone film was *Don Juan*, a prestige production released in the autumn of 1926 and starring John Barrymore, one of the leading movie actors of the era. It was shown at Warners' best cinemas and ticket prices were hiked up to remind customers that this was a special treat. There was no talking, only music and sound effects. *Don Juan* did well, but without breaking box-office records – a worry for a studio that had already committed a small fortune to converting its cinemas to sound.

WAIT A MINUTE – YOU AIN'T HEARD NOTHIN' YET

Sound was an expensive business. Warner Bros invested over $3 million in equipping its theatres to show Vitaphone movies – and posted big losses in

above This Vitaphone studio has been adapted to produce the first sound pictures. Note the amount of cumbersome equipment.

DISC ERROR – SOME TEETHING PROBLEMS

Vitaphone's method of recording sound on a separate disc did have its advantages, as well as its flaws. Filmmakers were able to cut between scenes in a fluid way, whereas recording directly onto film posed far more problems. Primitive sound-on-film techniques required the sound to be recorded onto the negative several frames ahead of the picture, and that made cutting all but impossible – one of the reasons that so many of the early talkies were static. The drawback with Vitaphone was that it was well-nigh impossible to stop a scene to shoot from a different angle without ruining the recording. The only solution – an expensive one – was to shoot with several cameras at once. By 1931, sound-on-film systems had finally become reliable, and sound-on-disc began to seem risky and old-fashioned. Warner Bros therefore abandoned Vitaphone as an unsafe bet in the same year.

1925 and 1926. Nevertheless, it is a myth that the studio was teetering on the edge of bankruptcy before rescuing itself with *The Jazz Singer* (1927). The brothers and their Wall Street backers had accepted that converting to sound would result in short-term debt.

The Jazz Singer was adapted for the screen from Samson Raphaelson's hit play, a cornball yarn about the son of a Jewish cantor who, rather than sing in the synagogue as his father demands, wants to ply his trade on the stage. After George Jessel, who had played the role on Broadway, and Eddie Cantor had turned it down, the part was eventually offered to Al Jolson. Given that Jolson's own father was a cantor and that he had sung in a synagogue as a child himself, he was ideal casting. Nor was he new to sound. He had already performed a few songs in *April Showers* (1926), an experimental Warner Bros Vitaphone short.

Warners had very high hopes for *The Jazz Singer*, which, with a budget of $500,000, was the most expensive film in the studio's history. On 6 October 1927, it premièred at Warners' Theatre in New York City. The songs, as the studio executives had predicted, were ecstatically received, and the film as a whole was a huge hit. The surprise was that audiences warmed to more than just the music. They also relished the few snatches of dialogue – the cantor's father (Warner Oland) yelling 'Stop!' when Jolson breaks into a jazz number while on a visit home, and Jolson's trademark, improvised introductions to his songs. 'Wait a minute, wait a minute – you ain't heard nothin' yet,' he prophetically announced before one of his ditties.

Jolson is so inextricably linked with the success of *The Jazz Singer* that it is impossible to guess whether or not the film would have worked without him. Nobody minded about his poor acting – that was never the point. In *The Jazz Singer*, he put across his songs – including the ludicrously mawkish 'Mammy' – with such élan that audiences were bowled over. It is overstating it to suggest that he single-handedly ushered in the talkies, but without him to galvanize the other studios, the new technology would have taken longer to catch hold. *The Jazz Singer* grossed a remarkable $3,000,000 and Warners' first all-out talkie, *Lights of New York*, released in 1928, cost a fraction of the price to make and did almost as well. Warners' rivals belatedly realized that talking pictures could not be ignored.

ANNA CHRISTIE

'Gimme a viskey, ginger ale on the side and don't be stingy,' a strange-looking floozy in a waterfront bar intoned in a gruff, European accent. It was hard to tell what was more surprising – the role or the voice. In *Anna Christie* (1929), her first talkie, Greta Garbo was playing a bedraggled, hard-drinking ex-prostitute, and the audiences loved her throaty voice. Generally, MGM displayed Garbo as if she were the prize good in the shop window, but here she was slumming it. The primitive sound technology complements what was one of her earthiest, least characteristic performances. 'GARBO TALKS!' shrieked the posters and whether or not she did it well was immaterial; what mattered was that she did at all. The film became a huge hit and was acclaimed by critics for its gritty realism.

below 'Give me a viskey, ginger ale on the side.' Greta Garbo as the drunken floozy in *Anna Christie* (1930), her first talkie.

right Hitchcock (pictured with the book on his lap) makes his customary cameo in *Blackmail* (1929), the first British talkie.

BLIMPS AND BLIPS

The transition to sound was not quite as difficult as myth suggests, and the notion that Hollywood gave up on what it had learned over two decades of making silent movies and started again from scratch is absurd. Cutting remained central to the way the studios made films; they didn't just place the camera in front of the actors and record. To get around the limitations placed upon them by noisy, unwieldy equipment, filmmakers used more than just one camera.

During the early talkie era, films were still made using awkward, highly dangerous carbon arc lights that gave off a whistling noise that the microphone could pick up. Filmmakers now had to go to extraordinary lengths to soundproof the sets and the studios therefore had to invest in expensive, less noisy, new equipment. The cameras, too, made a din and had to be housed in soundproof booths. Engineers quickly designed blimps (soundproof covers) which allowed the camera to be liberated from the booths. Squeak- and creak-proof tracks were introduced on which the camera could be mounted and moved.

HITCHCOCK'S *BLACKMAIL*

The most famous early British talkie was made on the sly, by the mischievous young sorcerer's apprentice, Alfred Hitchcock, at Elstree Studios in 1929. 'See & Hear it,' proclaimed the trade poster. 'Our mother tongue as it should be – SPOKEN! 100% Talkie. 100% Entertainment. Hold everything till you've heard this one!'

Blackmail was based on a hit West End play by Charles Bennett, a regular collaborator with Hitchcock. The backers, British International Pictures (BIP) were under the impression that Hitchcock was shooting a silent film that would have some sound sequences in it. 'I suspected the producers might change their minds and eventually want an all-sound picture. I worked it out that way,' the director later told François Truffaut. 'We utilized the technique of talkies, but without sound. Then, when the picture was complete, I raised objections to the part-sound version and they gave me carte blanche to shoot some of the scenes over.' Many critics considered dialogue simply as a novelty – and one which would not last. 'Every now and then the human voice helps the pictorial action,' one reviewer wrote of *Blackmail*. 'For the most part it is merely a delaying, harsh, unmusical and often ridiculous force.'

Hitchcock, of course, was interested in much more than just recording people's voices. For him, sound was an expressionistic tool, as important as production design, cinematography or lighting, and right from the outset he used it inventively. He dubbed the voice of the heroine, the Polish-born Anny Ondra, who plays a working-class Englishwoman who kills a man after he tries to rape her. This was partly because of necessity – Ondra's heavy Eastern European accent would have seemed wildly incongruous in a London-set crime thriller – but the director also wanted to show off his mastery of sound and to prove that he was a consummate magician, able to conjure up voices and effects.

In one famous sequence, not long after Ondra has stabbed to death her assailant, she is at breakfast with her parents next to the shop they run. She hears a customer talking about the killing. The customer keeps on using the word 'knife'. The sound gradually becomes amplified. She is asked to cut some bread but by now she is frantic. All she can hear is 'knife! knife! knife!'. She is so traumatized that she suddenly flings the knife away. Her parents, who have been chattering away like humming birds, are utterly bewildered.

FLESH AND THE DEVIL

The most high-profile casualty of the early talkie era was John Gilbert. Whether it was his voice which destroyed his career, or his self-destructive behaviour, or a feud with MGM boss Louis B. Mayer, remains a matter of contention among film historians. But no one disputes that Gilbert, born in Utah in 1897, was one of the great matinée idols of the silent era. He was handsome, dashing, charismatic, and by the time Irving Thalberg put him under contract at MGM in the mid-1920s he was already a veteran of dozens of movies, some of which he had starred in, some of which he had even written. His new bosses regarded him as the natural successor to Valentino and groomed him accordingly.

His greatest hit was in King Vidor's wartime melodrama, *The Big Parade* (1925), which saw him doing his patriotic bit for Uncle Sam in World War I Europe. He registered strongly opposite Lillian Gish in *La Bohème* (1925), and as a rakish aristocrat opposite Mae Murray in *The Merry Widow* (also 1925). The following year he was cast for the first time with Greta Garbo in the deliriously overcooked melodrama, *Flesh and the Devil*. She was the *femme fatale*, he was her prey – the handsome military man who fights duels with not one but two of her cuckolded husbands. The main interest for the public – something which MGM hyped to the hilt – was the rumour of an affair between the two stars. They appeared together again a few months later in an adaptation of *Anna Karenina* which the studio publicists decided to call simply *Love*. This meant that they could plaster 'Garbo and Gilbert in Love' on the posters and theatre fronts without anyone complaining that they were exploiting their stars' private lives.

In 1929, Gilbert made his first full-length sound film, *His Glorious Night*, following a brief talkie sequence in *The Hollywood Revue of 1929*. But whereas fans had adored Garbo despite her bizarrely throaty, European accent in *Anna Christie*, they had no time for Gilbert and *His Glorious Night* flopped ignominiously. There were rumours that his voice had been sabotaged and that the studio had failed to market the film properly.

Gilbert, it is frequently pointed out, had a perfectly pleasant speaking voice, but he was in an invidious position. Audiences accustomed to seeing him playing dashing officers and seducers could not help being disappointed when he opened his mouth and spoke in a light baritone. He sounded like any other American actor, and his aura was lost. As his career went into decline, at least Garbo stayed loyal to him and she insisted that he was cast in the male lead, Don Antonio, in *Queen Christina* (1933). Young British actor Laurence Olivier, who had been lined up to play the Don, was dropped from the production because Garbo refused to accept anyone else except her old co-star. There was still a spark between her and Gilbert: he was her perfect foil and she gave one of her greatest performances as the 17th-century Swedish queen. The role did nothing to help his career, though, and after years of heavy drinking, he died of a heart attack in 1936.

below The brief talking sequence in *Hollywood Revue of 1929* (below), was a precursor to Gilbert's first full-length sound film *His Glorious Night* (1929) which flopped at the box office.

above Thanks to his mellifluous voice, English matinée idol Ronald Colman (seen here for once without his trademark moustache, opposite the much more smartly dressed Donald Woods in the 1935 *Tale Of Two Cities*) enjoyed a new lease of life in the talkie era.

opposite Charlie Chaplin and Paulette Goddard walk off into the horizon in *Modern Times* (1936), a movie which he insisted on shooting as a silent.

MARION DAVIES – THE STAMMERING STAR

There were many reasons why stars' careers stalled at the beginning of the talkie era. Mabel Poulton, one of the best-known British actresses of the late 1920s, was a victim of the inveterate snobbery that characterized the British film industry of that time. 'She had the face of a lovely flower, but a cockney accent which no amount of elocution lessons would eradicate,' remembered her contemporary, Chilli Bouchier. Outside broad comedy roles, British screen actors were not allowed to have regional accents.

The career of ex-showgirl Marion Davies might have gone the same way as Poulton's, if it had not been for the money and influence of her lover, the newspaper magnate, William Randolph Hearst. Davies' problem was that she had a slight stammer. MGM overcame this by casting her in *Marianne* (1929), a musical in which she played a Frenchwoman who could only speak in broken English. The stammer, therefore, seemed completely in keeping with her role.

Davies was as popular in Hollywood as the notorious Hearst was disliked. It was her misfortune that Orson Welles' 1941 masterpiece, *Citizen Kane*, is so barbed at Hearst's expense. In the movie, Welles suggests that Kane – all too obviously based on Hearst – used his influence to further his mistress's career. Susan (Dorothy Coningmore), the Davies character, is conspicuously without talent and she shrieks rather than sings. At the beginning of the film, we hear Kane, close to death, whisper the word 'rosebud'. It is revealed much later in the film that this was the name of a sledge that Kane had had as a child. But the other explanation often advanced is that 'rosebud' was Hearst's private nickname for Marion Davies' clitoris, and if so it is little wonder that Hearst tried so hard to suppress the film.

Davies was clearly more talented than Susan in the film, but Hearst controlled her career in exactly the way that Welles suggested. She was a popular enough comedienne, but not even Hearst could convince the American public to take her seriously in straight roles. In a fit of pique, when Irving Thalberg passed her over for the lead part in *The Barretts of Wimpole Street*, Hearst took Davies from MGM to Warner Bros. It is a measure of his influence that she was immediately given a contract, but she was no more successful there than she had been at Metro.

IT'S A FAR, FAR BETTER THING I DO...

Fawning on classically trained stage actors was nothing new. Long before the talkies, both British and American producers had offered theatrical luminaries vast fortunes to appear in front of the cameras. Obviously, talkies made these thespians that much more employable, and one to benefit from the coming of sound was English actor Ronald Colman (1891–1958). A conspicuous failure in British films after World War I, he had enjoyed a fair measure of success in Hollywood silent melodramas, often playing dashing leads opposite Hungarian-born Vilma Banky's *femmes fatales*. In the talkie era, although he was already close to 40, his career blossomed anew. His sonorous, slightly gloomy voice made him ideal casting as a world-weary roué in *A Tale of Two Cities*, an amnesiac, upper-class army officer in *Random Harvest* and the jaded diplomat in search of his own pet Shangri-La in *Lost Horizon*.

Colman was one of a handful of mellifluous-voiced British actors to cut a swathe through 1930s Hollywood. Others who appeared in studio movies in the early talkie era include Basil Rathbone (1892–1967), the best-known screen Sherlock Holmes, Charles Laughton (1899–1962), who won an Oscar in 1933 for his outrageously hammy turn as the Tudor king in Alexander Korda's production of *The Private Life of Henry VIII*, C. Aubrey-Smith (1863–1948), the ex-England cricketer who excelled at playing gentlemanly patriarchs, and the ethereal Leslie Howard (1893–1943), who played Ashley Wilkes in *Gone with the Wind*.

MODERN TIMES

Charles Chaplin viewed talkies as 'spoiling the oldest art in the world – the art of pantomime. They are ruining the great beauty of silence.' His *Modern Times* (1936) could be regarded as the last, great silent movie, although it was not a silent film as such: it has a soundtrack full of burps, rumbles and comic noises. At one stage, Chaplin (as a performing waiter) even breaks into song – but the words that come out of his mouth are absolute gibberish.

The symbolism of this film is obvious: Chaplin's factory is a soulless, dehumanizing place and once the machinery begins to belch and rumble, he is sucked up into its bowels. His mindlessly repetitive job is to tighten bolts, and the production line is extended to his lunch break, when he is fed by a huge contraption that hurls food at him and then dabs at his mouth with a giant napkin.

Paradoxically, although Chaplin relied on technology as much as any other filmmaker, in *Modern Times* he seemed to be blaming the modern world for all the ills of the Depression. His rage against the machine was not just an expression of his dissatisfaction with talkies, but against mass production in general. As he put it: 'Machinery should benefit mankind. It should not spell tragedy and throw it out of work. Something is wrong. Things have been badly managed if five million men are out of work in the richest country in the world.' In making *Modern Times*, you half guess that Chaplin was trying to remind cinema-goers of what they were losing with the coming of the talkies. Film historians have gone to great lengths to prove that talkies were just as fluidly shot and just as reliant on editing as the silent films which had preceded them. Nevertheless, something hard to pinpoint was lost. Silent movies had an aura, a universality, and an exoticism which the prosaic, earthbound talkies simply could not match.

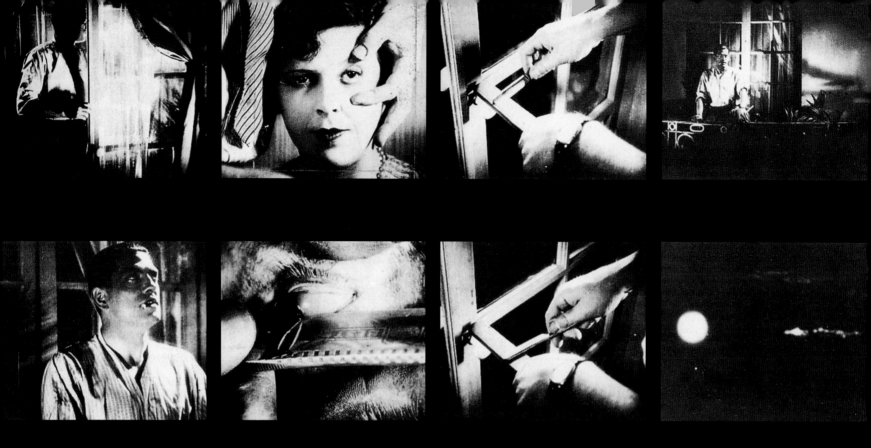

The Surreal & the Avant-garde

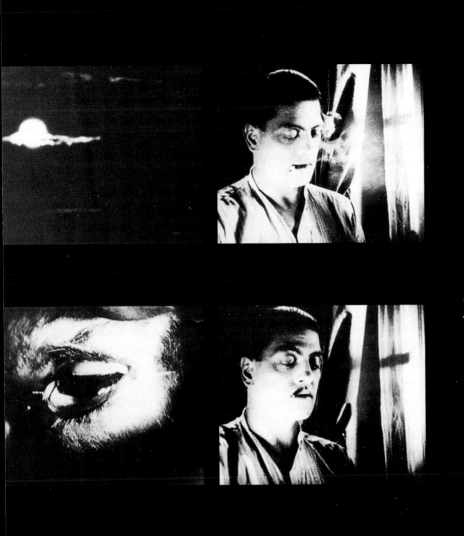

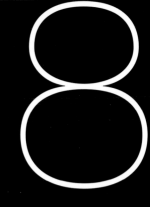

Un Chien Andalou
1928

Apart from his cherished dry martinis – whose concoction he likened to the Immaculate Conception – Luis Buñuel's greatest passion in life was dreaming. 'Give me two hours a day of activity, and I'll take the other 22 in dreams – provided I can remember them,' the Spanish director (1900–1983) once remarked.

It is not surprising, then, that Buñuel's first film, the Surrealist classic *Un Chien Andalou* (1928), financed with money from his mother and co-directed with artist Salvador Dalí, had its roots in a dream, in which 'a long, tapering cloud sliced the moon in half, like a razor blade slicing through an eye'. He confided the details of the dream to Dalí, who responded by describing his own dream of the previous night in which he had seen 'a hand crawling with ants'.

Buñuel and Dalí improvised *Un Chien Andalou* around these two images. 'Our only rule was very simple,' Buñuel confides in his autobiography *My Last Breath*. 'No idea or image that might lend itself to a rational explanation of any kind would be accepted. We had to open all doors to the irrational and keep only those images that surprised us, without trying to explain why.'

Predictably, Dalí claimed that all the best ideas were his. This, he said, was 'a film of adolescence and death', which he was going to 'plunge right into the heart of witty, elegant and intellectualized Paris, with all the reality and all the weight of the Iberian dagger whose holt is made of the blood-red and petrified soil of our prehistory, and whose blade is made of the inquisatorial flames of the Holy Catholic Inquisition mingled with the canticles of turgescent and red-hot steel of the resurrection of the flesh'.

This may be boasting, but *Chien Andalou* does have one of the most arresting openings in all films. To the accompaniment of stirring tango music (hand cranked on a record player behind the screen by Buñuel at the very first screening in Paris) a man sharpens a razor. There is a close-up of a woman's face. A cloud crosses the moon. The man takes his razor to the woman's eye. Eventually, we see her eyeball slit with blood and yolky fluid oozing out. Buñuel used a calf's eye for this now notorious shot.

AN APPEAL TO MURDER

Although the film dispenses with conventional narrative, it has a warped, dreamlike logic all of its own. Heavy on symbolism, it has been interpreted in myriad different ways by critics: they see it either as the perfect film for the age of Freud (who was also obsessed with dreams), as a savage anti-bourgeois satire, as a valuable record of decadent, bohemian 1920s Paris, or as a modernist in-joke. Whatever else, *Chien Andalou* proved that filmmakers did not have to subject themselves to the tyranny of plot, character and causality. Cinema could also be surreal, playful, provocative or – as Buñuel would put it – 'a desperate and passionate appeal to murder'.

The director attended the first screening armed with stones in his pockets in case matters became riotous. In the event, the film went off without a hitch, but its successor, *L'Age d'Or* (1930) provoked a rather more heated response. The Anti-Semitic League and The League of Patriots infiltrated the screening – at which many Surrealists were present – and attacked spectators, let off stink bombs, and even threw ink at the screen. Buñuel seems to have enjoyed this response enormously.

MESHES OF THE AFTERNOON

Maya Deren's *Meshes of the Afternoon* (1943) uses jump cuts, slow motion and haunting poetic symbolism to create a mood both dreamlike and deeply unsettling. The picture unfolds in what seems to be a typical Californian house. The very familiarity of the setting makes the film seem that much more sinister. Everyday objects – a key, a kitchen knife, a mirror, a flower – suddenly begin to seem threatening. As in a dream, there is no dialogue. The heroine of the film (played by Deren herself) is seen walking up a staircase, like a figure in a trance.

Deren (1917–1961), who was born Eleanora Derenkowsky, left her homeland Russia as a child when her family fled to escape anti-Jewish persecution. She chose the new name 'Maya', meaning 'illusion' in Hindu philosophy, at the time she made *Meshes of the Afternoon*. A theorist as well as a filmmaker, she liked to boast that her movies cost less than Hollywood spent on lipstick. A key figure in the New York intellectual world of the late 1940s, she distributed and promoted independent films as well as making them. None of her subsequent work matched *Meshes of the Afternoon*, an instant classic of avant-garde filmmaking. Later in her career, she became obsessed with Haitian culture – dance and voodoo in particular. The footage she shot on the island was later edited into the film, *Divine Horsemen: the Living Gods of Haiti* (1947–1951). This is a superb documentary, lyrical and brutal by turns, and in its way, every bit as unsettling as *Meshes of the Afternoon*.

MOTHLIGHT

Whoever said that you needed cameras to make films? In *Mothlight* (1963), Stan Brakhage glued tiny pieces of leaf, moth wings, and crystals onto translucent tape which he projected through an optical printer. That was only one of his many ruses as he attempted to escape the tyranny of mainstream cinema. He would spit on or hand-paint the film, scratch the lens, or do anything else he could think of to make the eye see in a new way. He has sometimes shot on Super-8 (most commonly used for home movies) and at other times has used 70mm IMAX, the ultimate blockbuster format. The problem, as he sees it, is that audiences do not question or reflect on what is in front of their noses. 'Most people can't see,' he once proclaimed. 'Children can – they have a much wider range of visual awareness – because their eyes haven't been tutored to death by man-made laws of perspective or compositional logic.'

opposite right A bourgeois woman basking in the Mediterranean sun in Jean Vigo's playful, satirical *A Propos De Nice* (1930).

opposite left Stan Brakhage's *Mothlight* (1963), a film made without a camera.

below A haunting still from Maya Deren's avant-garde classic, *Meshes of the Afternoon* (1943).

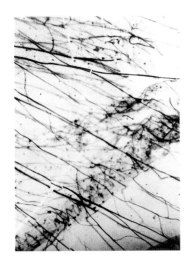

Brakhage was born in Kansas in 1933. He grew up in Denver, where he made his first film, *Interim*, when still a teenager. In his early 20s, he went 'on the road', roaming all over the US, 'making films in such diverse places as Colorado ghost towns and the Lower East Side of New York'. In the late 1950s, he made his permanent base in an old cabin in the mountains of Colorado and since then he has shot, improvised or patched together well over 300 films. 'Regardless of how you count,' author Paul Arthur comments of him, 'he has doubtless pieced together more images than anyone in the history of the medium.' He has made films about birth, sex, and religion; he has made documentaries, studies of landscapes and lyrical meditations on his own life, films about journeys round the world and about trips to town.

Do not expect Brakhage's work to share the pristine (but in his eyes ersatz) clarity of the typical studio film. 'People for years attacked the variety of focus in my films,' he told fellow filmmaker Jonas Mekas. 'At some point, I said, "look, we are trained to pay conscious attention to what we are focused upon. But just try for an instant to pay attention to what you are not focused upon. And suddenly, if one really consciously does that, it's perfectly obvious that most of your seeing is unfocused.'

A PROPOS DE NICE

Tourists, ancient monuments, elegant women on wicker chairs (with or without their clothes), cars, gamblers, old women with umbrellas, gypsies, beggars, street cleaners, cripples – these are all images that appear in *A Propos De Nice*, the Surrealist documentary shot in 1929 by young avant-garde filmmaker Jean Vigo. He and his cameraman Boris Kaufman prowled the streets of the French resort town with a hidden camera, capturing it in its full opulence and vulgarity. 'A city, a way of life is put on trial,' he said after a screening in Paris. 'As soon as the atmosphere of Nice and the kind of life lived there… has been suggested, the film develops into a generalized view of the vulgar pleasures that come under the sign of the grotesque, of the flesh and of death. These pleasures are the last gasp of a society so lost in its escapism that it sickens you and makes you sympathetic to a revolutionary solution.'

Vigo (1905–1934) is the *poète maudit* of French cinema – its answer to the equally precocious and subversive Arthur Rimbaud. His father was a French anarchist who was murdered in his prison cell in 1917. He was a tubercular child, dogged by ill health throughout his life, but every film he made was exceptional. He followed up *A Propos de Nice* with *Zéro de Conduite* (1933), about boys fighting back against their authoritarian teachers in a boarding school. Next came his masterpiece, *L'Atalante*, a lyrical but barbed love story about the turbulent marriage between a barge captain and his young bride. The couple's relationship oscillates wildly; the wife runs off, the husband pursues her. The movie was butchered by its original distributors Gaumont, who could not see any commercial possibilities in a film about a chequered romance between an ordinary, working-class French couple, and was only restored many years after its director's death. Lyrical and warm-hearted, it is a magical piece of filmmaking which transcends its own deceptively simple screenplay.

below and bottom Eye-popping shots from two movies that can best be described as symphonies of a city: Walter Ruttmann's *Berlin, Symphony of a City* (1927), and Dziga Vertov's *Man with the Movie Camera* (1929).

CITY SYMPHONIES

Attempting to capture a day in the life of a city is a challenge that has enraptured and exasperated filmmakers in equal measure since the silent era. In 1927, when he was making his impressionistic documentary, *Berlin, Symphony of a City*, German modernist Walter Ruttmann used hundreds and hundreds of index cards instead of a conventional script. His film follows Berlin from before dawn, 'the dead hours', until late at night. Appropriately enough, given that he is trying to show the frantic, protean quality of city life 'with its millionfold moving molecules', the documentary culminates in an enormous, late-night fireworks display. In between, Ruttmann and his cameraman shoot Berliners as they go about their daily business: en route to work, at clubs, dance halls, sports stadiums, cinemas and cafes. Ruttmann shows the streets deserted and the city asleep. He also shows it at its busiest. The city, he said, was like a machine; its movements were intoxicating. 'If I have succeeded in making people swing with this movement in my film symphony and to let them experience Berlin in this way, then I have achieved my ambitions and proved my theories right.'

FROM BERLIN TO MOSCOW

Russian filmmaker Denis Kaufman (1896–1954) changed his name to Dziga Vertov for one reason only – he was in love with movement. 'Dziga' is adapted from a Ukrainian word for spinning top, 'Vertov' is from a Russian verb meaning 'to twist or rotate'. His superb 1929 film, *The Man with the Movie Camera*, offers a dawn-to-dusk panorama of Moscow. Its lead character is a cameraman who spins and rotates his way around the city. He is a cross between a Buster Keaton-like daredevil, who takes his camera onto railway tracks and bridges and shoots in the face of the oncoming traffic, and a chronicler of the brave new Soviet world. Vertov's goal was to escape the limitations of the human eye and rely instead on the camera eye, or, as he called it, the kino-eye. 'Kino-eye', he wrote, 'means the conquest of time... the possibility of seeing life processes in any temporal order or at any speed inaccessible to the human eye.' The idea was for the cameraman to plunge into the chaos of modern life in search of meaning. Every technique was permissible: acceleration, microscopy, reverse action, animation, 'the use of the most unexpected foreshortenings'. He was ready to 'break all the laws and conventions of film construction'.

Eisenstein dismissed *The Man with the Movie Camera* as 'a compendium of formalist jackstraws and unmotivated camera mischief'. Nevertheless, the film has had huge influence abroad. Its techniques and tricks are still used in experimental shorts and pop promos alike.

PEEPING TOM – MICHAEL POWELL AND THE DREAM OF TOTAL CINEMA

'Music, emotion, images and voices all blended together into a new and splendid whole' – this was the ideal that British director Michael Powell (1905–1990) pursued throughout his career. In 1960, he made easily his most controversial film, *Peeping Tom*, about a shy, duffle-coated loner (Carl Boehm) whose hobby is murdering women and filming the moment of their death. True, this is not a musical extravaganza like his earlier works, *The Red*

Shoes (1948), or *The Tales of Hoffmann* (1951), nor does it have the stylized flamboyance of *Black Narcissus* (1947), which re-created the Himalayas in a Home Counties studio. These films and many of Powell's other significant movies were made in collaboration with the brilliant Hungarian emigré, Emeric Pressburger while *Peeping Tom*'s morbidity probably owes much to its screenwriter Leo Marks. Nevertheless, this was arguably Powell's greatest stab at his goal of 'total cinema' in which all the formal elements are integrated. It is also a sort of love letter to cinema, as Powell traces the development of the medium using stills, silent black and white, and colour 35mm. In its obsession with sex, beauty and death, the film, set in 1950s London, shares the hallmarks of Baudelaire's symbolist poetry or Edgar Allan Poe's *Tales of the Grotesque and Arabesque*. It is as brave an attempt as any British filmmaker has made to draw the mainstream and avant-garde together.

How was the film greeted? With the most opprobrious reviews in recent memory. 'I was shocked to the core to find a director of his standing befouling the screen with such perverted nonsense,' wrote one review. 'The sickest and filthiest film I remember seeing,' said another. 'Shovel it up and flush it down the nearest sewer,' suggested a third. Powell was disgraced, and only a generation later, after the film had been enthusiastically championed by academics and by US director Martin Scorsese, was the director forgiven for making this 'blot' on the cinematic landscape.

above   Michael Powell's *Peeping Tom*, a film reviled by the British critics on its first release in 1960 but later recognized as a masterpiece.

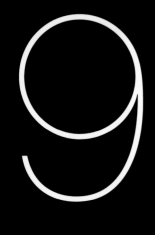

9

The Hays Code
1930

Censorship & Scandal

Will Hays and Fatty Arbuckle – you could not imagine two men less alike. William H. Hays, a lawyer and politician, was small and dapper, 'a prim-faced, bat-eared, mealy-mouthed political chiseler' according to film historian Kenneth Anger. A teetotal Presbyterian and member of the National Council of Boy Scouts, he was admitted to the bar before he was 20 and quickly rose in politics too, eventually becoming Postmaster-General in President Harding's government.

In contrast, Roscoe Conkling Arbuckle was a hard-living, overweight, generous-spirited hedonist with an appetite for booze. His movies were known for their joyous use of slapstick. Nobody could throw a custard pie quite like him. He could sing, and despite his weight – around 300 pounds – he was also extraordinarily nimble. He first appeared in bit parts in movies around 1908, and in 1913 he joined Mack Sennett's Keystone Cops. It was at Keystone that his reputation blossomed; his movies became immensely popular. On screen, Arbuckle was anarchic, gleeful, perverse – like an overgrown child, and the public loved him. He was – as critic J. Hoberman has observed, 'a somersault virtuoso, a hilarious female impersonator and a master of the food fight'. There was apparently nothing about him to dislike.

THE ALLEGED RAPE

What happened in the Hotel St Francis in San Francisco on 5 September 1921 has never been established. Arbuckle was in the city on a short break after shooting several films in succession. A drunken party was held in the rooms where he and his friends were staying. At the end of the party, one of the guests, an actress called Virginia Rappé, fell seriously ill and died a few days later. Arbuckle was charged with her murder, and, almost instantly, before any facts had been established, his adoring public turned against him. 'The newspapers had proved in less than a week that the public got a much greater thrill out of watching stars fall than out of watching them shine,' Arbuckle's old friend Gloria Swanson wrote in her autobiography. 'One day Fatty had been their most beloved comedian next to Chaplin; the next day they were screaming for his head.' There was no evidence to tie Arbuckle to Rappé's death, but within days, the press were charging him with every manner of monstrosity. It was reported that he had raped her with a block of ice, that he had used a champagne bottle, or even that with his vast bulk he had squashed her to death.

Arbuckle-baiting became a national pastime. His few movies in circulation were pilloried, and newspapers carried reports (later proved to be

above William H. Hays (1879–1954), the ex-Republican politician turned censorship Czar of Hollywood, 'a prim-faced, bat-eared, mealy-mouthed political chiseler,' as he was affectionately characterized by one film historian.

above right Virginia Rappé, the small-time actress who died in suspicious circumstances following a wild party in San Francisco in 1921 at which Fatty Arbuckle had been present.

opposite Two of cinema's most outrageous personalities, Mae West and W.C. Fields, appeared together in *My Little Chickadee* (1940).

fabricated) of Wyoming cowboys shooting at the screen when the films began to roll. 'From Atlantic to Pacific, the uproar grew, and even in Paris and London his pictures were greeted with hisses and cat-calls,' one of his obituaries later claimed. When Arbuckle was finally proclaimed innocent, his reputation was in shreds.

THE ROARING TWENTIES

Arbuckle was a victim of the times. This was the Jazz Age, the era of Prohibition, the beginning of the so-called Roaring Twenties – one of the most cynical, corrupt periods in American social history. For many religious groups, Hollywood was the symbol of all that was wrong in society. 'On every side we have seen the slipping and crumbling of social standards in national and community life,' fulminated the evangelical, LA-based Presbyterian minister, Dr Stewart MacLennan. 'Yet we think it strange that we find all this mirrored back from the silver screen.'

MacLennan's grumblings sound like the typical reaction of an old-timer to a society that was changing around him. The studio bosses would not have paid any attention to such sermonizing unless they felt fearful that they would be hit in the pocket. From their perspective, the worst thing about the Arbuckle scandal was that it was bad for business.

THE AFTERMATH – HOLLYWOOD PUTS ITS OWN HOUSE IN ORDER

Fearful that government committees might pass draconian new censorship laws, the Hollywood studios decided that the best idea was to police themselves. To do this credibly, they needed an outsider who commanded respect in Washington. Will Hays was just such a figure. In January 1922 he accepted the offer to head a new organization, The Motion Picture Producers and Distributors of America, Inc. (MPPDA). His influence over the next 30 years was to be immense. As one journalist noted (when Hays died in 1954), 'he had no authority from the State or from the Churches. He made up a moral code of his own. Any film that passed his code was safe. It could be shown anywhere. All over the western world now, moral means what Hays approved of. Immoral means what he condemned. Tens of millions of people think they are being moral when they are merely obeying the code of Will H. Hays.'

One of Hays's first actions on taking up the new post was to slap a lifetime ban on Arbuckle. This was a symbolic decision: it did not matter that Arbuckle had had nothing to do with Rappe's death, he still stood for the bad old Hollywood of drinking, promiscuity and conspicuous consumption that Hays was appointed to clean up. Nevertheless, the 'lifetime ban' was rescinded just months after had it been imposed in April 1922, and Hays was accused of capitulating to the studio bosses. At the time, Hollywood had almost 10,000 contracts in force for Arbuckle's pictures and stood to lose a small fortune if they were not released. There were half-hearted calls for Hays' resignation. Having taken the decision to ban Arbuckle, he now claimed to be acting in the name of natural justice. It made no difference to Arbuckle, whose reputation had been so sullied by the scandal that nobody wanted to see his movies or to hire him under his real name anyway. He died, penniless, of heart failure in 1933.

THE DEPRESSION BITES

In the early 1930s, as the Depression began to bite, an outcry was again being raised across America about falling moral standards in Tinseltown. Desperate to preserve profits, the studios were using sex, Mae West, the Marx Brothers and gangster movies as bait to lure audiences into cinemas. Just as Arbuckle was the symbol of Jazz Age excess, Mae West was the figurehead of what became known as Hollywood's 'golden age of turbulence'. Her outrageous persona scandalized Middle America and the double-entendre was the art form in which she specialized. As *Variety* put it, 'She has a way of making innocent lines sound dirty.' *I'm No Angel* (1933) was quintessential West, spawning such classic one-liners (most of them written by the actress) as: 'When I'm good, I'm very, very good, but when I'm bad, I'm better', 'It's not the men in my life that count, it's the life in my men' and 'She's the kind of girl who climbed the ladder of success, wrong by wrong'.

DRAWING UP THE CODE

In 1927, the MPPDA had drawn up a list of 'Don'ts' (venereal disease, ridicule of the clergy etc.). This had been followed in 1930 by the Production Code, a self-regulatory code of ethics, but it was clearly not working. In the heady early 1930s, the studios routinely flouted the code. This was the era of the Warners' gangster cycle, films like *Little Caesar*, *Scarface* and *Public Enemy*, in which

DOs & DON'Ts

The Hays Code is a fascinating mish-mash, the kind of battle plan that a prudish Sunday-school teacher might have dreamed up. Below are some of the pet rules:

'Revenge in modern times shall not be justified'
'Methods of crime shall not be explicitly presented'
'Illegal drug traffic must never be presented'
'The sanctity of the institution of marriage and the home shall be upheld'
'Pictures shall not infer that low forms of sex relationships are the accepted or common thing'
'Scenes of passion should not be introduced when not essential to the plot'
'Excessive and lustful kissing, lustful embracing, suggestive postures and gestures, are not to be shown'
'Seduction or rape should be never more than suggested...'
'Ministers of religion... should not be used as comic characters or as villains'

The Production Code enforcers were not just preoccupied with maintaining moral standards. They wanted to ensure that the Hollywood studios who paid their bills had a competitive advantage over rival film industries. Hays had not been appointed just to scold Hollywood: he also represented the interests of the studios both at home and abroad. When the Hays office objected to the amount of cleavage that Margaret Lockwood was showing in the British bodice-ripping costume melodrama, *The Wicked Lady* (1945), it helped sabotage the US box-office fortunes of a film that had broken records in the UK. The same complaints had been made about Anna Neagle in *Nell Gwyn* (1934) a decade before.

gun-toting antiheroes got all the best lines. Many comedies, not just those made by Mae West, were sexually suggestive. It seemed that Hollywood was making a monkey out of Hays, and Church leaders were again complaining about the collapse of moral standards. Hays felt his job and reputation were under threat, and he responded by clamping down. From July 1934, the Production Code began to be enforced far more strictly than ever before under Hays' protégé, Joseph Breen, who was director of the Code Administration. Any studio that violated the Code was subject to hefty fines.

BIRTH OF THE SCREWBALL

Many of the Production Office's strictures verged on the absurd. Husbands and wives were not to be shown together in bed; a kiss should not last longer than ten seconds; men and women could embrace standing up, sitting down was just about passable, but getting horizontal was absolutely forbidden. Hays inadvertently gave Hollywood a licence to tease and paved the way for the emergence of a new genre, screwball comedy, in the 1930s. The challenge now was to deal with the battlefield of relationships in ever more oblique and imaginative ways. 'Since sex could not even be implied,' noted historian Molly Haskell, 'it was sublimated into the furor of one-on-one combat in which the double standard itself was overturned in a noisy contest of verbal assault and insult battery, with women the aggressors as often as the men.' An intricate new game was played by the filmmakers and the censors. The former would submit their scripts to the Production office, where Breen and his boys were liberal with their use of the red pen. The trick was to hoodwink the censors – to smuggle in action and dialogue that had a completely different meaning (or at least subtext) from what Breen imagined.

In screwball comedies, the hero and heroine express their affection for one another with barbed one-liners and vicious slapstick. Often, the male is ritually humiliated and emasculated. This happens most viciously in Howard Hawks's *I was a Male War Bride* (1949). 'Demented sexual frustration' (in critic David Thompson's phrase) is what propels the French officer hero Rochard, played by Cary Grant, through the film. He suffers every manner of indignity: he is splashed with paint, left hanging by his fingernails over a waterfall, is arrested, soaked, taunted by kids, and, as a final blow to his self-esteem, forced to dress in drag – and all because he loves Lt Catherine Gates (Ann Sheridan). He is also turfed out of bed after bed. He is even interrupted on his wedding night. There is nothing unusual about the hero being put through the wringer – in this film it is the extent of his suffering which is startling. Cary Grant's character is a hapless, impotent figure; he gets the girl, but has to suffer multiple humiliations first.

SOME CASE STUDIES IN SCANDAL

HEDY LAMARR IN *ECSTASY* Scandal may have ruined Arbuckle but it was the making of Hedy Lamarr. In 1933, the Vienna-born actress appeared, credited as Hedy Keisler, in Gustav Machaty's *Ecstasy*. This naive, rustic tale was a *succès de scandale* largely because she took off her clothes and was seen swimming naked. The Pope denounced the film, which was banned in both Britain and the US. She played a beautiful young woman, married to a wealthy but impotent older man, who starts a reckless affair with a young

below Hedy Lamarr in Gustav Machaty's *Ecstasy* (1933), a *succès de scandale* which helped propel the actress all the way to Hollywood.

surveyor. Between close-ups of the star, there is much heavy-handed
symbolism of nature at its most fecund and of stallions and mares prancing
through the fields. Louis B. Mayer signed her up for MGM in 1937, and when
she arrived in Hollywood the following year, she was greeted by the press as
'the world's most beautiful woman'.

LAST TANGO IN PARIS **CHARGED WITH OBSCENITY** Bernardo

Bertolucci's *Last Tango in Paris*, about the destructive relationship between a
middle-aged American widower (Marlon Brando) and a 20-year-old *ingénue*
(Maria Schneider), made history in Britain. It was the first film charged under
the Obscene Publications Act. In 1974, the distributors, United Artists, were
charged with contravening the Act after Edward Shackleton, a retired,
Swindon-based, Salvation Army social worker, who had seen the film in
Leicester Square, brought a private prosecution. The film had been released
the previous year with an 'X' certificate. The prosecution failed.

EMMANUELLE – **PORNOGRAPHIC BUT TASTEFUL** The filmmakers'

ambitions for *Emmanuelle* were relatively high: the script was written by Jean-
Louis Richard, who had written François Truffaut's Oscar-winning *Day for Night*
the year before; it co-starred Alain Cluny, one of the most respected French
actors of his generation; and it was all very tastefully shot, in best Seventies
soft focus, by director Just Jaekin. Richard, formerly married to Jeanne
Moreau, had talent-spotted the film's star, young, red-headed Dutch model
Sylvia Kristel, on an audition tape the producers had been sent from Holland.

above Marlon Brando and Maria
Schneider in Bernardo Bertolucci's
Last Tango in Paris (1973).

left Sylvia Kristel in softcore porn
pic *Emmanuelle* (1974), a box-office
hit all around the world and still
reputedly the most successful film
ever released in Paris.

above The rape scene from Sam Peckinpah's *Straw Dogs* (1971).

above right Malcolm McDowell getting his eyes tested in Stanley Kubrick's *A Clockwork Orange* (1971), a film which the director himself withdrew from distribution in the UK after it had been linked to several youth crime cases.

Throughout the summer of 1974, when it was released, *Emmanuelle* did brisk business. Paris is relatively quiet in summer, when the wives and children are in the country or at the seaside, and Alain Siritzky, who had financed the movie, expected audiences would plummet in the autumn. To his amazement, the reverse happened: 'We were expecting a big drop, but when the women came back to Paris, they were asking their husbands, "did you hear about this film, *Emmanuelle*?" "No", the husbands would lie. "I think we should go and see it," the wives would suggest, so instead of dropping, the film in September picked up again.' It went on to rack up three and a half million admissions in Paris alone.

Soon the rest of the world began to hear about *Emmanuelle* too. The Japanese, in particular, adored her. Bus-loads of Japanese tourists turned up in Paris to see the film in its original cut – in Japan, it had been shown without any shots of pubic hair. Although censors all over the world tweaked it and there were various attempts to stop it being shown, Siritzky claims that there were hardly any protests by women's groups about the movie. *Emmanuelle*'s secret was that it was up-market and even relatively tasteful compared with the best-known porn films (like *Deep Throat*) that had preceded it in the 1970s. 'What made the difference was that it attracted women as well as men – it was very well photographed.'

STRAW DOGS AND *A CLOCKWORK ORANGE* – CINEMA ACCUSED OF PROMOTING CRIME

Straw Dogs featured probably the most controversial rape sequence in film history. A young bride (Susan George) is assaulted by her ex-boyfriend Venner (Del Henney) while her husband (Dustin Hoffman) is out on the moors, shooting with Venner's friends. She resists Venner, but eventually seems to succumb and even enjoy the rape. She is then assaulted far more brutally by a second man.

Straw Dogs was passed by censors in the US and the UK. The director Sam Peckinpah argued convincingly that his intention was to make the audience 'very, very uncomfortable about their own potential for violence', but certain critics felt it skirted close to celebrating sexual violence. James Ferman of the British Board of Film Classification claimed that the film was frequently cited as inspiration by men accused of rape. In 1977, a female patient at a psychiatric hospital was murdered a few weeks after *Straw Dogs* had been shown in the hospital. There was no direct evidence to link the film with the crime, but the incident served further to sully the film's reputation.

When *A Clockwork Orange* (1971) was rereleased in British cinemas in 2000, the response among audiences and critics was – why the fuss? The film had been withdrawn from British cinemas by its director Stanley Kubrick almost 30 years before, when it was linked to several youth crime cases. Kubrick refused to allow it to be shown in the UK while he was alive. He died in 1999. By then, the 'droogies' – gang members in braces and bowler hats – no longer seemed quite so threatening. British cinema-goers flocked to see the film on its reissue, but there was no more talk of copycat violence.

CRASH – OUTRAGE BRITISH-STYLE

'A movie beyond the bounds of depravity', fulminated London's *Evening Standard* about David Cronenberg's *Crash* (1996), 'a film that is immoral by any reasonable standard, unsafe at any speed'. The *Daily Mail* was even more hostile, calling the film a 'landmark in cinematic pornography' and arguing that 'it will encourage those who have a sadistic sexual bent to feel that they are not alone, that attractive people feel the same way and that no significant harm will come to others as a result of sadomasochistic acts... a damaging and irresponsible lie'. Religious groups signed a petition calling for consumers to boycott any goods associated with the film's distributors, Sony. The government's Heritage Secretary Virginia Bottomley waded into the debate, demanding 'significant cuts in screen violence' and calling for *Crash* to be banned, and Westminster Council refused to allow it to be shown in West End cinemas.

A film that had already opened successfully in Italy, Spain, France and Canada was thus still-born in the UK. Cronenberg's adaptation of J.G. Ballard's novel explored the links between sex and technology. Its characters were men and women who received an erotic thrill from car crashes. Cronenberg acknowledged that the film was 'difficult, disturbing and unrelenting', but pointed out again and again in interviews that 'the sexuality, odd as it is, is all consensual'. He complained that the film was being 'deliberately misunderstood by people who hadn't actually seen it'.

BAISE-MOI – THE FRENCH GET HOT UNDER THE COLLAR

A similar controversy occurred in France in the summer of 2000, when *Baise-Moi* (*Fuck Me*), Virginie Despentes' 'bad girl' road movie (adapted from her own novel) was released. The film, which stars porn actresses Karen Bach and Raffaela Anderson and features graphic sex and even more graphic violence, enjoyed a remarkably successful opening. Then the problems began. Protesters from Carpentras, a National Front stronghold in the South of France, challenged the 'PG-16' rating in court. The court, the Conseil d'Etat, decided to 'suspend' the certificate until further notice. Several exhibitors refused to withdraw the film. Not only was *Baise-Moi* doing good business – this was now about freedom of speech. The law had to be changed and the film given a new certificate – an '18' – before the outcry died down.

below David Cronenberg's *Crash* (1996) provoked an enormous outcry in the UK. Westminster Council banned it, thereby keeping it out of the key West End cinemas.

Musicals

LET'S CALL THE WHOLE THING OFF

It seems like a light-hearted, spontaneous frolic. Midway through *Shall We Dance* (1937), Fred Astaire and Ginger Rogers break into a roller-skating routine in the park. As ever with Astaire, the routine looks effortless – it used to be said of him that he was never more than a step away from a dance. He could improvise dances anywhere. In *The Band Wagon* (1953), his opening solo was inspired by the rhythm of a shoeshine boy's brush on leather; in *Shall We Dance*, his jig around the ship deck is inspired by the noise made by a ship's thudding, metronomic engine pistons. But the roller-skating routine is something else: watching it, you get the impression that he and Rogers are just fooling around for the sake of it. Both have broad smiles on their face and they give every impression of enjoying themselves enormously.

In fact, the routine was agony to film and perform. What seems like such light-hearted fun entailed skating in excess of 80 miles, and if one of them made an error, they would have to start again from scratch. Most of the Astaire and Rogers routines were shot in only one or two takes, with their full bodies in view. There are no special effects or editing tricks. As Astaire tartly put it, 'either the camera dances or I do'. His employers at RKO, who once insured his legs for £200,000, were not about to argue. Their technicians even fashioned a new piece of equipment just for him: the 'Astaire dolly', as it was called, was a little wagon with wheels, only 2ft off the ground, on which the camera could be placed. It ensured that Astaire's most elaborate routines could be shot from a low enough angle to keep his whole body in frame.

In the course of his career, Astaire broke dozens of canes; sweated his way through innumerable changes of shirt; and wore out close to a thousand pairs of those shiny, jet-black dancing shoes. He was a perfectionist, who worked himself to exhaustion to make his dances appear effortless. 'My routines may look easy,' he once said, 'but they are nothing you throw away while shaving. It's always murder to get that easy effect.'

Back in 1928, when Fred and his sister and first dancing partner, Adele, auditioned for Paramount after conquering Broadway and London's West End, a myopic talent scout came up with the following assessment of Astaire's screen potential: 'Can't act, can't sing, balding, can dance a little'. This cruel, blinkered judgement hints at what made Astaire such a star – not so much ability or looks, but sheer hard work. All the critics preferred Adele, and he was simply regarded as her partner and straight man – there to ensure that she looked good. This was how his deceptively casual style developed: as if to compensate for always being eclipsed by her, he took to pretending that he

above The famous roller-skating routine from *Shall We Dance* (1937). What seems like such light-hearted fun entailed Rogers and Astaire skating in excess of 80 miles.

above right Fred Astaire and Cyd Charise in *The Band Wagon* (1953), a film hailed as an instant classic – 'one of the best musical films ever made,' according to the New York Times.

was not even trying, an illusion of carefree effortlessness that eventually made him a huge star. Fred and Adele were superb ballroom dancers, but they also knew tap and jazz dancing and even a little ballet. Using his training as the foundation, Astaire went on to elaborate what he called his 'outlaw style', which combined steps and ideas from all three forms.

It was only with the retirement of his sister, who quit show business to marry English aristocrat, Lord Charles Cavendish, in 1932, that Fred Astaire became appreciated as a dancer in his own right. His film career began in faltering fashion. He was first paired with Rogers in the RKO musical, *Flying Down to Rio* (1933). They were not the main stars, but their carioca routine stole the movie. Astaire thought he looked awful in it, but evidently the public did not agree. He reportedly did not think much of Rogers either and asked not to be paired with her again, not so much because of her shortcomings but because of his own relentless perfectionism. No partner could match that. As his choreographer Hermes Pan put it: 'Of course, it would have been impossible for him not to have danced with a partner, but I think probably he would have preferred to dance alone because then he would be more free to do what he wanted. Naturally a partner placed a certain amount of limitations on him.'

Rogers found working with him exhausting. He loved to rehearse, but she endured it grimly. If he pushed himself to the limits, he was just as harsh with her. In one of their best films, *Swing Time* (1936), he forced her to perform a particularly tricky dance again and again. By the fortieth take, her feet were beginning to bleed into her satin slippers. Perhaps this was his revenge for the famous 'Cheek to Cheek' routine in *Top Hat* (1936), in which her dress, covered in ostrich feathers, tormented him beyond endurance, making him sneeze so violently that he insisted on being allowed to have final say on his partners' costumes thereafter. He drew up strict rules: no feathers, no sequins, no wide skirts that might trip him up, and no beads. Little wonder that Rogers, after an especially gruelling shoot, quipped to reporters that she was going to take a holiday – digging in the salt mines.

After years of playing second fiddle to Adele, Astaire did not want to be overshadowed by yet another partner. Rogers, however, was his perfect foil. In an interview in 1934, he described himself as 'a sort of a character actor' whom audiences had difficulty believing in as a leading man. Rogers helped get him out from under his shell. 'He gave her class, she gave him sex,' was how Katharine Hepburn characterized their partnership. Rogers was earthy and sensuous, whereas Astaire was nimble and ethereal. He had a host of other leading ladies, many of them more technically accomplished dancers than Rogers, but it was his partnership with her that defined the era.

GENE KELLY – SINGIN' AND DANCIN' IN THE RAIN

Don Lockwood, Gene Kelly's character in *Singin' in the Rain* (1952), is shuffling down the street, humming to himself. The rain is falling around him. We know he is feeling happy. He is in love, and not even a Hollywood monsoon can dampen his high spirits. With his hat pulled down over his head and his umbrella as his main prop, he starts one of the most famous musical routines of all. As the rain grows heavier, his exhilaration grows. He ends up wrapping himself around a lamppost, singing his heart out as a bemused policeman in a

below left *Singin' in the Rain* (1952). Gene Kelly wraps himself round the lamppost in one of the best-loved sequences in movie history.

below right Not many partners could steal a scene from Gene Kelly. One who managed it effortlessly was Jerry the Mouse in *Anchors Aweigh* (1945).

cape looks on. With just a hint of embarrassment, he gives the umbrella to a passer-by and sidles off down the street.

Thirteen years younger than Astaire, Gene Kelly was the antithesis of the older dancer. Whereas Astaire wore top hats and tails, Kelly was more likely to be seen in a battered suit or a sailor's outfit, and he was a far more muscular and physical dancer. 'With Fred the sweat never showed,' Kelly once acknowledged. 'He is the aristocrat and I am the truck driver.' He broke the rules by taking a film unit out on location to the streets of New York to film *On the Town*. He would dance with anybody or anything, himself included – one of the most famous sequences in *Cover Girl* is 'The Alter Ego', in which, as his character bemoans the loss of a girl, he dances with his own reflection. In *Anchors Aweigh*, he has Tom and Jerry as partners. In *It's Always Fair Weather*, he and his co-stars hoof their way through a street scene with dustbin lids on their feet, making the kind of clatter that would have driven Astaire wild. The *Singin' in the Rain* routine is quintessential Kelly. This is no random jig in the puddles, the routine reflects what the character is feeling – exultation over getting the girl.

Kelly resented enormously the idea that dancers were in any way effete. For him, the profession was as manly an activity as baseball or boxing. 'I remember when I was a kid my mother would drag me and my brother screaming and crying to a local dancing school in Pittsburgh,' the Irish-American star once told a newspaper. 'We'd have to fight all the neighborhood kids until in the end we just quit. It was only in my late teens, at college, that I got back into it. I said, wait a second, the girls like a feller who's a good dancer.' His first major role – the one that landed him a Hollywood contract – was in a stage production of *Pal Joey*. He was cast true to type as the restless, amoral hero, desperate to be successful in show business, prepared to tread over anybody – lover, rival – who stands in his way. He was the MGM musical's answer to the new generation of actors that emerged in Hollywood after the war. He once even described himself as 'the Brando of dance'. Astaire was a figurehead for the Depression era, when audiences craved escapism. Kelly was a symbol for the post-war years, when affluence and introspection seemed to go side by side.

There is a hint of irony and pathos about his role as the movie star in *Singin' in the Rain*. He was 39 when he made the film, not young for a dancer. Set in the dying days of the silent era, it is itself a kind of valediction – one of the last flourishes of the old-style studio system. It is as if Kelly and Co. are dancing themselves towards extinction. 'The furious energy,' novelist John Updike wrote in the *New Yorker*, 'has something desperate about it; it is like Cinerama and the 50s biblical epics, trying to outshout and outdazzle the little home screen.'

The classical Hollywood musical was not a genre that could be revived. Despite the later experiments of filmmakers such as Bob Fosse (*All That Jazz*), Woody Allen (*Everyone Says I Love You*) and even Kenneth Branagh (*Love's Labour's Lost*), there was no one who could match Astaire and Kelly. 'Could there be? I think it's unlikely,' says Stanley Donen, who co-directed *Singin' in the Rain* with Kelly. He points out that it is impossible to serve the right kind of apprenticeship. 'Kelly came from vaudeville, theatre, Broadway, nightclubs, singing, dancing, and Astaire the same. That garden doesn't exist any more. It's possible, but I don't know where those people are going to come from – they don't have any place to polish their art.'

SATURDAY NIGHT FEVER

The golden era of the Hollywood musical is long since past, but the myth of the 'ordinary Joe' transformed by his fancy footwork is as potent as ever. Dancing, like the movies themselves, is a means of escape. Look at Tony Manero (John Travolta) in *Saturday Night Fever* (1977). He lives a deadbeat existence, working as a clerk in a Brooklyn paint store. Come the weekend, though, he is king of the disco. As we watch him strut his way across the rainbow-coloured squares, performing the hustle, the freak and the dolphin roll, we too are transported.

WALTZING DOWN UNDER

'A life lived in fear is only half a life.' This old Spanish proverb, quoted in Baz Luhrmann's *Strictly Ballroom* (1992) sums up in a nutshell why dance works so well in the movies. Dance is about living to the full, about risk and romance – a combination cinema finds irresistible. Luhrmann's own heroine, Fran (Tara Morice) is the proof of the pudding. She starts the film as a timorous, dowdy damsel with two left feet, who waltzes with all the grace of a short-sighted elephant. But, by the final reel, she has become a smouldering Hispanic beauty. Her partner Scott (Paul Mercurio), decked out in full Matador gear, circles round her as they perform a paso doble. It is a fiery, magnificent routine. Dance Federation officials, appalled that the couple are deviating from the official steps, stop the music. Fran and Scott are not fazed in the slightest. They take their rhythm from the claps of the audience instead, and finish their

below 'A life lived in fear is only half a life.' That was the motto of the lead character (Paul Mercurio), a dancer always prepared to do the unexpected, in *Strictly Ballroom* (1992).

dance to wildly enthusiastic applause. So ends the most magical moment in a magical movie. Cast off your shackles, forget your inhibitions, *Strictly Ballroom* tells us, and anything is possible.

JIM CARREY LET LOOSE IN THE CONGO BONGO

Stanley Ipkiss (Jim Carrey) in *The Mask* (1994) is another, more recent example of the hero redeemed by hoofing. A mild-mannered bank teller, he lacks the gumption to ask the gorgeous Tina Carlyle the time, let alone for a date. But when he puts on his green mask, he turns into the hottest shaker this side of Ramon Navarro. He takes to the floor of the Congo Bongo, grabs Tina, and leads her through a heady Latin American routine – a mish-mash of lambada, tango and salsa, with a bit of jitterbug thrown in for good measure. Admittedly, he is more cartoon character than real human – not many of us can throw our partners as high as the ceiling and spin them like gyroscopes – but we're intoxicated by the fantasy all the same.

SOME COMIC HOOFERS

Of all the ballroom dances featured in the movies, the tango is the most common, and it is not hard to see why: it combines arrogance and sensitivity with raw sexuality. It originated in the slums of Buenos Aires in the late 19th century, but soon spread right across Europe. Little wonder, then, that in its travels round the world, and into the movies, the tango underwent many refinements and modifications. Sometimes, it was milked for laughs: the ridiculous steps Groucho Marx danced with plump and matronly Margaret Dumont are as far removed from the sultry, violent movements of the original Buenos Aires pimps and prostitutes as it is possible to get. Charlie Chaplin used the routine to sentimental effect in *City Lights* (1931). Arnold Schwarzenegger, looking more like a mobile cement mixer than a Latin lover, did his own version of the dance with Tia Carrere at the start of *True Lies* (1994). In recent years, perhaps only Al Pacino in *Scent of a Woman* (1992) has been true to the original spirit of tango. As the grizzled, sightless army veteran who takes beautiful Gabrielle Anwar in his arms, he dances with a passion and longing that easily transcends his technical limitations.

RUDY'S TANGO LESSON

If you want to know where Carrey learned his best moves, you have to go right back to 1921. That was the year Rudolph Valentino starred in *Four Horsemen of the Apocalypse* and caused a million women's hearts to flutter with the most sensuous, erotic, and downright dangerous dance steps cinema has ever seen. Valentino appears in close-up, dressed in Argentine gaucho costume. He is chewing on a cigarillo, with the smoke swirling around his face. He takes a shine to a woman on the dance floor, marches up to her partner, taps him on the shoulder, and suddenly beats him to the ground with his bolas. Then he grabs the girl in his arms and leads her through a languorous but highly charged tango.

MAMBO AND LAMBADA

Tango may have been the main South American dance exported to Hollywood and beyond, but it was by no means the only one. After World War II, mambo and rumba caught on in the USA, especially in the Hispanic communities.

LEARNING THE LINDY HOP
One night in the summer of 1928, George 'Shorty' Snowden was competing in a four-day dance marathon at the Manhattan Casino, a huge ballroom in New York. He broke away from his partner and improvised a few, wild solo steps of his own. The jitterbug, or Lindy Hop as it is also called (after pioneer aviator Lindbergh's 'hop' across the Atlantic), was born. Harlem became the centre of this new style of jazz dance. With Fletcher Henderson, Earl Hines, Duke Ellington and their orchestras setting a breakneck tempo, hoofing speeded up out of all recognition. These riotous early days are celebrated in Francis Ford Coppola's lavish *The Cotton Club* (1984).

Not long afterward, Benny Goodman appeared on the scene and swing grew into a nationwide craze. Arguably, every subsequent American dance fad, from rock and roll in the 1950s to the twist in the early 1960s, disco in the 1970s, and even hip hop in the 1980s, has its roots in swing. Movies from *Rock Around the Clock* to *Twist Around the Clock*, from *Grease* to *Beat Street*, celebrate the youthful exuberance and madcap energy that each new generation of footloose kids brought to the floor. Not everybody was happy with the way Hollywood embraced youth culture. For those who preferred their dance films 'strictly ballroom', jitterbug marked the beginning of the end.

Traditional Latin American rhythms fused with jazz and early rock and roll to create something sultry, new and accessible. Arne Glimcher's film, *The Mambo Kings* (1991), celebrates the rowdy, freewheeling lives of two Cuban brothers who start up a mambo band during this heady, if short-lived period. Perhaps the greatest mambo dancer ever seen on screen was the beautiful Italian star, Silvana Mangano. She enlivens *Bitter Rice* (1948), an earnest drama about the trials of various women toiling in the rice fields, with a superb exhibition of the dance, and also displays her skills in Robert Rossen's 1954 comedy-romance, *Mambo*.

Meaning 'slap' or 'rapid shot' in Portuguese, the lambada is a bastard dance, an Afro-Brazilian-Caribbean hybrid that mixes salsa, merengue and rock. Big-city dwellers dismissed it as crude and provincial, and it was only really popular in the poor, rural regions of Brazil. However, Kenny Ortega's choreography for *Dirty Dancing* (1987) borrowed some of its moves and ensured its revival, at least on celluloid. Rival producers tried to cash in on the new craze with such pictures as *Lambada*, *Lambada the Forbidden Dance*, *Naked Lambada*, *Blame it on the Lambada*, and *Lambada the Sound of Love*, but few of these earned a dime. The difference with *Dirty Dancing* was its two sizzling star performances from Patrick Swayze and Jennifer Grey, and a nostalgic script that evoked the lost innocence of the early 1960s. The dances themselves owed as much to rock and roll and the twist as they did to Latin rhythms.

opposite Jim Carrey (with Cameron Diaz as partner) shows that anything Valentino can do, he can do better in *The Mask* (1994).

below Cynthia Rhodes, Jennifer Grey and Patrick Swayze in *Dirty Dancing* (1987), the film which sparked off a popular revival of the lambada.

11

Radio City Music Hall
1970

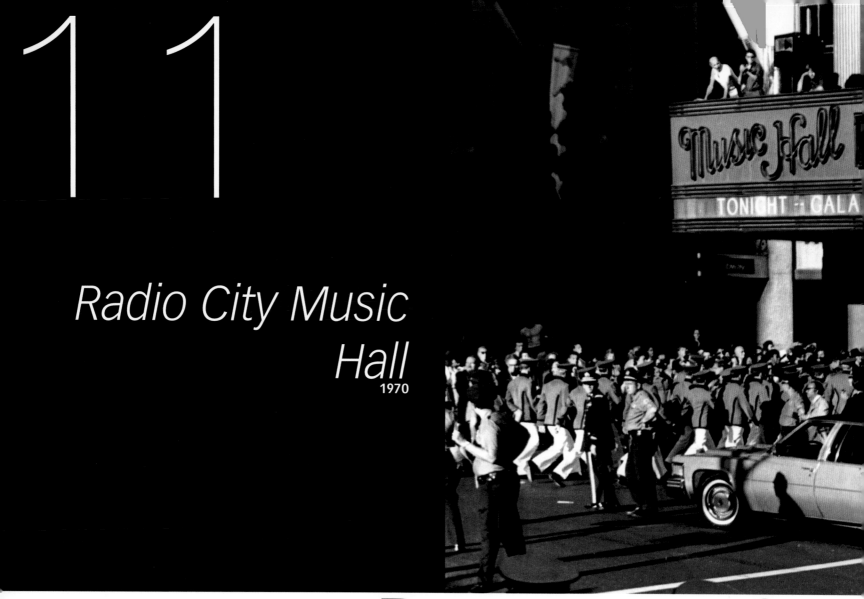

Popcorn &
Showmanship

Chicago hustler Charles Cretors did not 'invent' popcorn, but by building the first popcorn machine in 1885 he turned it into one of the most popular fast foods of the modern age. Cretors' machine was mobile, and vendors could now go in pursuit of the crowds in parks and at fairgrounds. At some point, popcorn machines moved from the streets and into the cinema foyers, probably during the Depression. In the dog days of the 1930s, popcorn was cheap enough to be affordable even for the most cash-strapped families, something that cinema managers were not slow to notice. 'Before then, the theaters considered themselves to be above food vending. They considered it a little bit tacky,' Charles Cretors (Cretors' namesake and great-grandson) told *American Film Magazine* on the 100th anniversary of the first popcorn machine. 'But with the Depression, they found that the guy on the street was making more money than they ever were, so movie exhibitors developed the concession stand, and popcorn was a major part of it.'

PICTURE PALACES

To audiences accustomed to multiplexes or to the fleapit-style cinemas that became all too common in the 1970s and 1980s, it is hard to credit just how opulent some cinemas used to be. In Britain in the 1920s and 1930s, the doyen

of cinema designers was Theodore Komisarjevsky, an ex-Moscow theatre designer who had moved to Britain in 1919 to escape the Bolshevik regime. Komisarjevsky's watchword was extravagance. His theatres, many of them designed for Sidney Bernstein's Granada chain, were luxurious and brightly lit. 'The masses who frequent cinemas usually come to the theatre tired out after hard work, probably in not too cheerful surroundings,' he noted. 'The picture theatre supplies these folk with the flavour of romance for which they crave. The richly decorated theatre, the comfort with which they are surrounded, and the efficiency of the service contribute to an atmosphere and a sense of wellbeing of which the majority have hitherto only imagined.'

His Granadas in humble London neighbourhoods like Tooting and Woolwich were settings fit for Medici princes. They boasted mirrors, sweeping staircases, elaborately embossed ceilings, pillars, murals, chandeliers – the idea being both to pamper cinema-goers and to fill them with a sense of awe.

AIR CONDITIONING

During humid Chicago summers from 1917 onwards, cinema-goers were not just thinking about what movies they wanted to see – a more important consideration was getting out of the heat. This is what Balaban and Katz's

SWEETIES

Audiences had been buying sweets and popcorn for years before the cinemas started stocking them. Exhibitors who were too haughty to sell such treats themselves could not stop cinema-goers from arriving at the theatre already laden with their own mini-picnics, and eventually they woke up to the profits they could make by getting in on the act. Soon the food and drink concessions became as important to exhibitors as the films themselves. If you bought a helping of salty, butter-drenched popcorn, you would almost certainly want a soda with which to wash it down. The new food had its own distinctive aroma – one that soon became instantly recognizable to all cinema-goers.

By World War II, American audiences were eating more popcorn than ever. Sugar was dispatched overseas for the US troops, which meant that there was not much left over for candy, and popcorn was the obvious replacement for hungry cinema-goers. Although sales declined in the 1950s as audiences dwindled in the face of the new rival, television, they soon picked up again. In 2000, it was calculated that Americans consumed 17.3 billion quarts of popped popcorn every year. Cinemas alone made around $1.4 billion per annum from popcorn sales, more – the magazine *Sight and Sound* recently pointed out – 'than three times the US gross of *Jurassic Park*'.

Central Park Theatre enabled them to do. 'It was the first mechanically air-cooled theatre in the world,' notes film historian Douglas Gomery. The technology that Barney Balaban used to keep his audiences comfortable was ultra-reliable: Chicago's meat packers had been using it for years.

DRIVE-IN CINEMAS

Cars and movies were a twin obsession in 20th-century America. What better way to combine them than through the 'Drive-In Cinema'? The earliest drive-ins date back to the early 1930s, and 20 years later, as car ownership became more widespread, the drive-in spree began in earnest. Every summer evening, millions would motor down to their local drive-in. By the mid-1950s, there were 4,000 such theatres dotted across the country. As countless teen movies later chronicled, the drive-in was the perfect dating arena.

THE DUBIOUS ART OF SHOWMANSHIP

In the days before anyone realized how strongly movies would take hold of the public's imagination, film displays were seen as a tool for advertising live performance. 'The more the appetites of those who support the variety theatre and musical comedy and drama are whetted by witnessing potted versions of star turns and popular pieces on film, the more successful will each flourish,' suggested one trade paper. 'The man, woman or child who has witnessed an exceptionally good performance on screen will never rest content until he or she has made a closer personal acquaintance with the artistes in the flesh in their own particular sphere.' But it soon became obvious even to the most ostrich-headed theatre-owners that film would eclipse music hall and variety, and showmen began to devise ever more elaborate ruses for boosting the new medium. Circus-like advertising, film magazines, personal appearances and star stunts were used to entice audiences.

Visionaries like the theatre designer Komisarjevsky were the respectable face of the exhibition business, but there were others altogether less scrupulous. One of the most important figures in getting a movie across to its public was the 'Ballyhoo Man'. His job was to plan the Ballyhoo campaign, which encompassed star lookalike contests, fashion clinics and popular mother competitions, devising slogans, coordinating star appearances, wooing everybody from local politicians to the local press, arranging tie-in competitions with local shops, and generally hyping any given movie to the high heavens.

Part of the Ballyhoo merchant's brief was to transform the cinema foyer into a never-never land mirroring the world portrayed on screen. If there was a Western screening, this might mean putting up a cactus here and there and (perhaps) having a few cowboys in stirrups milling around the ticket booth. If it was a sword-and-sandal epic, the emphasis would obviously be on laurel wreaths and togas.

The Ballyhoo men worked in tandem with press agents, who were every bit as imaginative and unscrupulous as they were. Universal boss Carl Laemmle details one occasion on which an agent, keen to promote a new Tarzan film, hired a lion from the local zoo and booked it into a hotel room under the name T.R. Zann. The lion arrived concealed in a piano box (the hotel was told in advance that Mr Zann liked to tinkle on the keys). The stunt blew up in the agent's face when the house detective became suspicious about the amount of sirloin steak that the surprisingly carnivorous Mr Zann was consuming. Both lion and agent were turfed out of the hotel. They got plenty of column inches in the press, but even so the movie they were hawking failed to attract the customers.

WILLIAM CASTLE –
THE BIGGEST BALLYHOO MERCHANT OF ALL

Audiences at William Castle's 1959 film, *The Tingler*, were shocked. This is not a matter of opinion, but of brute fact. The ever-enterprising Castle (1914–1977) had decided that it was time to galvanize spectators and, with this in mind, he bought hundreds of little electric motors from war surplus stores at $3 a time. He sent them out to exhibitors along with instructions to place them under the audience's seats. At strategic moments during the screening (generally whenever Vincent Price was around), mini-bolts of electricity shot through spectators. They must have enjoyed the sensation because there is no record of any complaints.

Electrocuting the audience was mild by comparison with some of the other stunts that Castle dreamed up. He once paid Lloyds of London a small fortune to insure himself against anybody dying from fright during one of his movies. In truth, this was not likely to happen – his movies generally provoked as much mirth as terror – but it was a brilliant marketing trick. Like the old ham he was, he took to appearing at the beginning of his movies in order to warn audiences of the trauma that was about to descend on them. He proclaims at the beginning of his 1961 opus *Mr Sardonicus*, that what follows is a 'tale full of gallantry, graciousness and ghouls'. For reasons impossible to fathom, he is standing on the fog-shrouded streets of London (or, at least, a Hollywood B-studio's re-creation of it) as he makes his announcement, even though the film is actually set in Eastern Europe – where a British scientist ventures to meet the disfigured Baron Sardonicus, 'a man so evil... his face could stop a

opposite *Mixed company* (1974). Young girls with popcorn at a baseball game.

below Legendary showman and B-horror movie director William Castle (1914–1977) tries to bribe a chimp with a cigar.

below right William Castle arranged for audiences at his 1959 film *The Tingler* to be given an electric shock midway through screenings.

heart'. Sometimes, as if concerned that audiences could not tell that they were watching a horror movie, Castle would dangle glow-in-the-dark skeletons from the ceilings. He devised special spectacles through which audiences could – if they chose – see ghosts on the screen.

BUILDING ON CASTLE

Castle's influence continues to be felt. He was the inspiration behind Joe Dante's *Matinee* (1993), a nostalgic yarn set during the Cuban missile crisis in which a flamboyant, Castle-like showman Lawrence Woolsey (beautifully played by John Goodman) rolls up in a Florida town with his brand new production, *The Mant*. Woolsey's film – and the stunts he stages – stoke up the already simmering emotions of the local adolescents to boiling point. Their hormones are raging, there is the threat of Armageddon, and this mad movie maverick is unleashing what seem to be real-life monsters in their backyard.

HITCHCOCK AND *PSYCHO*

'No one… BUT NO ONE… will be admitted to the theatre after the start of each performance of PSYCHO,' ran the instruction given out from Alfred Hitchcock to exhibitors showing his 1960 horror movie. He also implored audiences not to give the end away – 'It's the only one we have,' he joked. Hitchcock, it seems, was as astute a showman as William Castle and he knew that these injunctions would tantalize and tease the public. 'No admission after the film has begun: none till a minute or so before; and the consequent baffled queues which block the traffic in Lower Regent Street are innocently flaunted as free advertisement,' noted critic David Robinson when the film was first released in London.

Hitchcock's ultra-strict door policy was not simply a matter of hype. Janet Leigh, the ostensible star of the movie, has her fatal shower at the Bates Motel relatively early on in proceedings. Hitchcock realized that latecomers arriving just after (or indeed just before) she was killed would be baffled. He also loved the idea of locking in the audience for the entire duration of one of his most macabre films. This was a filmmaker who relished practical jokes. Once, his biographer John Russell Taylor notes, he paid a studio prop man a pound to let himself be handcuffed overnight 'then immediately before gave him a drink liberally mixed with a strong laxative'. With *Psycho*, he targeted an entire audience – albeit not with laxatives.

HORROR MOVIES – AN EXCUSE TO PRINT MONEY

Psycho was shot in black and white double-quick time with the crew Hitchcock normally used for his television series. He had noticed that many two-bit production companies were turning out low-budget horror pictures and making a fortune with them. He wanted to share in these profits and relished the challenge of making a full-length feature film under the same conditions as a TV show. He also realized tastes were changing and that censors were prepared to let scenes pass that only a few years before would have been cut out instantly. It was not just the famous shower sequence that broke new ground; equally daring was the overture to the movie, in which the camera glides through a hotel window to peep on Leigh and John Gavin during an illicit afternoon tryst in a hotel room.

opposite left Jamie Lee Curtis is put through the wringer in John Carpenter's creepy teen horror pic, *Halloween* (1978).

opposite right *Star Wars* (1977) was less a triumph of filmmaking than one of marketing and merchandising.

below Janet Leigh's notorious shower scene occurs relatively early in *Psycho* (1960). It was considered a great risk for Hitchcock to kill off his leading lady so quickly, but the film was still a huge box-office success.

Afternoon sex was one thing, lavatories were quite another. John Russell Taylor argues that the biggest taboo that Hitchcock broke in *Psycho* was the unwritten one that dictated that no filmmaker should ever refer to bodily functions. In a key scene, we see Leigh flush her notes down the loo. According to Taylor, 'the censors found the very sight of a toilet offensive'.

STAR WARS AND THE MERCHANDISING BUG

The movie that revolutionized Hollywood's approach to merchandising was George Lucas's *Star Wars* (1977). The tie-in products went hand in hand with the film itself. 'In a way, this film was designed around toys,' the director commented not long after the movie's release. 'I actually make toys. If I make money, it will be from the toys.'

As Lucas went on to shoot more and more sequels, his licensing company, LucasArts Licensing, earned a fortune not only from toys, but from confectionery, comics, board games, video games, computer games, drinks and stationery. It was calculated by one analyst that *Star Wars* products had tallied up sales of more than $2.5 billion by the late 1990s. This was before the release of *The Phantom Menace* in 1999 shot that merchandising figure even higher.

Before Lucas, Hollywood's attitude toward merchandising was acutely wary. Whereas popular TV series played for years, films came and went. Nobody wanted to risk mass-producing toys or comic books inspired by figures in movies that the public were already beginning to lose patience with or forget. *Star Wars*, however, was something new – not so much a movie as a

"HOLLYWOOD COME IN ... YOUR TIME IS UP
TRAINSPOTTING IS HERE AND IT'S TOE-CURLINGLY GOOD"
★★★★★
EMPIRE

#1 BEGBIE #2 DIANE #3 SICK BOY #4 SPUD #5 RENTON

Trainspotting 18

CHANNEL FOUR FILMS PRESENT A FIGMENT FILM IN ASSOCIATION WITH THE NOEL GAY MOTION PICTURE COMPANY TRAINSPOTTING EWAN MCGREGOR EWEN BREMNER JONNY LEE MILLER KEVIN MCKIDD AND ROBERT CARLYLE AS BEGBIE INTRODUCING KELLY MACDONALD COSTUMES RACHAEL FLEMING PRODUCTION DESIGN KAVE QUINN EDITOR MASAHIRO HIRAKUBO DIRECTOR OF PHOTOGRAPHY BRIAN TUFANO B.S.C. BASED ON A NOVEL BY IRVINE WELSH SCREENPLAY JOHN HODGE PRODUCER ANDREW MACDONALD DIRECTOR DANNY BOYLE

left Danny Boyle's *Trainspotting* (1996) was one of the most imaginatively marketed European films of the 1990s. Somehow, PolyGram made a film about low-life Edinburgh drug addicts seem hip.

franchise. Its success opened the way for other filmmakers and studios to start hawking their products in the same way. Toy Rambos, toy Batman figures, toy Superman figures all soon began to clog a market which Hollywood had not even realized existed.

TRAINSPOTTING

Generally, Europeans are far more reticent about hawking their movie wares than their Hollywood counterparts. One company which bucked this trend in the 1990s was PolyGram Filmed Entertainment. PFE's idea – novel for Britain – was to tout its movies in the same brazen and aggressive way that record companies promoted pop albums. Its most groundbreaking campaign was the one it mounted for *Trainspotting* (1996).

'This film is expected to arrive... 23:02:96.' In the weeks leading up to *Trainspotting*'s release in British cinemas, cryptic posters and teaser advertisements began to appear all over the place: on billboards, bus shelters, in newspapers and in magazines. At first glance, it was not quite clear what was being marketed. Five youngsters, each photographed in sleek black and white, stared out aggressively at passers-by. Gaudy orange lettering revealed the characters they played in the film, but none were stars. Many must have assumed that they were advertising trainers, soft drinks or some new compilation LP.

The confusion, producer Andrew Macdonald later claimed, was deliberate. 'I was very sure that I wanted it to be a buddy movie; I wanted the imagery to be young and fashionable – to have an attitude.'

A scabrous, low-life novel about heroin addicts in an Edinburgh suburb did not immediately seem to lend itself to an upbeat campaign. However, the marketing reflected the filmmakers' intentions: they set out to harness the vitality and humour in Irving Welsh's hugely popular novel on which the film was based, and not just to 'make a dull drugs movie'. They signed up many of the leading Britpop bands of the time – Blur, Elastica and Primal Scream among them – to contribute original music. Not only did this guarantee endless column inches in style and music magazines, it also helped lure young cinema-goers who generally give low-budget British films a very wide berth.

The *Trainspotting* campaign encompassed a tie-in screenplay, a reissue of Welsh's novel, and an original soundtrack album. The marketing team also looked for whatever merchandising opportunities they could find. Obviously, it was not possible to sell toys on the back of a movie about heroin addiction, but T-shirts bearing Irving Welsh's words of wisdom 'It's shite being Scottish' did a roaring trade as did *Trainspotting* mugs. The general success of the marketing campaign was underlined by the number of imitators it inspired. Spoof *Trainspotting* posters were used to promote the rereleased *Withnail And I*, Cobra shoes ran a 'Trainerspotting' campaign, and even Andrew Lloyd-Webber's musical, *Starlight Express*, mimicked the Polygram approach.

Of course, all the marketing ingenuity in the world would count for nothing if the film was no good. *Trainspotting* was a rare example of a British-produced film which really did live up to its own immense hype. It also proved how far marketing had moved on since the days when William Castle used to dangle skeletons from the screen.

THE BLAIR WITCH

In the autumn of 1994, three young Americans hitchhiked into Maryland's Black Hill Forest to make a documentary about a local legend, the Blair Witch. They have never been heard from again. In 1995, their footage was found, detailing their journey through the forest and capturing the terrifying events leading up to their disappearance.

This, at least, is the story that was told on the 'Blair Witch' Web site. Months before the movie it was promoting was released, 'Blair Witch' had already become a cult. Surfers did not know whether the story was true, or simply an elaborate hoax. By the summer of 1999, the 'Blair Witch' site was receiving over two million hits a day. The movie was a low-budget horror film, directed by a group of unknown students from the University of Central Florida. It was not a star-driven action adventure with a huge marketing budget behind it, and boasted no monsters or state-of-the-art special effects. Slime on rucksacks, rags, teeth and twisted sticks are the main props the filmmakers use to scare the audience out of its wits. The film was shot on colour camcorder and in grungy black and white. Its production values were no better than those of a well-made home movie. Nevertheless, thanks to ingenious 'guerilla marketing tactics', *The Blair Witch Project* became a full-blown phenomenon. Its screen average ($26,528) broke the record ($21,822) set by *Star Wars: Episode 1, The Phantom Menace* only a few weeks before. It topped box-office charts in the US and throughout the world. The 'biggest little film of all time', as it was characterized, was a triumph that the old-fashioned Ballyhoo merchants would surely have cherished.

below *The Blair Witch Project* (1999) owed much of its phenomenal success to its groundbreaking use of the internet as a marketing tool.

The Western

12
Monument Valley
1939

'In a western state, far from the present haunts of man, there is a stately valley of great monuments of stone... men come and live their hour and go away, but the mighty stage remains.' **(Intertitles from George B. Seitz's silent Western, *The Vanishing American*.)**

INTO THE VALLEY

Monument Valley stands in the centre of the Colorado Plateau, nestling between two states, Utah (to the north) and Arizona (to the south). It is a majestic and forbidding wilderness. Looming above the parched ground are rocks of every conceivable size and shape. There are aiguilles – long needle-thin peaks which look as brittle as Giacometti sculptures; there are mesas – high, rocky plateaux with steep sides; and buttes – isolated, cliffy mounds. This is a geologist's paradise. The valley has also become the most recognizable symbol of the one film genre that the Americans invented all on their own.

'I have always claimed that the Western movie is one of the few art forms the Americans can lay claim to, next to jazz,' Clint Eastwood once observed. That art form's spiritual home is here, next to these gigantic rocks which are as instantly familiar to the public as Easter Island's mysterious statues.

Monument Valley has been used not just in movies, but in cigarette ads ('come to where the flavor is!') and even Chanel commercials.

Monument Valley with Yosemite Valley and the Grand Canyon are what old-timers in Hollywood films might call 'God's own country'. It is the kind of sublime wilderness celebrated by 19th-century poets like Philip Freneau (a place 'where Nature's wildest genius reigns'), artists like Asher Durand, Albert Bierstadt and Thomas Moran, who painted vast canvases depicting unspoiled American landscapes, and novelists like James Fennimore Cooper, whose *Leather-Stocking Tales* created one of the first fiction heroes of the frontier West in the quaintly named Natty Bumppo, hero of *The Pioneers* (1823).

JOHN FORD COUNTRY

John Ford was not the first filmmaker to visit Monument Valley, nor did he make as many of his movies there as is commonly believed. Nevertheless, he is so strongly associated with the area that you could be forgiven for thinking he was born in its shadow.

There was a revealing television interview done by Peter Bogdanovich with Ford towards the end of the latter's career. Ford is shown sitting in his director's chair with the valley as his backdrop. He is wearing a baseball cap and chewing

above Zane Grey had begun his career as a dentist in New York but went on to immortalize the West in his novels, many of them set in Monument Valley and many of them later filmed by Hollywood.

a cigar. Bogdanovich remarks that Ford's films have become increasingly melancholic with the years. Ford replies gruffly, 'I don't know what you're talking about.' Bogdanovich tries to draw him out on ideas and themes in his films, but Ford waves him away contemptuously, muttering 'cut!' at the camera. It was clear what he meant: he was a professional, directing was his job, and he saw no reason why he should talk about it for the sake of some pretentious film historian (Bogdanovich went on to become a director). 'My name is John Ford. I make Westerns,' he once remarked, as if that was all he ever did and all he needed to say. Real cowboys do not talk much and orotund rhetoric would not have been appropriate in Monument Valley. The place was like a church. 'In the Western,' historian Ed Buscombe notes, 'mountain scenery could be said to function as a substitute for religion, a way of introducing a secular, spiritual dimension.' It was awe-inspiring – not a stage for frivolity.

THE DENTIST GOES WEST

Often, the roots of the biggest-growing Hollywood myths are all too prosaic. The first 'artist' to be inspired directly by Monument Valley was a dentist by profession. Zane Grey (1875–1939) had been to Flagstaff and the Grand Canyon as early as 1907 and his visit there led him to write his first best-seller, *The Heritage of the Desert*. Ohio-born Grey never was much good at filling teeth, and even when he was practising dentistry in New York, he was far more interested in baseball, writing and deep-sea fishing.

Grey had long wanted to become a novelist, but only after many years of obscurity did his work become successful. His first novel, *Betty Zane* (1903), was loosely based on the heroics of one of his own ancestors, who had defied British and Indians alike to liberate a fort under siege in 1782. It was not a success. The 1907 trip out west, ostensibly to catch mountain lions, was the turning-point in his career. He was awestruck by the Arizona and Colorado landscapes, and from then on made them the setting for his fiction. It was the wealth of local detail in his work that seemed to inspire readers. Soon Grey was topping best-seller lists. Over 60 of the 90 or so books he wrote were Westerns, mostly set on the Colorado Plateau.

Grey was not the first to take cowboys as his heroes. Owen Wister's influential *The Virginian* had been published in 1902, newspapers had gleefully charted Billy the Kid's bloody adventures, and Buffalo Bill was a national hero. Dime novels about Western heroes were published by the bucketload during the late 19th century. The difference with Grey was that he revered the West. His name became indelibly associated with the landscapes he was describing. Tourist associations still call parts of Arizona and Colorado 'Zane Grey Country'. Other writers saw the lawless, untamed West as a mythical world that no longer really existed.

By the early 20th century, the genre already seemed steeped in nostalgia. Many Westerns are elegiac affairs in which cars, churches, East Coast businessmen, great snaking railway lines and industrial machinery slowly stifled the life out of the old world. Grey, almost alone amongst his contemporaries, refused to accept the march of time. In his fiction, the modern world hardly intrudes: the West remains as lawless and remote – and as unspoiled – as ever, and his characters remain utterly in awe of the landscapes they encounter.

HOLLYWOOD DISCOVERS THE VALLEY

More than 100 films have been inspired by Grey's fiction. He insisted that the filmmakers used the locations he had been describing and was thus responsible for leading Hollywood by the nose to Monument Valley and its environs. *The Riders of the Purple Sage*, *Nevada*, *The Rainbow Trail*, *Red Canyon*, *Rangle River*, *The Mysterious Rider*, *The Lone Star Ranger* – the list of Grey-inspired Westerns is extensive. Some are B-pictures, some are big budget studio efforts. Actors from John Wayne to Robert Mitchum, from Tom Mix to George Montgomery appeared in them. Grey discovered Monument Valley in 1913, and the first filmmaker to follow him there was George B. Seitz, who made *The Vanishing American*, adapted from a Grey novel, in the valley in 1925. John Ford arrived in 1939, to make *Stagecoach*.

Ford can be described, not too fancifully, as Hollywood's answer to Zane Grey. Just as Grey's reverential approach helped revive the cowboy novel, *Stagecoach* ensured that Westerns would again be taken seriously. In the 1930s, there had been a plethora of B-oaters, many featuring John Wayne, whose stock had fallen since his first important role in Raoul Walsh's epic, *The Big Trail* (1930). This was the era of *Hopalong Cassidy*, starring William Boyd, *The Three Mesquiteers*, and the singing cowboy, Gene Autry (who was followed a generation later by Roy Rogers).

Stagecoach was Ford's first Western since *Three Bad Men* (1926). The film was loosely based on Ernest Haycox's *The Stage to Lordsburg*, a short story published in *Collier's Magazine* in 1937. Intriguingly, Ford later claimed that the real inspiration was the Maupassant story, *Boule de Suif*, which

below John Ford seen here directing Tom Holt and the cavalry in Monument Valley for the film *Stagecoach* (1939).

right John Carradine, Louise Platt
and John Wayne in John Ford's
Stagecoach (1939), the film which
helped revive the Western as a
serious genre.

below Singing cowboy Gene Autry
and his beloved horse, Champion.

describes a coach journey across Prussian-occupied France. In that story,
the travellers are held up at an inn. The most generous and kind-hearted of
them is a prostitute, nicknamed Boule de Suif. The other travellers force her
to sleep with their captor so that they can resume their journey. Once she
does so, they immediately shun her – although she was only doing what
they demanded.

Stagecoach is not as barbed or bleak as the Maupassant story.
Appropriately for a film which kick-started the Western genre, it is a story
of redemption. In the course of their perilous journey across Indian
country, the passengers overcome their own chequered pasts. The
drunken, disgraced surgeon Dr Boone (Thomas Mitchell) delivers a baby in
perilous circumstances; Dallas (Claire Trevor), the Boule de Suif-like
prostitute, proves her mettle by helping the baby's mother; rugged outlaw
the Ringo Kid (John Wayne), whom Dallas loves, performs heroics during
the Indian attack, and then avenges the death of his father at the hands of
the Plummer gang. In addition to outstanding performances, *Stagecoach*
combined spectacular scenery, vivid characterization and daredevil stunts
– including one famous scene in which legendary stuntman Yakima
Canutt, playing an Apache, falls in front of the coach and is run over by it.
The dialogue by Dudley Nichols, a regular collaborator with Ford,
is infinitely more sophisticated than the gnomic 'aw shucks'-style one-
liners found in the B-Westerns of the time. All these elements together
ensured the film's box-office success, and revived Hollywood's interest in
the genre.

VALLEY BOYS

Some of the major film companies were making Westerns as early as 1907. By 1910, around one-fifth of all films made in Hollywood were Westerns. The new genre's unofficial muse was the former dentist Grey and its first big star was the one-time travelling salesman, Gilbert M. (Broncho Billy) Anderson, who could not even ride a horse. Not that this is necessarily a disqualification – a much later Western hero Clint Eastwood is also uncomfortable in the saddle. Anderson had appeared in Edwin S. Porter's *The Great Train Robbery* (1903), which is often described as the very first Western (slightly misleadingly, because it was shot on the East Coast). He launched himself as Broncho Billy in 1907 and began to make a film a week, chronicling Billy's adventures. He was by then a producer and only played Billy himself because he was unable to find any other actor to do the part. Nevertheless, the public warmed to him. Over the next seven years, he made around 400 Broncho Billy Westerns.

Thomas Ince (1882–1924) arrived in California a few years after Anderson, in 1911. He is the producer credited with inventing the studio system – of putting actors and directors under contract, employing script development consultants, and mass producing films in the same systematic way that Henry Ford made motor cars. Inceville, as his production operation became known, was heavily dependent on the Western. In 1912, his company Bison bought a ranch and a Wild West show, complete with all its props and performers. He also gave the first big break to arguably the greatest Western star of the silent era, William S. Hart (1870–1946). Hart was not the conventional juvenile lead. He was already in his mid-40s when Ince, who was a friend of his, began to give him work. He had a successful stage career behind him in which he had appeared in various Western dramas. Nevertheless, his emergence as a matinée idol took everyone by surprise. The studios, then as now, placed an extraordinary emphasis on youth, whereas Hart was wrinkled and weatherbeaten. Ince used him first of all as a villain, but soon realized he could play starring roles.

Hart had the look of authenticity about him. He too was a Monument Valley type. In his youth, he had travelled widely in the American West, accompanying his father, who was an itinerant labourer. He was plausible as a cowboy in a way Broncho Billy never was. His defining quality was his gravity: Hart took himself and his roles extraordinarily seriously. Look at old stills of his films and you will never see the hint of a smile. He introduced psychological complexity to the Western, and the characters he played were seldom straightforward heroes. Often they began with evil motives and only slowly became swayed to doing good.

As if to prove that he did have a sense of humour, he set one of his Westerns, *Branding Broadway* (1918) in modern-day New York. This was the same trick that Clint Eastwood and Don Siegel performed 50 years later in *Coogan's Bluff*. On the whole, though, his films are firmly set in the harsh and unforgiving West. Just as British Shakespearean actor Sir Johnston Forbes-Robertson (a dead ringer for Hart) continued playing Hamlet in his 60s, Hart remained in the saddle into late middle age. He bickered constantly with his bosses, whether Ince or United Artists, who produced his last film, *Tumbleweeds* (1925). His other defining trait, alongside his extreme seriousness, was his sentimentality: in his films, the hearts of even the most truculent cowboys are melted by beautiful women.

below Ex-Shakespearian actor William S. Hart (1870–1946), the most sombre cowboy star of his generation, in his 1925 vehicle, *Tumble weeds*.

WILLIAM FOX PRESENTS
TOM MIX IN
THE CYCLONE

above Tom Mix (1880–1940) was the silent Western's answer to Jackie Chan, clean-living, respectful toward women and very acrobatic. Here he's seen in his 1920 film, *The Cyclone*.

TOM MIX

Compared to the saturnine Hart, the other great star of the era, Tom Mix (1880–1940), was all cheeriness and youthful swagger. Like Hart, he claimed to be an authentic Westerner. The publicists dreamed up an extravagant biography for him. It was claimed he was the son of a US cavalryman and that he had been educated at a top-flight military academy. The truth was more mundane: his father was a lumberman, and young Tom himself was a high-school dropout and army deserter. Nevertheless, he had briefly served as a Texas Ranger and, having won various rodeo competitions and performed in Wild West shows, he certainly knew how to ride.

There was little psychological depth to his Westerns: their selling point was the virtuoso stunt work (largely performed by Mix himself) and the star's irrepressibly cheerful personality. As historian Clyde Jeavons notes in his book on the Western (Hamlyn, 1972), Mix was the most wholesome of screen presences. 'He didn't drink, swear, treat women disrespectfully or engage in unnecessary violence; and he refrained from killing his foes, rarely even wounding them unless forced to do so.' He was the silent Western's answer to Hong Kong's greatest star of the modern era, Jackie Chan. Like Chan, he often produced and directed his own films, first for the Selig Company (1911–1917) and then for Fox (1917–1928), and sustained numerous injuries as he flung himself hither and thither in the name of his art.

FORD AND HIS EVER-CHANGING MOODS

After Mix and the singing cowboys of the 1930s, none of whom would look at home against as austere a backdrop as Monument Valley, the Western needed its gravitas restored. That was where John Ford came in. His links to the Western stretch right back to the early silent days. His brother Francis started directing films for Thomas Ince in 1912. John, then known as Jack, joined him in California in 1914, and was directing Westerns himself by 1917. Many starred (and were co-written) by Harry Carey, who played a character called Cheyenne Harry.

The most ambitious film of this early part of Ford's career was *The Iron Horse* (1924), a big-budget yarn about the building of the Union Pacific Railroad. As in *Stagecoach*, the lead characters endure every kind of discomfort and danger. Although attacked by Indians, swindled by rapacious landowners, and buffeted by blizzards, they get the job done. The film was made in response to James Cruze's *The Covered Wagon* (1923), an epic account of settlers heading west.

Ford loved to make Westerns. However, there was a 13-year hiatus between *Three Bad Men* (1926) and the time he first set up his camera in Monument Valley. He made seven films in the valley: *Stagecoach* (1939), *My Darling Clementine* (1946), *Fort Apache* (1948), *She Wore a Yellow Ribbon* (1949), *The Searchers* (1956), *Sergeant Rutledge* (1960) and *Cheyenne Autumn* (1964).

They differ widely in tone. Some are elegiac, some action-driven shoot-'em ups. In some, the Native Americans are invested with pathos and dignity. In some, they are whoopin' hollerin' Red Indians, the Wild West's very own version of pantomime villains. Despite sharing the same location, the films all look radically different from one another. In *The*

Searchers, as Ethan Edwards (John Wayne), the Ahab-like loner, relentlessly hunts down his niece (Natalie Wood), who has been kidnapped and raised by the same Comanches that massacred her parents, the skies are grey and full of foreboding, and the valley seems utterly desolate. In the much warmer, more sentimental *She Wore a Yellow Ribbon*, in which Wayne stars as a bluff old cavalry captain on the verge of retirement, Winton C. Hoch's Oscar-winning cinematography bathes the valley in a glowing, twilight red and manages to make it look almost inviting in the process.

Filmmakers are still going to Monument Valley today. In late 2000, two new movies featured it – Neil LaBute's *Nurse Betty* and Chris McQuarrie's *Way of the Gun*. And no, the valley had not changed in the slightest – it was still the same imposing wilderness that had so attracted Ford and Grey all those years before.

below Laying tracks in John Ford's silent epic about the building of the Union Pacific Railroad, *The Iron Horse* (1924).

SPAGHETTI WESTERNS

One latecomer to Monument Valley was the paunchy Italian director, Sergio Leone, who arrived to film part of his epic 1968 film, *Once Upon a Time in the West*. He had been drawn there both by the myth of John Ford and the desire to escape his tag as a director of spaghetti Westerns. According to the popular definition, spaghetti Westerns were low-budget, infra dig affairs, shot in Spain or Italy. By moving to the 'real' West, Leone was staking his claim to be taken as seriously as any of the Hollywood directors he so admired.

Leone's biographer Christopher Frayling notes that the Italian was fairly irritated by the name 'spaghetti Western' when he first heard it. 'I thought it was quite subtle – maybe the spaghetti had replaced the lasso,' Leone joked. It was not so much the phrase itself that annoyed him as the sense that his work would be lumped together in critics' and audiences' eyes with the derivative Westerns made by so many other, lesser Italian directors. His great trilogy of the mid-1960s, *A Fistful of Dollars* (1964), *For a Few Dollars More* (1965) and *The Good, the Bad and the Ugly* (1966), as he was the first to boast, was far superior to the work done by his imitators.

Leone was a jackdaw talent who drew his inspiration from all sorts of unlikely sources. His Westerns did not just pay homage to the classics of Ford, Raoul Walsh and co. *A Fistful of Dollars* also owed a considerable debt to Akira Kurosawa's samurai warrior classic, *Yojimbo* (1961), and to the Dashiell Hammett crime novel, *Red Harvest*. It was based around a bracingly simple idea – that of the lone gunman who rides into a town where two gangs are feuding and plays each off against the other. His desire to make such a movie owed much to his distrust of the modern, psychological Western. As he once remarked, 'the cowboy picture has got lost in psychology...the west was made by violent, uncomplicated men, and it is this strength and simplicity that I try to recapture in my picture'. Such a sentiment ran contrary to the conventional wisdom that the reason the genre stuttered was precisely because its code of morality was too simple-minded for post-war audiences.

In *A Fistful of Dollars*, as in the sequels, the emphasis is on blood, violence and picaresque humour. Leone and his collaborators were formalists who paid minute attention to detail: sound editing, music, perfecting the widescreen close-up, and choreographing the gunfights in as flamboyant a way as possible. There is something wonderfully chaotic and haphazard about the gestation of the film. The casting of Clint Eastwood owed much to accident. 'The man with a vacant look on his face in an unwatchable film about cows?' Leone exclaimed at the idea of making Eastwood the star of *Magnificent Stranger* (the film's original title). He had seen Eastwood in an episode of *Rawhide*, and had been far from bowled over. His vision of the West as lawless terrain, full of ugly 'sons of bitches', didn't allow much scope for matinée hero types like Rowdy Yates (Eastwood's character in *Rawhide*). Henry Fonda (whose agent didn't even show him the screenplay), Charles Bronson and James Coburn were all higher up Leone's wish list than Eastwood, whose main recommendation was that, at $15,000, he came cheap.

The film's troubled production history and struggle to reach an audience have long since become part of its myth. In flatly contradictory accounts of

below Leone's spaghetti Westerns were characterized by their picaresque humour. Here, a smirking Eli Wallach mistakenly thinks he has the upper hand on Eastwood in *The Good, the Bad and the Ugly* (1966).

the making of the movie, both star and director claim the credit for the evolution of the dusty, bestubbled, poncho-wearing, cigar-chewing 'man with no name'. Whoever was responsible, Eastwood's dialogue was pared down to a minimum ('he's one of the few actors in film history to have fought for fewer lines,' Frayling notes), thereby increasing his mystique and rendering his lapidary little one-liners ('my mule don't like people laughing') all the more memorable.

To richen the mix, Leone cheerfully threw in references to the West of *Shane* and John Ford with Christian symbolism and pantomime-style imagery which rightly belonged in commedia dell'arte. He was helped immeasurably by Ennio Morricone's riveting music. To dismiss his Westerns, as some have done, as glorified comic strips is patronizing and unjust. *The Good, the Bad and the Ugly*, the most ambitious of the trilogy, contains some of the most haunting imagery of the US Civil War ever committed to film. In among the jokes and gunfights, it shows up the absurdity, squalor and pathos of war in a way that can't help but move even the most hardbitten and cynical of audiences.

13

Brief Encounter
1946

British Cinema's Golden Era

'One of the most adult films in years, it is the story of an affair between a respectable British matron (Celia Johnson) and a doctor (Trevor Howard).' This was how the *New Yorker* magazine summarized the plot of David Lean's *Brief Encounter* (1946). Lean disliked the description and objected to the use of 'adult' and 'matron'. Given that the majority of cinema-goers in both the UK and US were teenagers, he surmised that an adult film about a matron would be box-office poison.

Whatever its status as a classic now, *Brief Encounter* performed disappointingly on its initial release. It had no stars and its ending was downbeat. Even so, the film perfectly illustrated the new-found confidence of British cinema in the 1940s. Lean and screenwriter Noel Coward treated a humdrum romance between a middle-class couple in suburbia as if they were making a full-blown *Anna Karenina*-like tragedy. The pounding Rachmaninov music on the soundtrack, the heroine's emotionally fraught voice-over, and the juddering shots of trains disappearing down tunnels transformed what might otherwise have seemed a timid domestic melodrama.

The war years were a golden era in British cinema. In 1939, the government had threatened to close down the industry and only intense lobbying kept it open. Manpower and resources were scarce, and cinema-going became an intensely perilous activity: 160 theatres were destroyed by German bombs between 1939 and 1945. Nevertheless, audiences increased rather than decreased during the war, and tastes also changed. People did not only want Hollywood escapism; British escapism would do just as well. They also had a new-found appetite for more challenging fare. The filmmakers in turn had stumbled on subject-matter – namely the war itself – which they could address from first-hand experience. No longer did they need to ape American crime movies or thrillers. What was happening in their own backyard suddenly seemed far more exciting. By 1946, for the first and only time, British movies outperformed their Hollywood counterparts at the UK box-office.

ON THE PLATFORM

The symbolism in *Brief Encounter* is not subtle. Laura (Celia Johnson), on the platform of a small-town railway station, waiting to go home to her husband and children, gets a speck in her eye. A stranger, Alec (Trevor Howard), helps to dab it out. The speck seems to have been put there by Cupid. By the time it is removed, she is besotted with the stranger. Lean lets us know that Laura is obsessed with romantic fiction. She is spotted with a novel by Kate O'Brien, a writer who specialized in stories about middle-class women haunted by religious guilt. She also loves the cinema, and the encounter with Alec enables her to become like a character in one of the movies or novels she so cherishes. Johnson, a slight, bird-like actress with a nervous demeanour and mournful eyes, captures Laura's guilt and indecision perfectly. She is ostensibly devoted to her bluff husband (Cyril Raymond) and kids, but she craves more.

Brief Encounter was made by Cineguild, one of the production companies under the umbrella of Independent Producers Ltd, the organization set up by J. Arthur Rank for the 'elite' filmmakers of the day. Rank's idea was to give the privileged few complete creative freedom in the hope that they would repay him with the best films possible – films that he could go on and sell in the all-important American market.

'We can make any subject we wish, with as much money as we think that subject should have spent on it. We can cast whichever actors we choose and we have no interference with the way the film is made,' Lean wrote not long after the completion of *Brief Encounter*. This idyllic state of affairs, unheard of in British film history, lasted not much longer than Laura's illicit relationship with Alec. Nevertheless, it yielded many of the gilt-edged classics of British cinema, films like *The Red Shoes*, *A Matter of Life and Death*, *Oliver Twist* and *Black Narcissus*.

LOVE DASHED

Laura and Alec were not the only frustrated lovers around. As if echoing the real-life separations and travails of the war years, British films of the 1940s are full of couples split apart in the cruellest and most outlandish circumstances. There was always something in the way of the perfect relationship, whether illness, death, the law, or the nasty neighbours.

Similar thematically, but in an altogether different register to *Brief Encounter* was Leslie Arliss's weepie, *Love Story* (1944), one of the many melodramas that Gainsborough Studios made in the 1940s. The director had no qualms about the sentimentality of a story hinging on a wartime affair between a classical pianist and a mining engineer. As if worried that cinema-goers would not get the point otherwise, Arliss makes sure they both have terrible afflictions. The pianist (played by Margaret Lockwood) has a terminal illness, while the engineer (Stewart Granger) is going blind. The fact that one of the protagonists is a musician allows Arliss to complement the story with a swirling, emotive classical soundtrack. 'It will no doubt get audiences so dizzy that they must fall off their seats,' suggested one critic. 'A sleepy pear masked with thick warm sauce,' ventured another when asked to characterize the film.

THE WICKED LADY

From playing an ailing pianist, it was but a small step for Margaret Lockwood – the most popular British star of the era – to become a lusty highwaywoman in a low-cut dress (too low-cut for the American censors) in *The Wicked Lady* (1945), the biggest British box-office hit of the 1940s. Arliss was again the writer-director. 'I like wicked women – on the screen,' he told *Picturegoer* magazine. 'They are so much more interesting than the average heroine type. They've got more colour and fire – and they're more human.'

left Margaret Lockwood and Stewart Granger in Gainsborough Studios' unashamedly maudlin tearjerker, *Love Story* (1944).

In *Brief Encounter*, Laura's loyalty to husband and home, and fear of upsetting the status quo stymies her relationship with Alec. In Gainsborough melodramas, affairs tended to end in a far more bloody way. In *The Man in Grey* (1943), a scowling James Mason beat Lockwood to death – a shocking denouement, but one which failed to put off British audiences. In *The Wicked Lady*, she and Mason are again illicit lovers, she a society woman turned thief, he a Dick Turpin-type figure. 'Spectacle and sex, a dash of sadism, near-the-knuckle lines and an end where virtue is rewarded,' was how one newspaper characterized Arliss's pet formula for bodice-ripping costume pictures.

above left Margaret Lockwood, the most popular British star of the 1940s, as a highwaywoman in bodice-ripping box-office smash, *The Wicked Lady* (1945).

above right Gordon Jackson and Patricia Roc in British wartime classic, *Millions Like Us* (1943), a film made all the more moving by its understatement.

MILLIONS LIKE US

If the war years saw the flourishing of Gainsborough melodramas, they also yielded many documentary-style films which dealt with the romances and disappointments of 'ordinary people' in understated style. One of the strongest was Launder and Gilliat's *Millions Like Us* (1943) detailing the love affair between an airman (Gordon Jackson) and a factory worker (Patricia Roc). The couple are shown as part of a community, not simply as individuals, and when the airman is killed in action the filmmakers do not resort to lachrymose music or flashy close-ups to underline Roc's grief. Their refusal to resort to cheap melodramatic tricks impressed British cinema-goers, many of whom had taken to complaining about Hollywood gimmickry in the fan papers. 'We are sick and tired of having American films (chiefly second rate) rammed down our throats,' wrote T.H. Martin, an RAF man, in *Picturegoer*. 'They may be slick of production and technically sound, but they are filled with oomph-oozing women, their bodies covered or uncovered to stimulate the sexual rather than the artistic senses... what refreshing contrasts are provided by British films full, as they invariably are, of superb acting by people full of character, and in which one can almost exist, so realistically and vividly are they portrayed.' (*Picturegoer*, 16 March 1946).

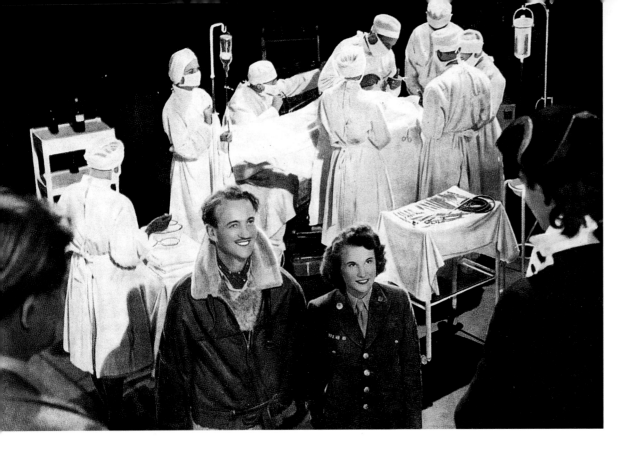

STAIRWAY TO HEAVEN

Not even death could get in the way of British movie romances of the 1940s. In Powell and Pressburger's 1945 classic, *A Matter of Life and Death*, the hero, Squadron-Leader Peter Carter (David Niven) does not set eyes on the beautiful US radio controller June (Kim Hunter), until after his fatal plane crash.

The film begins in spectacular style, with Carter in the cockpit as the aircraft – in flames – hurtles down towards the ground. He is the only member of the crew still alive. He blithely chats up June, reciting poetry to her, before telling her that he is about to bail out. 'But there's a catch – I've got no parachute. I'd rather jump than fry.'

Thanks to some celestial bungling, Carter does not die. The emissary from heaven (Marius Goring), a

perfumed fop dressed like an eighteenth-century French aristocrat, is very disappointed that Carter has escaped the net. The fantastical plot entails Carter going up to heaven on a gigantic stairway to argue his case with the celestial court. By a neat twist, whereas earth is in 'glorious Technicolor', heaven is monochrome, and very bureaucratic. There is one remarkable shot in which the camera seems to venture beyond Carter's eyelid and into his imagination as he lies under anaesthetic having a dangerous operation. While the doctors pore over his body on earth, he is fighting for his life – and for his love of June – with the court. Inevitably, the climax comes on that gigantic stairway – itself a testament to the artistry and ingenuity of British film technicians of the time.

A REPUBLICAN LASS

British filmmakers generally steer clear of making movies touching on the vexed issue of relations between the UK and Ireland. When they do make such films, they tend to be either sombre, solemn affairs bemoaning the rift between two cultures so close together, or high-testosterone action-thrillers using the 'Troubles' as an excuse for staging lots of gunfights. One film which avoids these clichés is Launder and Gilliat's comedy-thriller, *I See a Dark Stranger* (1946). The premise is provocative: the heroine Bridie Quilty (Deborah Kerr) is a colleen who detests the Brits so much that she prefers to work for the Nazis. Trevor Howard plays an English officer who falls in love with her, and sets out to overcome her acute Anglophobia. A ripping yarn, playful and witty, this is another tale of love across a divide – one which proves that (at least some) British filmmakers were flexible and imaginative enough to re-examine old stereotypes.

TAKING COALS TO NEWCASTLE… AND SAND TO EGYPT

You cannot help but admire the sheer chutzpah of Hungarian producer-director Gabriel Pascal, who inveigled British tycoon J. Arthur Rank into backing his wildly, wilfully extravagant film adaptation of George Bernard Shaw's *Caesar and Cleopatra* (1945). It was the most expensive British film ever made, costing more than *Gone with the Wind* (1939), whose star, Vivien Leigh, Pascal had picked to play the old crocodile of the Nile alongside Claude Rains's Caesar.

Pascal, the only film producer trusted by Shaw, built his own full-scale Sphinx (he deemed the one in Egypt not up to scratch) and let money slip through his hands like the consignments of sand with which he filled up Denham Studios. He shot both in the Middle East and in the UK, and re-created ancient Alexandria, complete with peacocks, camels and even a baby leopard, on the studio lot. As well as the stars, he assembled a huge cast of bit actors and extras. The film was originally scheduled to shoot for two months, but ended up taking 80 weeks to complete. His 'spend, spend, spend' philosophy antagonized other film producers working for Rank who were not allowed to go a penny over budget, and it also rankled with the British public. This, after all, was a time of shortages and rationing.

When the film was finally released in cinemas decked out to look like Egyptian palaces, it was – almost inevitably – an enormous anticlimax. 'A dismal ordeal,' complained one critic. 'It costs over a million and a quarter pounds, took two and a half years to make, and well and truly bored one spectator for two and a quarter hours.' Another grumbled that George Bernard Shaw's intentions had been completely ignored. He wrote the play as a protest against spectacle and stage pageants, but Pascal had mounted it in the most lavish way imaginable. The film did surprisingly well in the US, but had cost too much ever to make a profit. Pascal was never to work in the UK again.

THE RED SHOES

Largely because of their experiences with Pascal, Rank and his executives became very wary about financing big-budget, prestige productions. The Rank Organization was haemorrhaging money. Post-war British audiences had now lost their appetite for home-produced fare, and wanted Hollywood movies once more. The freedom granted Powell and Pressburger, David Lean and a few others at Independent Producers Ltd was therefore withdrawn. The last movie that Powell and Pressburger made at IPL was *The Red Shoes* (1948), a £700,000 extravaganza set in the esoteric world of European ballet, which was precisely the kind of project to raise Rank's hackles. When the tycoon saw the film for the first time, he thought he had lost his shirt. Rank was convinced the film would be an expensive flop and chose a damage-limitation approach – to

opposite David Niven and Kim Hunter confront the celestial powers in Powell and Pressburger's *A Matter of Life and Death* (1945), a film set between earth and heaven.

below left Claude Rains is Caesar to Vivien Leigh's Cleopatra in Gabriel Pascal's ill-fated *Caesar and Cleopatra* (1945), the wildly extravagant film adaptation of George Bernard Shaw's play.

below right Moira Shearer in the breathtaking ballet sequence which rounds off Powell and Pressburger's 1948 classic, *The Red Shoes*.

release it as cheaply as possible and to be rid of it. Sure enough, the film performed poorly in the UK, but in the US it was a different matter: after a slow start, it became one of the most successful films ever in the US market. Both Martin Scorsese and Brian De Palma cite it as one of their favourite movies. 'Why do you dance?' the ballet dancer Vicky Page (Moira Shearer) is asked by the Diaghilev-like entrepreneur (Anton Walbrook) recruiting for his ballet company. 'Why do you live?' is her reply. The answer captures perfectly the obsessive perfectionism of the true artist.

GREAT EXPECTATIONS

Great Expectations was a prophetic title for a film made in 1946, just as the Attlee government swept to power. These were seismic years: the establishment of the National Health Service, the passing of the Butler Education Act (1944), and the promise of 'Homes For All' (the title of a popular documentary of the era) suggested a new egalitarianism in British society. David Lean's adaptation of Charles Dickens's great novel tapped into the national mood. This was a story about a young man from a humble background, Pip (John Mills), who is suddenly and mysteriously given unimaginable opportunities in life. The film is full of symbols of the old and new. The ancient, dried-up Miss Havisham (Martita Hunt) lives in a dusty house, where the curtains are always closed, pining for the suitor who deserted her on her wedding day. She is a symbol of the old England, characterized by privilege, snobbery and cruelty. Pip, his guardian Joe Gargery (Bernard Miles) and his ex-convict benefactor Magwitch (Finlay Currie) are from a new and kinder world.

Set-pieces were always Lean's forte. While *Brief Encounter* had its famous tryst on the railway platform, *Great Expectations* boasts an even more bravura sequence. Pip (played as a boy by Anthony Wager) encounters Magwitch for the first time when the convict has just escaped a prison ship and is on the run from a posse of soldiers. Shaven-headed, as ugly as a gorgon, he looks as if he has just wandered off the set of one of James Whale's Frankenstein movies. The mist and sound effects add to the sense of foreboding, but Pip, however frightened he is of the convict, treats him with kindness and generosity, stealing food and drink on his behalf.

The film ends with the shutters of Miss Havisham's ghastly Gothic pile being thrown open, sunlight pouring in. This, it seemed, was to be a new dawn for everyone – British filmmakers included. Of course, the new world turned out to be far less idyllic than David Lean and his contemporaries had hoped. Nevertheless, their energy and optimism is present in every frame of the film.

RUTHERFORD PONTIFICATES

British cinema of the 1940s was not just about brief encounters and stiff-upper-lipped heroism. This was the decade in which Ealing Studios began to mine a rich seam of humour in its quizzical comedies. In the 1930s, Ealing had made many knockabout films with stars like George Formby and Gracie Fields. Under production boss Michael Balcon (1896–1977), who took over at Ealing in 1938, the emphasis changed. During the war years, Balcon and his team concentrated on turning out such patriotic, character actor-driven fare as

below David Lean's *Great Expectations* (1946) is still considered one of the greatest screen adaptations of Dickens. It gave plum roles to John Mills and Alec Guinness while also providing veteran character actor Finlay Currie with his best-known part as the convict, Magwitch.

left Much to the consternation of the big, bad bureaucrats from Whitehall, a small London community declared it was no longer part of Britain in Ealing classic, *Passport to Pimlico* (1949).

below Alexander Mackendrick's *The Ladykillers* (1955) was one of the last of the great Ealing comedies. Despite brilliant performances from Herbert Lom, Peter Sellers, and Alec Guinness, the real scene-stealing turn here came from the octogenarian Katie Johnson as the little old lady who has the thieves to stay in her boarding house.

The Foreman went to France, *Next of Kin*, *Went the Day Well* and *San Demetrio London* – all films about heroism and self-sacrifice. It was only after the war that Balcon steered the studio towards comedies reflecting 'the country's moods, social conditions and aspirations'. Unlike far-fetched 1930s farces starring the likes of Will Hay and The Crazy Gang, the films of the late 1940s were rooted in the realities of British post-war life. Charles Crichton's *Hue and Cry* (1947) was set in bomb-scarred London, but this was no grim social realist drama. As the film showed, bomb craters, mazes of rubble and derelict buildings provided a perfect playground for kids.

The best-known Ealing comedies, *Passport to Pimlico* (1949), *Whisky Galore* (1949), *The Lavender Hill Mob* (1951), *The Man in the White Suit* (1951), *The Titfield Thunderbolt* (1953) and *The Ladykillers* (1955) combined whimsical humour, social comment and superb character performances. These are all films portraying a mild but distinct rebelliousness, with small-timers cocking a snook at authority. Robert Hamer's *Kind Hearts and Coronets* (1949), about an unscrupulous, but supremely elegant, Oscar Wilde-like roué (Dennis Price) trying to murder his way to a family fortune, is, perhaps, the one exception.

In Ealing's tilted universe, the voices of eccentrics and outsiders carry more weight than those of the establishment. Thus, when the splendidly brusque bluestocking historian, Professor Hatton-Jones (Margaret Rutherford) goes to court in *Passport to Pimlico*, she is the one who lays down the law. She has in her hands the document proving that the little London community is part of the Duchy of Burgundy, and that there is nothing that the lawyers and civil servants can do about it.

Under Balcon, Ealing Studios was run like one of the proud, defiant little communities that its films so often portrayed. The emphasis was on character actors, not stars, on craftsmanship, not showy special effects. What mattered, both behind and in front of the cameras, was consensus, not individualism. Ealing under Balcon may have poked fun at the establishment, but it was also intensely patriotic. The famous plaque put up at Ealing when the studio was sold in 1955 describes perfectly what Balcon and his team were trying to achieve. 'Here during a quarter of a century,' it reads, 'many films were made projecting Britain and the British character.'

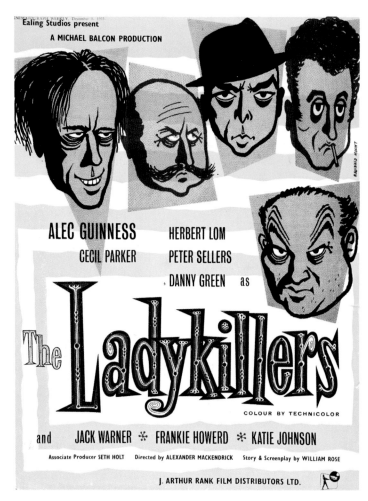

Teen Rebels

14

The Blue Lamp
1950

Sneering, tousle-haired Tom Riley (Dirk Bogarde) in *The Blue Lamp* (1950) and the boyish, razor-wielding thug Pinkie (Richard Attenborough) in *Brighton Rock* (1947) cannot exactly be described as teen rebels. They belong to a different but related British tradition – that of the post-war 'spiv'.

Spivs lived by their wits, not by holding down proper jobs. They were young, well-dressed men about town, whose standard uniform was sharp suits, felt hats and winkle-pickers. Spivs made their money on the black market, hawking luxury items that were hard to find in austere, ration-era Britain – nylon stockings and tobacco in particular. They tended to be obsessed with American consumer culture and their heroes were the glamorous low-lifes played by Cagney and Bogart in Warner Bros gangster movies. Spivs played at being tough without ever convincing anybody they really were. 'As flashy as neon, as exaggerated as the cut of their suits... they overcompensated for the drabness, becoming almost feminine in the process,' writer David Hughes observed, referring to their 'pansy braggadocio'.

The spiv was a specifically British phenomenon, but you can see him as the predecessor of the teen rebels that emerged in the US a few years later. Like the teen rebels, the spivs were engaged in an Oedipal battle against every kind of authority figure.

TO THE PUBLIC DANGER

British writer Patrick Hamilton, whose plays *Rope* and *Gaslight* were both made into successful films, was the supreme chronicler of 'spivdom'. Hamilton wrote the story on which Terence Fisher's 1948 short film, *To the Public Danger*, was based. The film was intended as a cautionary tale about the perils of drunk driving, but it shows how monotonous and claustrophobic post-war life was to young tearaways. Captain Cole (Dermot Walsh), a reckless, bored soldier-turned-spiv, out to have a good time, roars through the country in his car, stopping at every roadside pub for more alcohol. His companions try to stop him, but he is hell-bent on his drink-driving binge. Such self-destructiveness was to be the hallmark of many of the teen rebels that followed him a generation later.

P.C. DIXON TOPPLED

There is a watershed moment in *The Blue Lamp*: Tom Riley, in the midst of a bungled robbery attempt, is interrupted by P.C. Dixon (Jack Warner). In panic, he shoots Dixon and kills him. This was considered deeply shocking both by audiences and by the characters in the film. Just as the authorities and the criminal underworld had pooled resources to flush out the serial killer in Fritz

HUCK FINN AND SOME DEAD END KIDS

The term 'teen-ager' was hardly used before the mid-1940s, but within a decade had become the key word in US consumer culture. The post-war baby boom ensured that there were more teenagers around in the 1950s than ever before, and they had parents with unprecedented affluence. 'In the Nineteenth Century, young people had fuelled the Industrial Revolution with their labour,' historian Thomas Doherty observes in his book, *Teenagers and Teenpics*. 'In the Twentieth Century, they would fulfil a more enviable economic function as consumers, whose leisure vicariously validated their parents' affluence.'

Hollywood only really woke up to the new teenage phenomenon in the mid-1950s, when the studios belatedly realized that these youngsters had money to burn. There had been movies made about and for young audiences long before James Dean stumbled onto the scene. Cinema started as an immature medium and, many believed, never grew up. 'Movies sprung from minds essentially juvenile and adolescent,' Terry Ramsaye wrote in *A Million and One Nights*. But before *Rebel without a Cause*, youngsters (i.e. anybody from the age of about 8 to 18) were invariably portrayed as happy-go-lucky rascals.

Andy Hardy, the character played by Mickey Rooney in a series of anodyne but hugely popular films in the late 1930s, was from a well-to-do background: his high jinks got him into trouble, but his patient, kind-hearted father Judge Hardy was always on hand to steer him back onto the straight and narrow. The Dead End Kids were from the other side of the tracks – the tenement slums of New York – but these little tough guys were good lads at heart. They first appeared in *Dead End* (1937), a grim drama starring Humphrey Bogart about poverty and crime in the Big Apple. They stole the film with their wisecracking and japes, and went on to appear in dozens more movies, either as colourful support, as in *Angels with Dirty Faces* (1938), or heading up the cast. They were conceived as a sort of urban counterpart to Mark Twain's Huckleberry Finn, who has long since become the patron saint of teenage scamps.

Lang's *M*, Scotland Yard and London's underworld combine here to bring Riley to justice.

It is fascinating how the filmmakers treat Riley and his girlfriend (Peggy Evans). The young, gun-toting delinquent is, in the words of film historian Charles Barr, 'violent, hysterical... and sexy'. A few years later, he would have been portrayed as a glamorous antihero in the mould of Dean, Brando or Montgomery Clift. For young audiences, he must have seemed an infinitely more glamorous figure than the bluff young policemen who help hunt him down. Nevertheless, the filmmakers treat him as beneath contempt.

THE BLACKBOARD JUNGLE

Richard Brooks's 1955 film, *The Blackboard Jungle*, takes a more ambivalent approach to juvenile delinquency than *The Blue Lamp*. The filmmakers remain deeply distrustful of the young tearaways they are portraying. The new teacher (Glenn Ford) at North Manual High School in New York is a war veteran, but his experiences fighting the Nazis are no preparation for dealing with the worst that the American education system can throw at him. He is clean-cut, tolerant, kind-hearted – the rugged all-American type. His students, led by young street punk Artie West (Vic Morrow), come from another world where old ideas about respect and morality no longer apply. In one especially brutal scene, Ford is beaten up on the way home.

In the end, as in all good liberal wish-fulfilment fantasies, the teacher wins over his unruly charges. He is helped by the most charismatic boy in the school (Sidney Poitier), who can talk his classmates into behaving. As teacher and schoolkids are reconciled, the film eventually peters out; nevertheless, it is clear that Hollywood is beginning to understand that teenagers are not just something to be frightened of – they are consumers too. The choice of music – Bill Haley and the Comets perform 'Rock Around the Clock' over the opening credits – is significant. For all its pious homilies about the importance

of education, the film surreptitiously celebrates the raucousness and wild energy of its teenage heroes.

The Blackboard Jungle is fairly bland, but it still managed to appal mainstream America. Clare Boothe Luce, US Ambassador to Italy, refused to allow so sensationalist a film to be shown at the Venice Film Festival. A Senate committee pontificated that there were 'valid reasons for concluding that the film will have effects on youth other than the beneficial ones described by the producers'. That, of course, was the point. The Blackboard Jungle was a big box-office success, but this had nothing to do with its sanctimonious message about teenagers and teachers living in perfect harmony. What appealed to its audiences was the rebelliousness that the teacher played by Ford tried so hard to suppress. The film was released in the same year as Rebel without a Cause, and whatever its qualms about endorsing antisocial behaviour, Hollywood now realized that teenage revolt could be very lucrative indeed.

YOU'RE TEARING ME APART

'You're tearing me apart', Jim (James Dean) screeches in fury and self-pity at his parents early on in Rebel without a Cause (1955). The sentiment rang true with the teenage audience which clamoured to see the film. Jim is dismayed by the way his father is browbeaten by his mother, and the boy's own escapades – the fights, the drinking, the driving stunts – are not merely adolescent defiance: he is trying to prove he is tough and self-reliant in the way his father is not.

There is a paradox at the heart of Rebel without a Cause. Teenagers in the 1950s were in a much more privileged position than their parents had been, with no war or Depression to contend with, and money and consumer goods at their disposal. Nevertheless – if Dean's character in Nicholas Ray's movie was anything to go by – they were miserable. Hollywood was prepared to indulge the teen rebels in a way that would have been unthinkable a few years before. By 1959, the teen market was worth an astonishing $10 billion a year, but exploiting this new market was the last thing on maverick director Ray's mind. He had to fight Warner Bros for the right to use Dean. He had been hugely impressed by the young actor's performance as the Cain-like son in Elia Kazan's East of Eden, but the studio initially pressurized him to cast Tab Hunter and Jayne Mansfield (in the Natalie Wood role as Jim's girlfriend) instead. Dean was, in Kazan's words, 'a very, very neurotic kid... a sick kid' and his nervous energy and introspection brought an intensity to Rebel without a Cause that a more conventional, clean-cut young star could never have matched. His death in a road accident in the year the film was released added to his mystique. He was – as a 1975 documentary about him put it – 'the first American teenager'. In that film, an old friend of the actor remembered that Dean was driven throughout his career by 'a pathological desire for attention'. That was a trait he shared with many other disaffected teenagers and one that made him the greatest screen delinquent of all.

Ray's debut feature, They Live by Night (1949), romanticized its doomed young protagonists. Bowie (Farley Granger), ostensibly 23 but looking younger, and Keechie (Cathy O'Donnell) are lovers. They seem a perfect

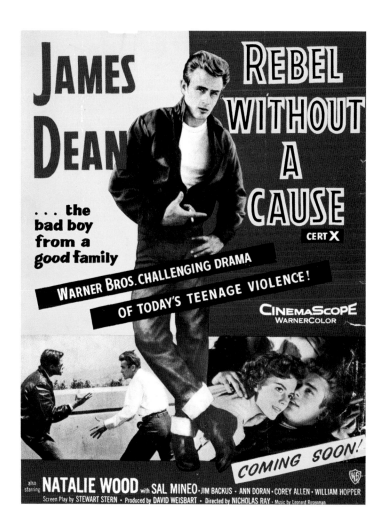

above James Dean (1932–1955) was perfectly cast as the mixed-up bad boy in Nicholas Ray's classic about teenage alienation, Rebel without a Cause (1955).

opposite left Dermot Walsh as the drunken spiv and Susan Shaw as the unfortunate woman along for the ride in British B-picture To the Public Danger (1948).

opposite right Teacher Glenn Ford confronts his most delinquent pupil, the sneering Vic Morrow, in Richard Brooks' The Blackboard Jungle (1955).

couple, but he is an escaped con-man and bank robber and it is only a matter of time until he gets his comeuppance. Rather than show him as a vicious mobster, Ray suggests he is a victim of the times – an innocent caught up in the Depression. 'This boy and girl were never properly introduced to the world we live in,' reads an introductory subtitle. Like the adolescent heroes and antiheroes of dozens of later teen movies, Bowie and his girlfriend are at odds with a harsh, adult world that doesn't even try to understand them.

THE WILD ONE

James Dean revered Brando's performance as the moody, leather-clad biker, causing havoc in a small town in *The Wild One* (1954). Laslo Benedek's film is more conventional than its reputation might suggest – a Western in which the outlaws ride motorbikes instead of horses. It is memorable, though, for two key moments. At one stage, Brando is asked: 'What are you rebelling against?' 'Whadda you got?' he fires back – the perfect teen rebel reply. Then there is his fight with a rival biker played by Lee Marvin (one of Hollywood's great screen heavies), a sock-it-to-him brawl that puts most cowboy shoot-outs to shame.

THE TEEN REBEL OUT WEST

If *The Wild One* was a Western in disguise, many Westerns of the 1950s and 1960s featured characters who seemed to have stumbled out of teen movies. Elvis Presley made his debut screen performance as the southern boy in love with the same woman as his brother in the Civil War drama, *Love Me Tender* (1956), while Ricky Nelson was the quick-on-the-draw Colorado Kid in *Rio Bravo* (1959).

Howard Hawks's *Red River* (1948) anticipates all those 1950s yarns about young tearaways pitted against their elders. In this case, Montgomery Clift (one of the supreme method actors) is the sensitive, self-reliant cowboy and John Wayne is the stubborn old patriarch he works for. The film ends in an explosion of fists as Clift finally takes on Wayne. It is an Oedipal battle: the two men are split by age, attitude – and even by acting style.

In Arthur Penn's *The Left-Handed Gun* (1958), Billy The Kid (Paul Newman) is presented to audiences 'as a juvenile delinquent in search of a father figure' (Martin Scorsese). Whereas most Westerns romanticize their protagonists, this one portrays the young outlaw as a sort of high plains counterpart to James Dean – a neurotic, brooding adolescent who is convinced that the adult world, in the shape of the lawmen and sheriffs, is against him.

PRESLEY ON SCREEN

King Creole (1958), adapted from the Harold Robbins novel *A Stone for Danny Fisher* and directed by Michael Curtiz (of *Casablanca* fame) is one of the few movies to do Elvis Presley justice. Nobody would argue that he was a match for Dean or Brando as an actor, but, given the chance, Presley could play mixed-up young rebels as well as anyone. Here, he is surrounded by a strong supporting cast, including Walter Matthau as a gangland leader and Vic Morrow (from *The Blackboard Jungle*) as the young punk who leads him astray. The film is shot (in black and white) by one of the

METHOD IN THEIR MADNESS

In 1947, Lee Strasberg, Robert Lewis, Cheryl Crawford and Elia Kazan formed the Actors' Studio in New York. They had been associated with the Group Theatre, the left-wing company which had revolutionized American theatre in the 1930s. The Group, in turn, was strongly influenced by the Russian theatre director, Stanislavsky, who had pioneered a new style of naturalistic acting in his productions – many of them Chekhov plays – at the Moscow Arts Theatre at the turn of the 20th century.

The 'method', as taught at the Actors' Studio, required actors to base their performances around personal experience. As one spokesperson put it, 'it identifies the actor's own personality not merely as a model for the creation of character, but as the mine from which all psychological truth must be dug.' In its distrust of big showy gestures and its move towards introspection, it was the perfect tool for a new generation of movie actor – and for any self-absorbed, would-be teen rebels. Its supreme exponent was Marlon Brando, who had trained extensively with another old Group Theatre alumnus, Stella Adler.

great Hollywood cinematographers, Russell Harlan. In such company, Presley sparkles. 'He has suddenly learned to act very well indeed, curbed his convulsions and cut off his sideboards,' one curmudgeonly British critic acknowledged after seeing the movie. It stands alongside *Wild in the Country* (1961), a sizzling southern melodrama scripted by Clifford Odets, and *Flaming Star* (1960), a Western directed by Don Siegel, as probably the best of the Presley movies. His other films may often have disappointed critics, but they invariably made money.

TEEN REBELS SANITIZED

There is a sense of Jekyll and Hyde about teen movies. For every mercurial, mixed-up kid played by a Brando or a Dean, there were always several squeaky-clean counterparts. Doris Day movies, like the beautifully crafted but very saccharine period piece *On Moonlight Bay* (1951) and *By the Light of the Silvery Moon* (1952), offered up a cosy, idyllic image of the typical American adolescent. Then there were the beach movies: whimsical, insubstantial yarns with stars like Frankie Avalon. The equivalent to such lightweight fare in the UK were the Cliff Richard movies. Genial, relentlessly upbeat films like *Summer Holiday* (1963), in which Cliff and his friends traverse the continent on a red London bus, exist as if in a time warp. They have more in common with Arthur Ransome adventures like *Swallows and Amazons* than with the world of *Rebel without a Cause* and *The Blackboard Jungle*. In them, the teen rebel is well and truly tamed.

left Paul Newman's Billy The Kid in Arthur Penn's *The Left-Handed Gun* (1958) was as much a mixed-up adolescent as a conventional Western antihero.

opposite Marlon Brando (centre) and Lee Marvin (on bike) confront one another in Laslo Benedek's *The Wild One* (1954).

below Walter Matthau as the hood and Elvis Presley as the New Orleans teen rebel in *King Creole* (1958).

Brits in Hollywood

It is a pleasing if hackneyed image: distinguished, statuesque character actor (and ex-England test match player) C. Aubrey Smith leading a team of tea-drinking, pipe-smoking, whisky-quaffing, flannel-trousered and blazer-wearing British exiles onto the field for their weekly cricket match in Hollywood. Smith was at the head of a small colony of ex-pats in Tinseltown who seemed to become more – not less – British the longer they spent abroad. Milling around during the heyday of the studios were writers, like P.G. Wodehouse, known as Plummy by his pals in Culver City, who was drawing a salary of $2,000 a week at MGM, scribbling dialogue for never-to-be-completed movies; character actors, including Melville Cooper, the man directors always turned to when they wanted to cast a butler; front-rank stars, among them Ronald Colman and Cary Grant; and plenty of directors.

A TOWN MADE UP OF OUTSIDERS

There was nothing especially unique about the British influence in Hollywood, which was a city made up of outsiders. There were, among many others, the Swedes Victor Sjöström and Greta Garbo, the German Ernst Lubitsch and the Austrian Billy Wilder, Russians, including Anatole Litvak and Maria Ouspenskaya, the French René Clair, Mexicans like Lupe

Velez, the Australian-born Errol Flynn and plenty of first- and second-generation émigrés from Eastern Europe. The Hollywood machine absorbed them all – on the condition that they made successful movies. Nationality was rarely an issue.

CHAPLIN AND HITCHCOCK

'I do not think the British are temperamentally equipped to make the best use of the movie camera,' Indian director Satyajit Ray once tartly observed. This is a familiar charge, echoed by everybody from François Truffaut to egregious US artist and filmmaker Julian Schnabel, both of whom complained that Britain's was a literary, not a visual, culture. Nevertheless, as film historian Charles Barr points out, during the 100-year history of cinema the two filmmakers who 'above all others have obtained worldwide recognition to the extent of becoming, at different periods, virtually synonymous with the notion of popular cinema' are Alfred Hitchcock and Charlie Chaplin – 'Londoners by birth, upbringing and cultural formation'.

Hitchcock (1899–1980) was unique – the only European director in Hollywood who had a bigger public profile than that of his stars. Of course, his cameos helped. The most cheeky of these was in *Lifeboat* (1944), in which a

scrap of newspaper is spotted with a 'before and after' advertisement for a wonder slimming drug. The model used is Hitchcock himself, who had recently lost seven stone in weight and wanted to show off his new waistline. Of course, the box-office success of his movies was another key reason for his fame. In the late 1940s, when he was still entangled with *Gone with the Wind* producer David O. Selznick, who had brought him over to Hollywood in the first place, he made a few box-office duds, *The Paradine Case* (1947) and *Under Capricorn* (1949) among them. In the 1950s, he flourished anew with substantial hits like *Rear Window* (1954), *To Catch a Thief* (1955) and *North by Northwest* (1959). In 1955, he started his television shows – 'Alfred Hitchcock presents...' – which boosted his profile still further. Whereas many of his contemporaries were eclipsed by the emergence of TV, he was able to adapt to the new medium and to combine small- and big-screen careers with a success nobody else came close to matching. His name also appeared on magazines and books. He was not simply a filmmaker but a full-blown brand name as well.

Hitchcock took out US citizenship in 1955. He worked in America, lived there, paid taxes there, and thought it only made sense to become an 'American'. His decision may have been influenced by the waves of criticism directed against him during the war years, when he was accused of abandoning Britain – and the British film industry – in its hour of need.

Unlike Hitchcock, Chaplin never became an American national and in 1952, after he had been to the UK for the première of *Limelight*, he was denied entry to the US altogether. This was the McCarthy era, and his politics counted

above Charlie Chaplin (seen here with Henry Daniell and Jack Oakie) played a dual role in *The Great Dictator* (1940): he was both a Jewish barber and the Hitler-like tyrant Adenoid Hynkel.

above right The old British master prepares to serve up more ghoulish gruel. Alfred Hitchcock wields the clapperboard on the set of *Psycho* (1960).

opposite Despite the title, much of Stan Laurel and Oliver Hardy's 1935 vehicle, *Bonnie Scotland*, is set in India where the bungling duo go as enlisted soldiers.

against him. The US press had objected to his film about a Bluebeard-like mass murderer, *Monsieur Verdoux* (1947), and was intensely suspicious of his contacts with communists. He proclaimed himself 'a citizen of the world', but it must still have hurt to be turned away from a country where, only a few years before, he had been adored by everyone.

Chaplin did not always receive a warm reception back in his home country either. In the early 1930s, when he made a brief visit back to the UK, the trade press accused him of being arrogant and standoffish, a charge levelled at various other filmmakers and actors who had been lured away to Tinseltown. The British have always been remarkably unsympathetic to anybody who has left the country to build a career abroad, whether in Hollywood or anywhere else.

THE BRITANNIA MUSIC HALL

Comedians have to start somewhere, and why not Bonnie Scotland? Stan Laurel (1890–1965), born Arthur Stanley Jefferson in Ulverston, Lancashire, was not offered much parental support when he announced his intention to go on stage. Given that his mother was an actress and his father worked as a manager in the theatre business, it is far from clear why they frowned on little Stanley's ambitions. He made his debut as a teenager at the Britannia Music Hall in Trongate, Glasgow, reportedly wearing a pair of his father's old breeches for his act. Little known to him, the old man, who ran another Glasgow theatre – the Metropole – was in the audience and was so impressed that he arranged for Stan to learn his craft with a travelling pantomime troupe. Eventually, the boy was signed up by Fred Karno, the entrepreneur who also gave a first big break to Chaplin.

In 1910, Stan toured the US in Fred Karno's troupe alongside Chaplin, acting as his understudy. Chaplin left the troupe to join Mack Sennett in 1913, and in the same year Laurel also quit – but his rise was less meteoric than that of the bowler-hatted tramp. He stayed in America, made his first film in 1916, married the first of his many wives – the domineering Mae Dahlberg – and slowly began to build a career as a screen comedian. He and Oliver Hardy crossed paths in 1917 on a comedy short called *A Lucky Dog* (which was released in 1922), but it was a decade later, when they were both under contract to producer Hal Roach, that their partnership began in earnest.

STAN'S THE MAN

Stan was extraordinarily versatile, and as well as performing he wrote, improvised gags and edited movies for Roach. His screen partnership with Hardy did not reflect their real working relationship at all. Stan may have been the browbeaten one on screen, but he was the galvanizing force behind their movies together. He was the one who thought up the gags, and battled with his boss Roach – with whom his partnership was stormy in the extreme – for more money and creative freedom. In contrast, the genial Hardy preferred playing golf and taking it easy when off camera.

Laurel's private life was turbulent. He was married and divorced many times and he was also caught up in well-nigh permanent battles with his employers, whether small outfits like Roach's or major studios like Fox, with whom he later worked. None of this turbulence filtered through into the

movies, which retain their childlike sense of innocence. Laurel may have quit England at the start of his career, but he and Hardy were more popular in the UK than anywhere else. They toured the UK in 1932, then again after the war in 1947 – when their stock in Hollywood was beginning to wane – and for a final time in 1953–1954, when both were dogged by ill-health. On every occasion, they were given a rapturous reception.

ARCHIE LEACH ON THE TRAPEZE

Stan Laurel was not the only film star to cut his teeth as a performer in an unprepossessing Glasgow music hall. That is how Archibald Leach started out as well – an inauspicious beginning for a man described by influential critic David Thomson as 'the best and most important actor in the history of the cinema'. Cary Grant (1904–1986), the smooth, unruffled leading man of countless screwball comedies and thrillers, was born in Bristol. His break – if it could be described as such – came when he was taken on as a singer and gymnast by Bob Pender's troupe of acrobats. He toured the US with Pender in 1920 and there he stayed – apart from a few years back in British theatre in the early 1920s – for ever after.

There was always something dark and saturnine about Grant's characters; a sense that beneath their frivolous, light-hearted exteriors, they were potentially violent or prey to melancholy. One of his favourites among his films was *None but the Lonely Heart* (1944), scripted by Clifford Odets. He plays Ernie Mott, a soured, cloth-capped Cockney everyman, embittered and restless, and eking out an existence in any way he can, legal or illegal, on the streets of London. He is cynical about everything, apart from his ailing mother (Ethel Barrymore at her most regal) whom he adores. Mott's story did not parallel Grant's own life, but the film was said to echo his own relationship with his mother. It also revealed that the carefree swagger he affected in so many of his movies was not as natural or spontaneous as it seemed. It was a persona that he had refined for the screen with precisely the same discipline and application he must have showed in his days as an acrobat.

Whereas many other English stars in Hollywood played up their nationality, Grant never made an issue of being English. His clipped, humorous delivery did not betray an upper-class accent (affected or otherwise). Nor did he behave in Hollywood as if he was there to bring culture and refinement to the natives – as many other British stars did. He fitted in and was the perfect consort. Whether cast opposite a sassy, wisecracking broad like Mae West or a refined East Coast type like Katharine Hepburn, he always looked at ease.

LOVELY LIZ

In May 2000, Elizabeth Taylor was appointed Dame Commander of the British Empire by the Queen at Buckingham Palace. This was an honour normally reserved for such patriotic stars of stage and screen as Edith Evans, Flora Robson, Peggy Ashcroft, Margaret Rutherford, Anna Neagle and Judi Dench, all of whom were regarded by the public as national mascots. Taylor's relationship with Britain was more complex. She was born in the UK in February 1932 and spent the first seven years of her life there, but her parents were American. The whole family returned to the US on the eve of World War II and set up home in Los Angeles.

'I love Britain,' she told the British press when she turned up at the Palace. She would live in the country, she proclaimed, if only she could bring her pet dog, Sugar, with her. The strict quarantine laws prevented that, and so she had to stay put in California. 'America is not a rabid country,' she protested. 'The people may be crazy, but the pets are not.'

It is easy to see why the British wanted to claim Taylor as one of their own. She had danced for the royal family at the ripe old age of three and she seemed like a showbusiness counterpart to Elizabeth II, who was roughly the same age. But while the Queen was prim and austere, Taylor was quite the opposite. She lived through eight failed marriages; went on spending blitzes; ate too much, drank too much; and, between times, graced the screen. Her most notable early films, made when she was very young, were with animals – Lassie in *Lassie Come Home* (1943) and the horse in *National Velvet* (1944). She was one of the few people ever to tell the all-powerful MGM boss, Louis B. Mayer, to go to hell (she was only 12 at the time). Much later, she was the first star to be paid $1 million – for *Cleopatra* in 1963. In short, she was the kind of star that the reticent, penny-pinching British studios were never able to create – and through birth, if nothing else, she was a true Brit.

opposite In one of his least characteristic roles, British-born Cary Grant played a cockney drifter in *None but the Lonely Heart* (1944).

below The Elizabeth Taylor who caught audiences' imaginations as a demure young child star in *National Velvet* (1945) was very different from the all-powerful star who seemed typecast as the Egyptian queen 20 years later in *Cleopatra* (1963).

"They'll never know I'm a girl... now!" Velvet sacrifices her hair... but her heart gave her courage to face the greatest moment of her life!

NATIONAL VELVET
CLARENCE BROWN
MICKEY ROONEY
A METRO-GOLDWYN-MAYER PICTURE

Happy & Not-So-Happy Families

'How can somebody with so much talent waste so much time in that greasy spoon?' Barbara Stanwyck once asked the great writer-director Preston Sturges (1898–1959) after visiting his Sunset Boulevard restaurant, The Players. Sturges blithely tossed money away on The Players, keeping the restaurant open 24 hours a day and employing a staff of over 150. The menu, which changed daily, was only intended as a list of suggestions. If any customer wanted something not listed, the top French chefs at work in the kitchen were duty-bound to rustle it up. If they did not have the right ingredients, they had to find them. Slowly but surely, The Players helped bankrupt Sturges and, by the late 1940s, his career was in decline. On paper, he was still fabulously wealthy, but the taxmen were after him, and every spare cent that they didn't grab was eaten up by the restaurant.

Money never interested Sturges very much: 'One should never have enough of it, or enough of a lack of it to allow of its playing a principal role,' he wrote in his journal not long before he died – broke – in New York in the late 1950s. During his life he experienced both enormous wealth and (relative) poverty. His stepfather was an immensely rich Chicago businessman, while his mother was best friends with the legendary dancer, Isidora Duncan, and led the kind of pampered and exotic lifestyle written about in Scott Fitzgerald novels. Sturges' own fortunes waxed and waned. Before he established himself as a playwright, he spent several years trying to run a kiss-proof lipstick business. He eloped with and married heiress, Eleanor Hutton, but the marriage did not last. He regarded whatever happened to him, whether good or bad, with an ironic air of detachment.

In his pomp in the late 1930s, Sturges was Paramount's golden-boy, the first man in Hollywood history successfully to combine the role of writer and director and to retain creative control of his movies. That gave him licence to spend money on cars, yachts and – above all – on his beloved restaurant.

The Players attracted a mixed crowd, 'not only the celebrated producers, directors, writers, agents and stars of Hollywood, but visiting admirals and generals and potentates and old Texas spenders on double-ended benders and the tourists who wanted to see them all,' as Sturges later wrote. It had its own room for live music and dancing, and eventually Sturges even added a small theatre. He liked to take his work into the restaurant and was always on hand to meet and greet customers. There are pictures of him scribbling at screenplays as diners mill around him. It was here that he plotted some of those comedies in which the characters enjoy similar reversals of fortune to his own.

RICH AND POOR

In Sturges' movies, characters ricochet between wealth and poverty, good luck and bad, in startling fashion. His screenplay for Mitchell Leisen's *Easy Living* (1937) showers benevolence on a penniless woman (Jean Arthur) in the shape of a sable coat. She is blithely sitting on the top of a bus when the fur – which has just been hurled out of a high window – lands on top of her. In *Sullivan's Travels* (1941), a big-shot Hollywood director, keen to make a film about the common man, goes on the road, has a series of misadventures, ends up a bum on a chain gang, and realizes that his attitude toward the noble, suffering poor is both patronizing and misguided. Once he gets back to Hollywood, he resolves to make movies to entertain the public rather than just to edify them. In *The Palm Beach Story* (1942), Claudette Colbert is at odds with her inventor husband and cannot even afford the rent on her grubby apartment, but is soon enjoying the high life in Palm Springs.

THE IMMACULATE CONCEPTION – SEXTUPLETS

The most subversive of Sturges' movies – and one that set the template for all the satires on cosy, small-town American family life that followed it – was *The Miracle of Morgan Creek* (1943). A good-time girl called Trudy Kockenlocker (Betty Hutton) becomes pregnant after a tryst with a soldier. She cannot remember anything about this brief encounter beyond the fact that her mysterious lover was called something like Ratsky-Watsky. He has gone off to war so, to ward off scandal, nervous bank clerk Norval Jones (Eddie Bracken) is named father in his stead. She goes on to give birth to sextuplets. Somehow, the censors failed to notice just how risqué and iconoclastic the movie really was, and audiences were too busy laughing at Sturges' gags to notice the film's full-blown assault on American family values.

Sturges' movies regularly gave vent to emotions and attitudes that mainstream Hollywood seldom went near. *Mad Wednesday* (1947), starring old silent star Harold Lloyd, celebrated the redemptive powers of alcohol. Lloyd's character, a humble, put-upon clerk, loses his job, takes his first drink,

and is transformed into a wise-cracking maverick who dresses in loud suits and cowboy hats, and whose pet hobby is borrowing animals from the zoo. Yes, he has hangovers, but they are nothing that cannot be cured by a few more highballs. In *The Lady Eve* (1941), the heroine Jean (Barbara Stanwyck) is a gold-digger and con artist who never hides her lust or appetite for money ('EVE SURE KNOWS HER APPLES', ran the logo on the poster). Her prey, millionaire explorer Charles Pike (Henry Fonda) is naive and unworldly, and obsessed with snakes – this is a film loaded with heavy-handed sexual symbolism. 'I need him like the axe needs the turkey,' Jean exclaims at one stage. In *Unfaithfully Yours* (1948), a conductor (Rex Harrison) is so sure that his wife (Linda Darnell) is unfaithful that he fantasizes about murdering her.

SMALL-TOWN HEROES

Frank Capra (1897–1991) was not as acidulous as Sturges. His movies did not come steeped in irony and double-entendres, but they presented an image of American life a long way removed from the glossy, make-believe world depicted in other Hollywood films of his era. In *It Happened One Night* (1934), made at the height of the Depression, he refused to fill the screen with the images of glamour and consumption found in Busby Berkeley musicals or other escapist fantasies. Instead, the film unfolds in the interiors of Greyhound buses, little Midwestern boarding-houses, or simply stretches of open road.

It Happened One Night played badly with smart, metropolitan audiences in the major cities. Fittingly, it only really became successful when it was released in small-town theatres. Audiences relished seeing characters like themselves up on the screen. 'Mr Capra, by resolutely shutting his eyes to the improbable and unimportant plot, gives us a very shrewd idea of how actors, when intelligently directed, can become as much like ourselves as our own humble photographs,' one critic noted.

There is a striking scene late in the film in which journalist Peter Warne (Clark Gable), in a borrowed car, stops at a level crossing. An old freight train rattles by with dozens of hobos packed into its carriages. Warne waves at

them and they wave back, as if they recognize that he too is a traveller, trying to keep himself alive as best he can. Claudette Colbert's character, a runaway heiress, only becomes sympathetic when she turns her back on her wealth. In one famous scene, Gable ridicules her inability to dunk her doughnut properly in her coffee. 'Where'd you learn to dunk?' he sneers. 'Finishing School? Forty million and you don't know how to dunk.' Colbert whimpers that she'd 'change places with a plumber's daughter any day'. The sheet hung between their beds when they reluctantly share a room – 'the wall of Jericho' as they nickname it – is not only there to titillate audiences. It also reminds them of the gaping social chasm between the hard-up hack and the rich man's daughter.

MR DEEDS

Clark Gable's journalist in *It Happened One Night* is a rougher-edged, more outspoken version of the American everyman, invariably played by either James Stewart or Gary Cooper, who became a regular fixture in Capra's later films. These follow a well-set formula: small towns are good, big cities are bad and the establishment – whether embodied by bankers, lawyers or politicians – is not to be trusted.

In Capra's 1936 effort *Mr Deeds Goes to Town*, Longfellow Deeds (Cooper) attempts to give away the $20 million he has just inherited from his uncle to farmers struggling in the Depression. Lawyers, importuning relatives and others try to prevent him and a sardonic woman journalist (Jean Arthur) makes fun of him in her paper as a yokel. He is sneered at and mocked in the same way that James Stewart's Jefferson Smith is when he takes up a position in the Senate in *Mr Smith Goes to Washington* (1939). In both cases, after much buffeting the everyman's idealism ends up carrying the day.

Much tougher and more ambiguous was Capra's 1941 feature, *Meet John Doe*. The hero is again an everyman (Gary Cooper), but he has no money to give away or political principles to stand up for. He is a minor-league baseball pitcher fallen on hard times. The plot is ingenious: another of Capra's sassy journalists, this time played by Barbara Stanwyck, is fired from her job when a new editor takes over. Her parting shot is to write a spoof letter, ostensibly from an ordinary reader who is so disgusted with the behaviour of the politicians that he has vowed to jump off the top of Radio City Music Hall on Christmas Eve. The letter, signed 'John Doe', causes a circulation rush, and readers send in money for Doe and write letters pleading with him to abandon his planned suicide. The editor is so impressed that he gives Stanwyck her job back and tells her to recruit a real-life John Doe. Enter Gary Cooper, who needs the money badly enough to agree to play John Doe. With Stanwyck manipulating the media, he becomes a national figure, revered by everyone for his plain speaking and homely maxims, all of them carefully scripted. The sting in the tail is that he is being manipulated by C.B. Norton, a neofascist tycoon who is trying to use him to grab political power.

By revealing that John Doe is a fake, Capra risks breaching his audiences' trust in the earlier films. Once you realize that there is a reactionary like Norton behind Cooper's everyman, Mr Deeds and Mr Smith become that much harder to take at face value.

above Gary Cooper (pictured here with Barnett Parker) can't get used to wealthy living in Frank Capra's *Mr Deeds Goes to Town* (1936).

opposite left Barbara Stanwyck as the gold-digger and Henry Fonda as the dopey millionaire in Preston Sturges' innuendo-filled screwball classic, *The Lady Eve* (1941).

opposite right Claudette Colbert, the runaway heiress, and Clark Gable, the cynical journalist in search of a story, erect a famous barrier (nicknamed the wall of Jericho) between them when they share a room on the road in Frank Capra's *It Happened One Night* (1934).

CLARENCE THE ANGEL

The barbed social comment in Capra's movies is often overlooked. Audiences are so used to the idea of *It's a Wonderful Life* (1946) as a perfect Christmas film that they risk failing to notice just how bleak much of its portrayal of small-town life in Bedford Falls really is. Before Clarence the angel (Henry Travers) pops up, the do-good everyman George Bailey (James Stewart) is in hock to the Savings and Loan Bank and contemplating suicide. The film's own fate matched that of its hero, and when it was first released, during a freezing winter, it performed poorly at the box-office. Only in the 1970s, when a copyright slip (perhaps engineered by Clarence) allowed TV stations to show the movie as often as they wanted, was it rediscovered and belatedly acclaimed as an all-American classic.

THE GRAPES OF WRATH

Capra's movies of the 1930s and early 1940s revealed a country still traumatized by the Depression. The image of cosy, stable family life presented in, say, MGM's Andy Hardy films, must have seemed false at a time when millions of Americans were having to leave home to find work. There is certainly no sign of little picket fences or neatly mown lawns in John Ford's *The Grapes of Wrath* (1940). Adapted from John Steinbeck's novel about dispossessed migrant farmers – 'Okies' as they were called – it follows the Joad family on their heart-rending journey towards California in search of work. Cameraman Gregg Toland shoots the film as if it is a documentary and the social comment is consequently hard-hitting. The filmmakers are railing against a society that treats its inhabitants in so callous a way. Nevertheless, Tom Joad (Henry Fonda) retains his dignity, and represents a far starker version of the kind of American everyman found in Capra's work.

Joad's famous speech on behalf of the common man rings out like a call to arms: 'Wherever there's a fight so hungry people can eat, wherever there's a cop beating up a guy, I'll be there'. The more the Joads and the other Okies

OPPORTUNITY FOR ALL

Capra's own life-story reads like a wish-fulfilment fantasy. He arrived in the US from Sicily as a very young child; couldn't speak the language and hated the country, but through sheer resourcefulness managed to make himself into one of the most famous movie directors in the world. En route to the top, he sold newspapers on street corners, tried to become an engineer, and endured every manner of hardship. The ambivalence in his movies about American society has its roots in his own experiences.

above Henry Fonda (seen here with Russell Simpson) played Tom Joad, the quintessential American everyman in John Ford's screen adaptation of John Steinbeck's *The Grapes of Wrath* (1940).

above left Madness strikes at the heart of suburbia as family man James Mason becomes ever more maniacal in Nick Ray's *Bigger than Life* (1956).

suffer, the more resilient they become. As they say: 'We keep on a comin'. We're the people that live. They can't wipe us out and they can't lick us. We'll go on forever, pa, because we're the people...'

TROUBLE IN PARADISE

Even in more prosperous times, long after the Depression was over, family life as portrayed by Hollywood was never as idyllic or as secure as stereotypes might suggest. Take the seemingly cosy suburbia of Nicholas Ray's *Bigger than Life* (1956). Shot in widescreen Technicolor, it slowly and slyly introduces madness and neurosis into the heart of the all-American home. The imp of the perverse is James Mason's character, seemingly an upstanding teacher and family man. There are hints that all is not quite well right at the outset. Happy homes don't come cheap. Mason is having to moonlight as a taxi driver, and working himself to the point of nervous exhaustion. The doctor prescribes him cortisone to pep him up – and then the madness begins. He browbeats and bullies his wife (Barbara Rush), picks fights with the milkman for clinking the bottles too loudly and – sounding more like Nietzsche than the typical small town pedagogue – begins expounding his strange new teaching philosophy. 'Childhood is a congenital disease,' he roars out at a parents' evening, 'the purpose of education is to cure it.' Not long after, he is seen going after his son with a knife. However bizarre Mason's behaviour, Ray's storytelling style remains deadpan. This is ostensibly a movie about the dangers of untested drugs, but it manages to make the cosy 1950s American homestead seem as threatening as a Gothic mansion in a horror picture. Not even David Lynch's *Blue Velvet* (1986), another famously warped look at suburbia, was as unsettling as this.

AMERICAN BEAUTY AND *HAPPINESS*

Sam Mendes' *American Beauty* (1999) performs exactly the same trick as Ray's *Bigger than Life*, surreptitiously introducing lust, madness and violence into a cocooned, brightly-coloured little corner of suburbia. Its satirical intentions are signalled right from the outset: as soon as Lester Burnham (Kevin Spacey), the family man, is shown masturbating in the shower, it is obvious that all is not well in the Burnham household.

right Kevin Spacey and Annette Bening are the unhappily married suburban couple in Sam Mendes' brilliant debut feature, *American Beauty* (1999).

There is an extraordinary moment halfway through Todd Solondz's *Happiness* (1998). Father and family man Bill Maplewood (Dylan Baker), a psychiatrist by profession, is watching a little-league baseball game when he suddenly becomes riveted by one of his son's classmates. Solondz shoots the scene with slow motion close-ups, as if this is the typical Hollywood case of love at first sight. The difference here, though, is that the object of the besotted suitor's gaze and affection is an 11-year-old boy. Between them, *American Beauty* and *Happiness* soiled the hoary old idealized image of the happy all-American household once and for all.

MONEY PROBLEMS

Debt was the constant, unstated fear in Hollywood's post-war family dramas. In the 1980s and 1990s, there were many yuppie-in-peril dramas in which middle-class American families were threatened by the looming spectres of drugs, disease, homicide and white-collar unemployment. Even a haunted house tale like *The Amityville Horror* (1979) was as much about negative equity as it was about witches and ghosts. All-American dad George (James Brolin) has bought it for $80,000 (a bargain for a six-bedroom house), but quickly realizes he cannot afford it. When he begins to slip into debt the brackish muck starts oozing out of the basins and lavatories and the ghouls begin to appear. There is even blood seeping through the walls – perfectly apt given that he has fallen so far into the red.

George retains at least vestiges of his sanity. The same cannot be said for Ned (Burt Lancaster) in Frank Perry's bizarre John Cheever adaptation, *The Swimmer* (1968). Another family man who has lost his money, Ned embarks on an epic journey home – via his neighbours' pools. The nearer he reaches his destination, the more obvious it becomes that there is something wrong with him. He has somehow, as he puts it, fallen out of 'his golden playpen'. His money is gone and his family have left him. We see him, still in his swimming trunks, trying to cross a busy road. His home, it turns out, has long since been taken away from him and is now boarded up and desolate. The image of the handsome, wisecracking all-American hero cast out of Eden is one that Preston Sturges would have recognized instantly.

17

The Big Heat
1953

Gangsters

'I don't think people believe in the devil with horn and fork tail,' **German director Fritz Lang once remarked**. *'They don't believe in punishment after they're dead. So my question is: what are people fearing?' The answer, he surmised, was physical pain. 'And physical pain comes from violence.'*

FRITZ LANG'S FRIGHT RECIPE

All Lang's post-war Hollywood films deal with violence in one form or another. In *The Big Heat* (1953), the heavy, Vince Stone (Lee Marvin), scalds his girlfriend, Debbie (Gloria Grahame), with a pot of coffee. This follows on from an opening in which happily married cop Glenn Ford is helpless to prevent his wife being blown up by a car bomb. Somehow the scene with the boiling coffee is much more shocking. A beautiful woman is disfigured almost on a whim. For the rest of the movie, she retreats into the shadows, her face swathed in bandages.

Lang's films invariably echoed what was going on in society around him. Long before Vince Stone, he had created one of the most intimidating screen villains of all in the evil genius Mabuse, first seen in *The Gambler* (1922). By returning to the character in *The Testament of Dr Mabuse* (1933), he was able to hint on screen at the turmoil convulsing Germany as Hitler came to power. Mabuse's ruthlessness and easy use of violence were in keeping with Nazi

practices, and even his language seemed familiar. 'People who endanger the organization will be annihilated,' Mabuse tells his followers. The criminal mastermind is first seen incarcerated in a mental asylum, scribbling pages and pages of notes. His doctors consider him mad, but from his cell, he is orchestrating a campaign of terror. His acolytes are bombing and burning factories, shops and banks.

The *Testament of Dr Mabuse* had all the qualities of an old-fashioned ripping detective yarn, with explosions, shootings and even a spectacular car chase. The detective (Otto Wernicke), a cheery, bulldog-like character who had appeared in Lang's *M* the year before, investigated Mabuse with a tenacity worthy of Scotland Yard's finest. But there was an unsettling undercurrent rarely found in escapist thrillers – a lingering sense that the Nazis were the biggest gangsters of all. Lang showed the queues of unemployed men at the Labour Exchange and captured that sense of blind loyalty that the Nazis showed their leader. 'You think too much – the boss don't like that,' one of the hoodlums is told when he questions Mabuse's plans.

Affluent, Eisenhower-era, 1950s America is a long way from Hitler's Germany, but working here in the twilight of his career, Lang was still exploring the same basic themes in his films as in his Mabuse days. Films like *Scarlet*

THE GANGSTER AS TRAGIC HERO

'America, as a social and political organization, is committed to a cheerful view of life. It could not be otherwise,' critic Robert Warshow wrote in a famous essay about gangster films. He argued that gangster movies were 'an expression of the part of the American psyche which... rejects Americanism'. In other words, they were made in opposition to the relentlessly cheerful, optimistic books, films and culture of mainstream America. The gangster allowed audiences to experience the thrill of kicking against the system, safe in the knowledge that he would be punished for his wrongdoing. 'We gain the double satisfaction of participating vicariously in the gangster's sadism and then seeing it turned against the gangster himself.'

'If you're interested in the real America, the real America has got a lot of blood in the soil,' writer/director Leonard Schrader once observed. One only has to read Herbert Asbury's 'informal history of the underworld', *The Gangs of New York* (1927) – which was made into a film by Martin Scorsese – to appreciate the all-pervasive nature of

violence in big American cities in the 19th century. 'Murders were frequent; it has been estimated that for almost 15 years, the Old Brewery averaged a murder a night,' Asbury claims. Movies were quick to harness this violence. *The Great Train Robbery* (1903) made a spectacle out of armed robbery, and D.W. Griffith's *The Musketeers of Pig Alley* (1912) and Raoul Walsh's *The Regeneration* (1915) depicted lawlessness and violence on the city streets. By the 1920s, the era of Prohibition, Al Capone and the St Valentine's Day Massacre, organized crime was such a factor in American life that Hollywood could hardly ignore it.

Street (1945), *Human Desire* (1954) and *Beyond a Reasonable Doubt* (1956) show that he remained apparently obsessed with violence. In *The Secret Beyond the Door* (1948), Joan Bennett is the heroine married to a neurotic and perhaps murderous architect (Michael Redgrave). With its heightened performances, use of chiaroscuro, shots of Bennett staring into a mirror, close-ups of keys turning in locks, and labyrinthine interiors, this film has a feverish, dreamlike quality. Set in the US and Mexico, and with an American heiress as its protagonist, it nevertheless seems reminiscent of the equally jarring, equally threatening silent movies made by Murnau and Robert Wiene. Expressionism was not just confined to Germany in the 1920s and the lines between gangster films and psychological thrillers in post-war Hollywood were often blurred.

PINT-SIZED GUNMEN

In *Little Caesar*, the casting is the key. Edward G. Robinson is the unlikely but brilliant choice to play Rico Bandello, the Capone-like gangster who murders and steals his way to prominence, but meets his downfall in spectacular fashion. This was the first of the classic Warners gangster cycle. Along with films like *The Public Enemy* and *Scarface*, it exercised an enormous influence on the noirish thrillers made in Hollywood after the war. Although Robinson hated the role – in real-life he was a mild-mannered, placid man, ill at ease firing machine guns – he ended up projecting a cold-hearted viciousness that more typical screen villains have seldom matched. Director Mervyn Le Roy put sticky tape on his eyebrows to stop him blinking and to make him look properly intimidating. The effect worked brilliantly.

For all the flamboyant violence shown in early 1930s gangster movies like *Little Caesar* and *Scarface* (1932), the most unsettling images – as Fritz Lang knew so well – were the least expected ones, where the aggression and madness spills out from the street into the home. William Wellman's *The Public Enemy* (1931) boasts several scenes infinitely more disturbing than the massacres and shoot-outs shown in other movies. The most notorious is the one in which, at the breakfast table, Tom Powers (James Cagney) smashes a grapefruit into the face of the floozy (Mae Clarke) he picked up a few days before. This was his way of ending the relationship. As with the coffee in *The Big Heat*, this burst of sadistic, misogynistic violence comes from nowhere, and is all the more startling for its unpredictability. Clarke reportedly knew nothing about the plan to really hit her in the face, and was expecting Wellman to use a trick shot. The way she grimaces with fury, pain and humiliation was not feigned. For years afterwards, every time Cagney went into a restaurant, some customer would be sure to offer him a grapefruit half as a joke.

Equally shocking, if only because of its morbidity, is the ending in which Tom finally gets his comeuppance. His corpse is delivered to his home, all trussed up in bandages; the doorbell rings, his brother Mike (Donald Cook) opens it, and in falls the cadaver with a bullet in its head.

In Abraham Polonsky's *Force of Evil* (1948), the violence is all-pervasive: it blights not only the lives of the gangsters, but those of their innocent relatives too. Joe Morse (John Garfield) is a slick mob lawyer who has lifted himself out of poverty, but is tormented by what has become of his brother, Leo (Tomas Gomez). Leo originally wanted to become a lawyer himself, but sacrificed his career for Joe's sake. He is now a middle-aged, overweight man with a heart problem, eking out a precarious existence in the numbers racket, winning tiny stakes from small-time gamblers. Joe tries to help him, but embroils him in his own nightmarish world, and Leo becomes a target for the gangsters. When they catch up with him, Polonsky uses elegiac classical music on the soundtrack to underline the shabby pathos of his needless death.

opposite A snarling James Cagney squashes a grapefruit in Mae Clarke's face in the classic Warner Bros gangster pic, *The Public Enemy* (1931).

below Abraham Polonsky's lyrical, doom-laden *Force of Evil* (1948) gave John Garfield (pictured here with Sid Tomack) a plum role as a lawyer who sells his soul to the mob.

WOMEN AS VILLAINS

Mae Clarke and Gloria Grahame were victims of male violence, but, just occasionally, women have been shown behaving equally brutally towards men. There is a shocking scene in John Stahl's melodrama, *Leave Her to Heaven* (1945) in which a possessive wife (Gene Tierney) lures her husband's paraplegic brother (Darryl Hickman) far out onto a lake. He wants to swim back to the shore, and she encourages him to do so, knowing he will not have the stamina to make it. Sure enough, he soon begins to struggle. She knows that he is drowning, but just sits in the canoe watching.

'I'm rotten to the heart,' Phyllis Dietrichson (Barbara Stanwyck) tells her lover and co-conspirator Walter Neff (Fred MacMurray) in *Double Indemnity* (1944) before casually flicking cigarette ash onto the carpet. Dietrichson is the quintessential film noir *femme fatale*, a sassy, hardboiled 'spider woman' who delights in entrapping her prey with the promise of sex and money. The first time Neff sees her, he marvels at her long, long legs as she descends a staircase. She is beautiful but provocative. The original story may have been written by James M. Cain, but scriptwriter Raymond Chandler clearly regards her as a sister figure to the sirens who flit in and out of his own novels.

Stanwyck adds an unexpected depth to the one-dimensional temptress that Chandler and director Billy Wilder believed Dietrichson to be. Her character is never exactly sympathetic, but she is at least honest in her ambition. In one key scene, she meets Neff at a supermarket after the murder of her husband. 'I loved you, Walter, and I hated him,' she tells her accomplice, 'but I wasn't going to do anything about it, not until I met you. You planned the whole thing. I only wanted him dead.' The question is, do we believe her? We are being told the story from Neff's perspective: he is the narrator, and according to his version of events Dietrichson is a double-crossing Medusa who has blighted his life. But there is a discrepancy between the phantom woman the flailing hero projects in his imagination

right 'I'm rotten to the heart,' *femme fatale* Phyllis Dietrichson (Barbara Stanwyck) tells her lover Walter Neff (Fred MacMurray) early on in Billy Wilder's *Double Indemnity* (1944). He knows it, but still can't resist her.

below Gene Tierney looks on impassively as her husband's crippled brother drowns in John Stahl's melodrama, *Leave Her to Heaven* (1945).

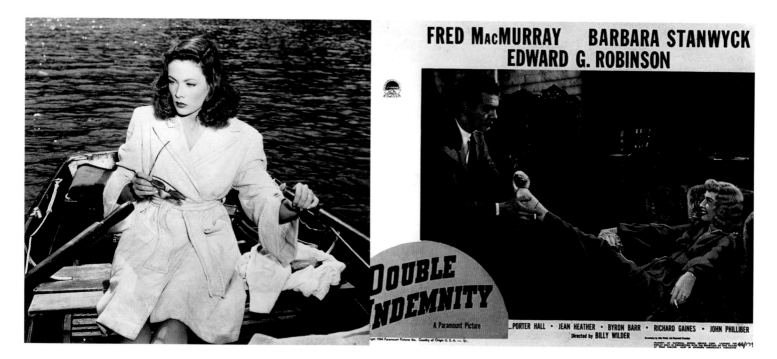

and the real character. Neff did indeed commit the crime, and perhaps Dietrichson is as much his victim as he is hers.

Japanese director Miike Takashi's thriller *Audition* (1998) shows a seemingly mild-mannered, very beautiful young woman (Eihi Shiina) taking female violence towards men to a horrifying new extreme. She breaks into the home of the widowed man (Ryo Ishibashi) who has been dating her, drugs him, and sets about torturing and maiming him. She puts stakes in his eyes and wraps butcher's wire tight round his ankle, severing his foot. The extreme, sadistic violence is all the more shocking because it comes at the end of a film that initially seems like a character-based love story. The British Board of Film Classification passed the film with an '18' certificate, thereby provoking accusations of double-standards. It was felt that if the violence had been inflicted on the woman by the man, the film would probably have been banned in the UK. However, the film turned the usual stereotypes of passive geishas on their head and, in doing so, helped avenge the indignities that countless women had suffered in Japanese cinema over the years.

DYING DON'T COME EASY

When a cowboy in a B-serial has a fist fight, he will throw a big haymaker of a punch. If he connects, the heavy is sure to collapse like a sack of potatoes. When he is in the stagecoach, being pursued by Apaches, he will lean out of the window and take pot shots at them, as if he is shooting clay pigeons. Every time he scores a direct hit, the Apache will tumble dead to the ground. This is stylized, make-believe violence, served up for matinée audiences.

Certain filmmakers always objected to the 'boys' own' action-adventure approach to screen fights and shoot-outs and tried to introduce an element of reality into their representations of screen violence. Again, Fritz Lang was a pioneer in this respect. In *Cloak and Dagger* (1946), he included a fight sequence of such unmitigated brutality that it shows up just how staged and artificial most screen violence is. When a nuclear scientist-turned-American spy (Gary Cooper) gets into a scrap with an enemy agent, it becomes a desperate, stamina-sapping fight between two men terrified of dying. The blows are inconclusive: they are trying to gouge, throttle or bite their opponents into submission. In real life, Lang is telling audiences, baddies do not obligingly fall down when you hit them on the chin. Killing somebody with your bare hands is squalid, back-breaking work.

The fight sequence in *Cloak and Dagger* is echoed in Hitchcock's *Torn Curtain* (1966). American scientist Paul Newman has a prolonged, very violent fight in a kitchen with a Soviet soldier who refuses to die. Newman pummels him, stabs him, chokes him, but still cannot squeeze the life out of him. In the end, the poor man's head is stuck inside a gas oven. Even as he is being asphyxiated, Hitchcock shows his fingers twitching. It is one of the most sordid and prolonged deaths in all of cinema.

GRANDSTAND FINISHES

As in *The Public Enemy*, gangsters are often given flamboyant send-offs. In the 1970s and 1980s, with less draconian censorship, death scenes became ever grander and more baroque. Sonny Corleone (James Caan), the wild, mercurial son in *The Godfather* (1971), is not simply killed: he is shot to pieces.

below Sonny Corelone (James Caan) dies in a hail of bullets at the toll booth in *The Godfather* (1971).

Ambushed at a toll-booth, he is caught in a hail of bullets. As if jealous of this macabre flourish, Brian De Palma ended his remake of *Scarface* (1983) in an even more extravagant and preposterous way. The defiant Cuban mobster antihero (Al Pacino) goes out all guns blazing, seemingly oblivious to the enemy gunfire pouring down on him. He is like a man caught in a storm without an umbrella who refuses to recognize that it is raining.

Contrast this with the lyricism of the gangster's death in John Huston's *The Asphalt Jungle*. Dix Handley (Sterling Hayden) had always yearned to buy back his father's Kentucky ranch, and that is why he became a criminal in the first place. Fatally wounded, he leaves the city far behind him and heads back out to the countryside he so cherishes. With his mistress (Jean Hagen) at his side, he drives all the way to the old ranch, but his strength is ebbing. With an almighty effort, he pulls himself out of the car and through the gate before collapsing.

SCORSESE THE BUTCHER

Martin Scorsese, natural heir to the Hollywood gangster tradition of the studio era, is often accused of glamorizing violence and of making heroes out of two-bit psychopaths. In fact, he depicts bloodshed and death with a frankness that would have been inconceivable in the era of *The Public Enemy* and *Scarface*. *Goodfellas* (1990), his adaptation of *Wise Guy*, Nicholas Pileggi's book about a real-life mobster, exposes a world in which violence is accepted as an everyday occurrence. The film begins with three friends stabbing and shooting a half-dead hoodlum locked in the boot of the car. They commit the killing as if it is an essential, albeit distasteful, chore that they have to complete as part of their professional duties. Rather than focus on epic gun battles and *Scarface*-like feats of flamboyance, Scorsese concentrates on the inner workings of the mob: the clothes the 'Wise Guys' wore, the food they ate, their own pet slang, what they did off-duty. In their working lives, glamour and banality exist side by side, and violence is simply something they do.

Scorsese takes the same matter-of-fact approach to violence in his later film, *Casino* (1995). But here, instead of the grey New Jersey of *Goodfellas*, the backdrop is gaudy, neon-lit Las Vegas, where money is king. When anybody steps out of line, or interrupts the cash flow, they are dealt with brutally, often by men who were formerly their friends and associates. Thus, when volatile, vicious gangster Nicky Santoro (Joe Pesci) offends the bosses, he ends up digging his own grave – and being buried alive in it.

NO HIDING-PLACE

In Greek tragedy, when a protagonist offends the gods, he releases 'the Furies' upon himself and wherever he goes, whatever he does, he is damned. Characters in film noir share this same fatalism: once tarred by violence, they cannot escape it. In Robert Siodmak's *The Killers* (1946), inspired by Ernest Hemingway's 1927 story of the same name, ex-boxer The Swede (Burt Lancaster) is hunted down in a small town by two professional assassins. 'Once I did something wrong,' he states, conscious that he is going to have to pay for it now. He accepts his death stoically, and the rest of the movie is concerned with insurance investigator Edmond O'Brien's attempts

to find out why he was killed. As the flashbacks begin, we soon learn that *femme fatale* Ava Gardner is at the heart of the mystery.

Jacques Tourneur's *Out of the Past* (1947), portrays an even more stoical former private eye (Robert Mitchum), holed up in a sleepy small town, working at the local petrol station. When hoodlums come to search for him, a complex, flashback-based narrative is set in motion. Again, a *femme fatale* (Jane Greer in this case) is at the root of his problems. He now sells gasoline for a living, buys his own groceries and has a nice, clean-living girlfriend (Virginia Huston), but we know that he will not be able to sustain this balmy, peaceful existence unless he first confronts his violent, double-crossing past.

The poor musician, Al (Tom Neal), in Edgar Ulmer's low-budget classic, *Detour* (1946), is an innocent dupe whom fate conspires against. Rather than escaping from violence, he is forced into it. While hitchhiking out to Los Angeles to join his fiancée in Hollywood, he is given a lift by a genial-seeming man. After eating a meal together, the man falls asleep and never wakes up. Rather than report his death, Al, who is broke, keeps the man's car and his money. It seems like a petty crime, but when he himself picks up a hitchhiker (Ann Savage), the 'Furies' come after him with a vengeance. She knows about the old man and thinks Al murdered him. Now, she plans to blackmail him. There is a nightmarish inevitability about what happens to him. As accident follows accident, quiet, unassuming, pacifistic Al turns into a killer for real. *Detour* was shot in six days on a budget of $20,000, but it takes much less time than that for Al's life to unravel around him. Violence intrudes into his life. It is not his fault, but he knows he can never escape its stigma.

above right Tom Neal gets that awful sinking feeling as he realizes just what he has done in Edgar Ulmer's low-budget classic, *Detour* (1945).

right It's one of the unwritten laws of film noir that you can never escape the past. Robert Mitchum soon discovers as much in Jacques Tourneur's masterful *Build My Gallows High* (a.k.a *Out of the Past*) (1947).

opposite If you're going to go down, go down in style. Al Pacino's gangster signs off in flamboyant fashion in the explosive finale to Brian De Palma's *Scarface* (1983).

Size Matters

18

The Robe
1953

CinemaScope, Fritz Lang once haughtily declared, 'was not meant for human beings... just for snakes and funerals'. His aversion to the wide-screen processes embraced by Hollywood in the 1950s was understandable. The majority of his great movies had been shot in 'Academy Ratio': that is to say, on 35mm film with a width-to-height ratio of 4:3 (or 1.33:1). He liked the almost square shape of the screen because in character-driven dramas you wanted to be able to have the actors next to one another, not at opposite ends of an artificially long screen.

This old-style 'aspect ratio' had one major symbolic drawback: it more or less matched the dimensions of the typical television screen. By the early 1950s, Hollywood had identified TV as the number-one enemy. Attendances were falling as more and more American families stayed at home to watch their TVs. One obvious way to entice cinema-goers back to the theatres was to offer them an experience that could not be replicated on the small screen.

GLORIOUS TECHNICOLOR, BREATHTAKING CINEMASCOPE, STEREOPHONIC SOUND...

Filmmakers had always been in love with size. Even in the silent era, the visions of D.W. Griffith, Cecil B. De Mille and Erich Von Stroheim were overwhelmingly grand and their movies boasted armies of extras populating the most lavish sets imaginable. Wide-screen formats were also tested far earlier than is commonly imagined. In 1927, the great French director Abel Gance made his epic movie *Napoléon* using a process known as Polyvision. This meant shooting the film with three synchronized cameras and then projecting it onto a screen three times the normal size. Whatever Lang may have thought, it was not only funerals and snakes that looked spectacular in wide screen – retreating armies and battle sequences also benefited from the format. Experiments in 3-D began as early as the 1920s and in the same decade Fox patented its own 'Grandeur' system – a format for projecting 70mm features. In the 1930s and 1940s, the main motives for Hollywood size kings making their movies bigger and brighter were vanity and ambition. By the early 1950s, thinking big was a matter of survival.

CINERAMA

In 1952, a few upmarket cinemas began using a process known as Cinerama to lure back audiences. The idea was roughly the same as that utilized by Gance on *Napoléon* 25 years before. Three synchronized cameras projected their images onto a huge, curved screen that gave the illusion of 3-D. The first

Cinerama shows were a great success, but they were expensive and few theatres were big enough to instal the right kind of screen. Not many filmmakers had the resources to work on this scale in any case, so Cinerama remained a novelty. The team behind Cinerama pooled resources with MGM in 1962 to make the epic Western, *How the West Was Won*. It was a huge hit, but that had little to do with the format: most of the profits came from cinemas that were not equipped to show the film in the right dimensions.

CINEMASCOPE

A much more successful innovation was CinemaScope, first introduced commercially by Fox in 1953. This was a wide-screen process based on a system developed by French scientist Henri Chrétien. It involved special lenses that squashed images during filming and then opened them out again during projection. The CinemaScope image, photographed on normal 35mm film, projects at an aspect ratio of 2.35:1 – in other words, the image is over twice as long as it is high.

The Robe, the first film made under the new system, opened at New York's Roxy Theater in September of 1953 . It was a sword-and-sandal, biblical epic – as were many other of the great 1950s wide-screen productions. The genre lent itself to the new format, allowing directors to fill the screen with thousands of extras in lavish period costumes.

The sheer scale of *The Robe* blinded many critics to its imperfections, and viewed half a century later it seems clumsy and inept. Richard Burton stars as Marcellus, a noble Roman converted to Christianity by the learned Pythagoras (Victor Mature). The storyline throws in romance, self-sacrifice, some very hammy dialogue, and costumes that barely reach down to the main actors' knees. Audiences adored the film, provoking Fox's rivals to devise their own wide-screen processes. WarnerScope, TechniScope, Todd A.O., PanaScope, Superscope and PanaVision were just some of the other formats developed.

Cecil B. de Mille's *The Ten Commandments* (1956) was shot for Paramount on 70mm VistaVision. Over 300,000 gallons of water were used in the scene showing the parting of the Red Sea. On wide screen, Charlton Heston's Moses was a truly formidable sight – an Old Testament prophet writ large. MGM struck the jackpot in 1959 with *Ben Hur*, also starring Heston, which made over $80 million worldwide in rentals, an astonishing figure for the period. The studio used its own wide-screen process, known as Camera 65 (the negative

SCRATCH AND SNIFF
The most startling of all the gimmicky new processes introduced by American B-movies was 'Odorama'. Baltimore-born auteur John Waters patented the system on his 1981 melodrama, *Polyester*. This time, cinema managers offered audiences scratch-and-sniff cards instead of magical spectacles. Numbers flashed up on the screen during the movie and audiences were supposed to respond by scratching and sniffing the appropriate numbers on their cards. Waters provided the full gamut of smells: a dedicated scratch and sniffer could get a whiff of everything from roses to dirty socks.

above Abel Gance's epic *Napoléon* (1927) pioneered a process known as Polyvision, using three synchronized cameras.

right Nobody could show righteous wrath like Charlton Heston. Here, as Moses in *The Ten Commandments* (1956).

far right Heston again, midway through the breathtaking chariot race in *Ben Hur* (1959).

was 65mm wide). Columbia made David Lean's *Lawrence of Arabia* with Super Panavision 70mm: an aspect ratio of 2.75:1, which made conventional CinemaScope look almost narrow. For *Spartacus* (1960), his tale about the slave/gladiator in ancient Rome, Stanley Kubrick used Super Technirama 70, a process developed by the Technicolor Company in the late 1950s.

As they made wide-screen blockbuster after wide-screen blockbuster, the studios risked spending themselves into a hole. Although there were several spectacular hits, there were also many expensive misfires. By the 1970s, Hollywood had largely abandoned shooting films on 65mm or 70mm. If a filmmaker wanted the wide-screen effect, it was cheaper to film on 35mm and then blow up the negative.

THE MARILYN EFFECT

CinemaScope was not the only trick Fox had in its bag to lure television watchers back to the cinemas. Another added attraction was the era's biggest sex symbol, Marilyn Monroe. The promotional campaign that Fox mounted for *Niagara* (1953), her first starring vehicle, went to absurd lengths to showcase her as a big-screen star, and she was treated less as an actress than as a force of nature. The studio publicists warned audiences to beware of 'the raging torrent of emotion' she was about to unleash on them; she was the star whose 'kisses fired men's souls'. Several of her subsequent star vehicles were shot in CinemaScope. In *How To Marry a Millionaire* (1953), her widescreen wiggles were not just for the benefit of potential sugar daddies and suitors on screen: they also helped mesmerize cinema-goers. In *The Seven Year Itch*, the famous scene in which her skirt is blown up almost over her head by a blast of air from the subway grating registers all the more strongly thanks to the CinemaScope and the De Luxe Color.

WIDE-SCREEN WIT

The wide-screen format was not just the preserve of Cecil B. de Mille and the biblical epic brigade, and occasionally it would be used much more subtly, in low-key, character-driven dramas. Cinematographer Conrad Hall shot *In Cold*

Blood (1967) in Panavision. Adapted from Truman Capote's book, this was a true story about two small-time punks who massacre a Kansas family in their farmhouse. Director Richard Brooks was determined to create an 'aura of reality' – not something that wide-screen photography is known for. The filming took place in exactly the locations that Capote had described, whether motel rooms, five-and-dime stores, gas stations or city streets. Seven of the original jurors featured in the court scenes and the two actors in the lead roles wore clothes identical to those of the actual killers. The Kansas police officers who had arrested the two killers were special advisers on the movie. To help the production, local newspapers reproduced exactly the same issues they had published on the case, but substituted the faces of the two actors for those of the killers. Brooks chose to shoot in black and white to give the film more of a documentary edge. For him, detail was all-important: by shooting in wide screen, he could fit more of it on the screen.

Woody Allen (and his cinematographer Gordon Willis) also used black and white Panavision in *Manhattan* (1979). They did so to capture the sheer beauty of the New York skyline and to make the city magical. Gershwin's *Rhapsody in Blue*, which plays over the opening sequence, sets the tone. This is an idealized vision of the city Allen loves so passionately. Seen in colour in Academy Ratio, New York simply would not have looked so entrancing.

3-D – A LION IN YOUR LAP

The wide-screen epics of the 1950s offered colour and scale that TV could not match, and another strategy adopted was to try to outwit the small screen with showmanship and gimmickry. This was the idea behind the commercial exploitation of 3-D, or 'stereoscopic cinema', as it was also known. It gave spectators the illusion of three-dimensional vision.

New 3-D processes, most of them unreliable, were tested throughout the silent and early talkie era. Only at the beginning of the 1950s, when TV emerged as a bugbear, did the novelty catch on in cinemas. *Bwana Devil* (1952), the first important 3-D feature, was a cheaply made, independently produced action-adventure about man-eating lions, and hardly an accomplished piece of

filmmaking. Nevertheless, it yielded a memorable tag line – 'A LION IN YOUR LAP! A LOVER IN YOUR ARMS!' – with which to attract attention. United Artists distributed the film in the US and made a small fortune as a result.

The other studios were now keen to jump on the 3-D bandwagon. Warners released their own 3-D horror picture, *House of Wax*, in 1953. This was directed by the flamboyant B-filmmaker Andre de Toth, who only had one eye (and wore an eyepatch) and was thus unable to enjoy the full benefits of stereophonic vision himself. A remake of a 1930s Warner Bros shocker, *The Mystery of the Wax Museum*, it was an enjoyably lurid yarn about a wax sculptor (Vincent Price) who declines to put a chamber of horrors in his museum. Instead, when the museum is burned down, he reopens it with real-life murder victims sealed in wax.

The main drawback with 3-D was the special red-and-green-lensed spectacles that cinema managers had to provide for their audiences. Unsurprisingly, young cinema-goers were not always inclined to give them back. 'Following the loss of 2000 Polaroid spectacles during the first run of *Bwana Devil* at the Theatre Royal, Dublin, plans to show 3-D films in Rank's Irish circuit cinemas have been scrapped,' a British trade magazine announced in 1953. 'This decision has been taken because patrons deliberately destroyed the glasses or had refused to surrender them' (*Kinematograph Weekly*, 25 June 1953). Most 3-D films were low-budget B-movies aimed at teen audiences, and perhaps the spectacles would have survived a little longer if the movies had also been aimed at adults. As it was, 3-D soon petered out.

IMAX

The birth of the multiplex in the early 1980s enhanced the cinema-going experience for millions. Instead of decaying old theatres audiences were offered shiny new picture palaces, each of them equipped with state-of-the-art sound systems. A single cinema could have a dozen or more screens, each showing different films. As more and more multiplexes were built, old cinemas were dismantled or converted. Auditoriums grew smaller and so, inevitably, did screens. The quality of projection may have improved but there were few cinemas left that could offer a real big-screen experience.

As if to satisfy the craving for size, a new wide-screen format was developed in the 1990s – IMAX, first presented at Expo '70 in Osaka. IMAX films cannot be shown in ordinary cinemas; they are shot with custom-built cameras on special film stock and projected on custom-built screens in custom-built theatres. IMAX is a giant-screen format that makes Cinerama and CinemaScope seem puny. The screens in IMAX cinemas are up to 10 times larger than the traditional cinema screen and are intended to fill the entire field of human vision. The films are projected on 15-perforation 70mm film, roughly three times the size of conventional 70mm CinemaScope frames.

The IMAX Corporation makes extravagant boasts about the image and sound quality of their system. 'The IMAX experience takes an image rich in clarity and definition and wraps the viewer in digital surround sound. You're not just watching a film. You're in it,' it boasts on its Web site. Nevertheless, IMAX has certain in-built problems, not least of which being that the films cost a fortune to make. There are also technical drawbacks: the screen is so big that editing has to be slowed down, as rapid cuts would disorientate spectators; and the sheer size creates massive problems in terms of light, close-ups and working with actors. The format is best at offering spectacle – often travel films set in exotic locations – rather than dramatic features. With the right subject-matter, the format works like a dream. A film like *Everest* (1998), a hugely successful documentary about an ill-fated mountain expedition, worked far better on IMAX than it would have done in a conventional cinema. The biggest screen format and the world's highest mountain complemented one another perfectly.

THE SWORD-AND-SANDAL EPIC REVIVED

By the 1970s, many thought that biblical yarns and sword-and-sandal historical romps had gone the way of the dinosaurs. They were prohibitively expensive to produce: nobody in the modern era was going to rebuild Babylon (as D.W. Griffith had in *Intolerance*) or part the Red Sea, or show Hannibal crossing the Alps.

The extraordinary box-office success of Ridley Scott's *Gladiator* in the summer of 2000 suggested that there was more mileage in historical epics than the sceptics had believed. Yes, this was a film on a massive scale, complete with armies of extras and mind-boggling battle sequences, but Scott was able to cut corners in a way that de Mille and Griffith could not. Thanks to CGI (Computer Generated Imagery), he could fill the Colosseum with massive crowds and stage spectacularly bloody set-pieces without having to bankrupt the studio – Universal in this case – in the process. As *Gladiator* and James Cameron's equally gargantuan *Titanic* (1998) proved, size mattered as much at the end of the 20th century as it had in D.W. Griffith's silent era heyday.

opposite One-eyed director Andre De Toth was unable to enjoy the full benefits of stereophonic vision, but that didn't stop him from directing one of the earliest 3-D films, *House of Wax* (1953), starring Vincent Price as the sinister embalmer.

below Just when critics were preparing to consign the sword-and-sandal epic to history, the genre made an unexpected comeback in Ridley Scott's Oscar-winning *Gladiator*, starring Russell Crowe.

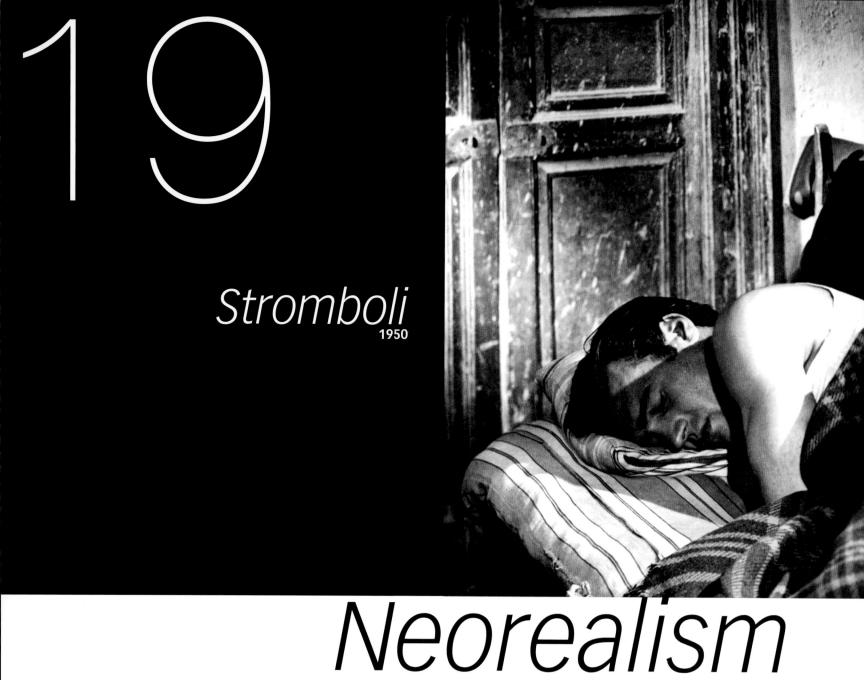

19

Stromboli
1950

Neorealism

VOYAGE TO ITALY

In 1949, Ingrid Bergman left her husband, Dr Peter Lindstrom, for the Italian filmmaker, Roberto Rossellini. The couple's relationship caused a huge scandal in Hollywood, where Bergman was a major star. She had written to Rossellini after seeing his films, *Rome, Open City* (1945) and *Paisa* (1946), offering her services to him. It would take seven years for the studios to forgive her. Whether they were more offended by her decision to work abroad or by her having an affair with a married man was impossible to tell.

In 1950, Bergman made *Stromboli*, the first of her six movies with Rossellini, whom she subsequently married. She admired the Italian director mainly because he did not make studio-bound, star-driven melodramas and was not interested in Hollywood hype. Nevertheless, *Stromboli* was presented to the world as if it were a bodice ripper along the lines of Selznick's Western *Duel in the Sun* (1946). 'Raging Island... Raging Passions? This is IT! The Place: Stromboli. The Star: Bergman,' shrieked the slogans on the lurid poster for the film's release in the US. Many American cities banned the movie, so outraged were they by Bergman's broken marriage and defection to Italy. The Boston Catholics who lobbied against *Stromboli* were only too aware that Bergman had just given birth to a child fathered by Rossellini. The notorious tycoon Howard Hughes, boss of

RKO (which was distributing *Stromboli*), relished this controversy. He handled the film's marketing with such skill that it grossed a small fortune in the US – something few other low-budget Italian films had done.

The fascination of Rossellini's *Stromboli* lies in the way it allows opposites to collide. It is, by dint of Bergman's casting, a star vehicle. It is also a story about an outsider intruding into a close-knit community. The world that she stumbles into is portrayed in the same unflinching way as the wrecked cities and ravaged countryside Rossellini showed in his earlier films.

Bergman plays a young Lithuanian émigrée who has married an Italian fisherman to escape the displaced persons' camp in which she has been interned since the ending of the war. The autobiographical resonances here are obvious: the actress had married Rossellini to escape Hollywood, a city which she had come to regard as purgatory. Stromboli is a bleak island dominated by a still-simmering volcano. The inhabitants are fishermen and their womenfolk, silent, truculent types who all seem to dress in black. Bergman is a complete outsider in the community, a modern woman in a society whose attitudes are still stuck in medieval times. Her husband barely speaks to her and nor does anybody else. She looks like precisely what she is – a beautiful Hollywood star adrift in a strange country where no one

GO OUT INTO THE STREETS

Neorealist cinema, of which Rossellini was considered one of the founding fathers, dealt with ordinary people and ordinary lives. Scriptwriter Cesare Zavattini once exhorted young Italian filmmakers not to sit at home, but to go out into the streets, onto buses and onto trams, and to 'steal' their stories and dialogue from the people they overheard. Generally, they followed his bidding, and throughout the late 1940s Italian movies abounded in accounts of ordinary folk struggling to come to terms with everyday problems. In De Sica's *The Bicycle Thief* (1948), scripted by Zavattini, the protagonist is a working man whose bicycle is stolen. What would seem no more than an annoyance in a Hollywood film threatens to unravel his entire life. Unemployment is high and if he does not get the bicycle back, he will not be able to ride to work and he will lose his job. But finding a stolen bicycle in Rome is

like looking for a needle in a haystack. In De Sica's other great neorealist film, *Umberto D* (1952), the protagonist is an old man with an inadequate pension who faces a huge struggle to survive, let alone maintain his dignity, in post-war Italy. Spotted begging by somebody he knows, he immediately turns his hand around as if he was checking to see if it was raining.

acknowledges her. There is a surreal, dreamlike quality to the film which was echoed a decade later in *L'Avventura* (1960), Antonioni's mystical, deeply unsettling fable about the disappearance of a young woman who is holidaying on a desolate island similar to the one shown in *Stromboli*.

OBSESSION

The roots of neorealism stretch back beyond Rossellini to the early 1940s, when the term was first coined by Italian critics. Long before that, filmmakers all around the world were shooting movies that conformed to neorealist tenets. Even certain Hollywood films of the 1930s could loosely be described as being in a neorealist vein. King Vidor's *Our Daily Bread* (1934) is a prime example. King Vidor mortgaged his home to pay for the movie, which tells of how an impoverished young city couple set up a collective farm at the height of the Depression. Their plans are threatened by drought and by the plotting of a woman who joins the collective, but they still manage to make a going concern of the farm. The final reel of the film is as dramatic as any in a melodrama or Western, but there is no shoot-out or reunion between star-crossed lovers: the tension comes from the farmworkers' desperate efforts to build the ditch they need to irrigate their crops.

Luchino Visconti's 1942 debut feature, *Ossessione* (*Obsession*) is generally regarded as the first neorealist film. An adaptation of James Cain's novel *The Postman Always Rings Twice* (later filmed in Hollywood in 1946 and remade in 1981), it eschews studio settings in favour of actual locations and has a grittiness about it that Hollywood movies of the period conspicuously lacked. While Visconti's movie was hardly seen abroad, *Rome, Open City* (1945) enjoyed better fortune. By the time Rossellini made it, the war was ending and audiences both in Italy and abroad were clamouring for films that dealt honestly with their events of the preceding difficult years.

Open City is the story of Catholic priest helping the Underground in its fight against the Nazis. It was inspired by the director's own experiences, hiding from Nazi patrols who were rounding up young Italians to fight as conscripts for the Fascists. Rossellini shot out on the streets with a largely nonprofessional cast. The city was still in chaos after the war and the sense of upheaval made even the simplest street scene seem unsettling and exciting. Rossellini made a virtue of the problems facing him: he had been given permission to make a documentary, not a feature, and could only get his hands on silent film stock (the sound was dubbed in later).

In his next two films, *Paisa* (1945), and *Germany, Year Zero* (1947), he refined his style. The former charts the events leading up to the Italian surrender of 1944. Again, the focus was on ordinary people rather than generals or heroes. Rossellini shows what they suffered and how they survived during these climactic years. *Germany, Year Zero* is set in an almost unrecognizable Berlin, where every second house is bombed. The remaining residents cower like pariahs in the face of the Allies who have taken over their city. The hero is a traumatized teenage boy, desperately trying to survive by selling goods on the black market. Again, the strength of the film lies in its use of real locations. No production designer could have fashioned a Berlin as woebegone and derelict as the one Rossellini found.

opposite left Lamberto Maggiorani and Enzo Staida in Vittorio De Sica's *The Bicycle Thief* (1948), one of the classics of Italian neorealist cinema.

opposite right In Roberto Rossellini's *Paisa* (1946), the lines between documentary and drama were blurred.

below The rubble-strewn streets of Berlin at the end of World War II made an eerie and evocative setting for Rossellini's *Germany, Year Zero (1947)*.

A dying city is also at the root of Rossellini's great 1953 film, *Voyage to Italy*, but almost a decade after the war his storytelling style was now very different. Bergman plays Katherine, an unhappily married Englishwoman who has just arrived in Naples with her husband (George Sanders). Their relationship seems close to breaking-point; they are unable to communicate and he treats her contemptuously. In *Stromboli*, a pregnant Bergman, startled by the ferocity of the volcano, experiences a moment of epiphany: suddenly, she is ready to embrace life on the island, however harsh and constrictive. There is an equally bizarre ending to *Voyage to Italy*, in which the bickering couple, after seeing the majestic landscapes around Naples, Vesuvius and the remains of Pompeii, somehow suddenly rediscover their love for another. The mystical, almost melodramatic finale in both films suggests that Rossellini was really far removed from the stereotype of the neorealist director who treated everything with documentary detachment.

THE YOUNG VEALS

In the 1950s, neorealist cinema in Italy gradually lost its way. Social conditions had changed and, in a more prosperous country with a more prosperous film industry, the documentary-style stories that Zavattini so relished seemed inappropriate. Rossellini's protégé Frederico Fellini had far more ambitious ideas. *I Vitelloni* (1953) was a key transitional film in his career, and arguably in Italian cinema. The film is about a group of small-town chancers – the title means 'veal calves' in English – who idle away their time drinking, womanizing and making mischief. Their loyalty to each other is unquestionable. In making

above Hector Babenco's horrifying *Pixote* (1981), the tale of a young Brazilian kid who becomes a pimp and a killer on the streets of Rio, was strongly influenced by the work of the Italian neorealists.

left *I Vitelloni* (1953), a tale about a group of young delinquents idling their lives away in a backwater town.

the film, Fellini is following Zavattini's injunction, portraying the kinds of ordinary Italians whose lives are depicted in other neorealist films. The difference here is that one of them (based on Fellini himself) is determined to leave. The film captures perfectly the director's ambivalence about his small-town roots, his nostalgia for the innocence and irresponsibility of his youth, and the gnawing sense of futility that so many young Italians felt then about a society that seemed to offer them no opportunities whatsoever.

THE SHOESHINE BOY

Neorealism may have died out in Italy, but its legacy was far-reaching. Many filmmakers in developing countries looked to Rossellini and his compatriots for inspiration as they tried to build up their own national cinemas. In Brazil in the 1960s, Cinema Novo acknowledged its debt to neorealism, not that it was an easy movement to categorize. 'Don't know where I'm going, but I know I'm not going over there,' Nelson Pereira Dos Santos, who directed the groundbreaking *Barren Lives* (1963), famously remarked. Meanwhile, Glauber Rocha, director of *Black God, White Devil*, coined the phrase: 'an idea in your head and a camera in your hand' to describe his improvisatory and flamboyant approach to filmmaking.

The Cinema Novo directors were confused but not cowed by the 1964 coup, which saw the overthrow of President Goulart's government by a military dictatorship. They continued to make movies in opposition to Hollywood; films that dealt with colonialism, militarism, and the quest for national identity. The political situation may have changed today, but the filmmakers' preoccupations remain largely the same. Their focus is still often on outsiders – migrants, prostitutes, orphans, thieves, or, sometimes, entire communities pushed to the margins of society. In Hector Babenco's *Pixote* (1981), the hero is a young homeless kid who becomes a pimp and a killer on the streets of Rio. The actor who played him, Fernando Ramos da Silva, was himself later murdered. The setting of *Pixote* may be very different, but the boy is confronted with many of the same problems as the teenager in *Germany, Year Zero*.

Walter Salles, director of the Golden Bear winner *Central do Brasil* (1998), freely acknowledged his debt to neorealism. He was making the film, he claimed, in opposition to the 'Neon Realism' of Hollywood. It tells of an epic journey into the heartland of Brazil. A retired Rio schoolteacher (Fernanda Montenegro) accompanies a nine-year-old street-kid (Vincius De Oliveira) in search of his father. The boy's quest stands in microcosm for the national quest for self-identity. 'All countries that have been colonized and then abandoned have this sense of the loss of the father figure,' Salles stated. The film's star, De Oliveira, true to neorealist principles, was a nonprofessional. Salles recruited the ten-year-old shoeshine boy after running into him at Rio airport on a wet morning. 'He was a little warrior fighting for survival, working – not stealing,' Salles said of him.

The child had always been central in neorealist cinema. Filmmakers like Rossellini and de Sica often used children as innocent witnesses, looking in on the corruption of adult life. 'Through the child's sense of time – lingering, intense and consecutive – they came to realize how film needed narrative structures that did not rely on the model of stage drama,' film historian Eric Rhode noted. 'In the child's spontaneity and freshness they recognized modes of behaviour that showed up by contrast the contrivance of the professional actor.'

*Death on the
Beach*

20

The Seventh Seal
1956

It is one of cinema's great clichés, endlessly parodied and imitated: under a louring twilight sky, a lean-jawed 14th-century knight (Max Von Sydow) plays chess on the beach with the Grim Reaper (Bengt Ekerot). The scene comes midway through Ingmar Bergman's *The Seventh Seal* (1956), a film that Bergman freely admitted is about 'the fear of death'.

The Seventh Seal began as a short play, *Wood Painting*, written by Bergman for his students when he was teaching at the drama school in Malmö in 1954. Its imagery – of the dance of death, of the chess match – was inspired by the director's long meditations on religious symbolism. As the son of a Lutheran pastor, Bergman (born in 1918) was a regular churchgoer and had plenty of opportunity to study the angels, devils, crucifixes and prophets depicted on stained-glass windows and murals. His relationship with his father was fraught, and his parents' marriage was turbulent. They stayed together 'for the sake of the children', as he put it in his autobiography. Bergman has talked at length of his religious doubts in the 1950s. 'For me, in those days, the great question was: does God exist? or doesn't God exist... what I believed in those days – and believed in for a long time – was the existence of a virulent evil, in no way dependent on environmental or hereditary factors.' These eschatological misgivings combined with the

memories of a troubled childhood and an obsession with Strindberg and Ibsen made a potent cocktail for a young filmmaker. With such a background, he was never likely to specialize in slapstick comedies.

Wild Strawberries (1957) is likewise warm and lyrical despite its seemingly downbeat subject-matter. The protagonist is an old professor (Victor Sjostrom), close to death. As if to signal that his time is short, he has a nightmare about being cast adrift in a city with empty, sinister streets and clocks without hands. The next day he embarks on a long journey to pick up a Lifetime Achievement award. En route, he looks back on his life. He rues missed opportunities, remembers how his wife cuckolded him and how his brother stole his first love. He learns that his son (whose wife accompanies him on the journey) resents him. The very process of analysing his life makes him better able to cope with its disappointments. In spite of them, the film ends on an affirmative and optimistic note.

THE MYTH OF SCANDINAVIAN GLOOM

The idea that Nordic filmmakers were obsessed by death and suffering predates Bergman. The best-known feature that actor-director Victor Sjostrom (later the star of *Wild Stawberries*) made during his stint in Hollywood

in the 1920s was *The Wind* (1928), starring Lillian Gish. It may have been set in Texas, but the storyline – encompassing murder, rape and insanity – was as overwrought as that of any Scandinavian play or melodrama.

Long before Bergman, Danish director Carl Theodor Dreyer (1889–1968) – another filmmaker from a strict Lutheran background – was dealing with martyrdom, religious guilt and unhappy marriages in his own, equally saturnine style. His *The Passion of Joan Of Arc* (1928) featured a performance of searing intensity by the Corsican-born actress Renée Falconetti as the Maid of Orléans. *Master of the House* (1925) sketched out the same battle territory that many of Bergman's later films would cover too: a tale of an unhappy marriage, it shows a young woman (Astrid Holm) chafing against the constraints placed on her by her bullying patriarch of a husband.

Dreyer's *Day Of Wrath* (1943) is every bit as powerful an indictment of religious bigotry and persecution as Arthur Miller's play, *The Crucible*. An otherwise tolerant community behaves with vicious cruelty toward old women in its midst accused of withcraft. Ann (Lisbeth Movin), the wife of the priest who oversees the burnings, bridles against her husband's unthinking sadism. The film's content of denouncements, conspiracies and torture made it deeply offensive to the Nazis then occupying Denmark. With *Ordet* (1954), Dreyer deals with faith and intolerance in a far starker way than Bergman does in *The Seventh Seal*. An austere tale about a family split apart by religious differences, it ends in astonishing fashion: a dead man comes to life and Dreyer is able to convince us that we have just seen a miracle.

In his last film, *Gertrud* (1964), Dreyer takes the kind of character familiar from Ibsen and Bergman – a beautiful but ageing woman (Nina Pens Rode) trapped in a marriage to a politician who treats her like a toy – and transforms her into a full-blown tragic heroine. Bergman, then, was not the only major Scandinavian director dealing with the rawest of private emotions.

TRUE IDENTITY
Bergman is a famously neurotic and self-obsessed director. Much of his autobiography is given over to discussing his stomach ailments and income-tax problems. Given the amount of his earnings the Swedish government wanted to grab, he had plenty of reason for looking down in the mouth. Nevertheless, the stereotype of Bergman as the quintessentially morose Scandinavian filmmaker does not altogether stand up to scrutiny. Alongside *The Seventh Seal* and *The Virgin Spring*, he was also making comedies like *Smiles of a Summer Night* (1955), a country-house drama set over one magical summer weekend at the turn of the 20th century, and high-spirited stories about young love like *Summer with Monika* (1952), which tells of a 17-year-old greengrocer's daughter ('mucky Monika' as she is nicknamed) who elopes by boat and spends an idyllic summer living in the wilds.

opposite top Max Von Sydow co-starred in Ingmar Bergman's stark, Middle Ages-set parable *The Virgin Spring* (1959).

opposite bottom Ingmar Bergman originally made *Scenes From A Marriage* (1973) for Swedish TV, but the 168-minute film version became an international art house success.

right Liv Ullmann, Gunnar Bjornstrand and Bibi Andersson pictures in Ingmar Bergman's haunting psychological drama, *Persona* (1966).

SCENES FROM A MARRIAGE

By the time his television drama *Scenes from a Marriage* (1973) had been edited down to feature length to be shown abroad, Bergman's reputation as the prince of Scandinavian gloom was well established. 'What is long, Swedish, deeply depressing, humourless and enormously boring?' the critic of the *Daily Express* asked. He could see no entertainment value whatsoever in Bergman's epic, unrelentingly intense slice of marital psychodrama.

It is easy to understand why the critic was discomfited. Bergman shoots much of the movie in tight close-ups, training his camera on the faces of his two leads, the bickering couple Johan (Erland Josephson) and Marianne (Liv Ullmann), and studying their features in the tiniest detail.

Despite hostile reviews in the popular press, up-market British audiences were fascinated by the film about the middle-class couple who drove a Volvo and lived in the kind of perfectly designed home that the British could only envy from afar (or read about in Habitat catalogues). There was something inspirational (and aspirational) about watching a well-adjusted couple tear strips off one another. Certain broadsheet critics were in raptures over the movie: 'Almost certainly one of the most important films ever made,' one wrote; 'Frankly incredible,' another enthused. Back in Sweden, the TV version of the film had emptied the streets, and there are stories of Bergman being stopped by couples who wanted him to advise them on their marital problems.

Bergman's great trick – and arguably what gave the film such resonance all over the world – was to create characters immediately recognizable both from real life and from popular soap operas of the time, and then treat them as if they were the 20th-century equivalents of the tortured lovers in Strindberg plays.

The tension between cosy domesticity and the hell of a relationship turned sour is spelled out in an early scene, when Johan and Marianne have dinner with another couple, Katarina and Peter. A quiet evening degenerates into a caustic slanging match – between Katarina and Peter. 'I wonder if there is anything more horrible than a man and wife who hate each other,' Peter says to himself, quoting Strindberg. The irony is palpable. Johan and Marianne, whom we know are at loggerheads, sit through their friends' spat as if they are a perfect model of marital harmony.

PERSONA

Two faces merge, two identities are subsumed within one another. This is the key moment in Bergman's 1966 film, *Persona*. An actress (Liv Ullmann) has become mute and been sent to a remote island to recover. There, she is tended by Nurse Alma (Bibi Andersson). Nurse and patient look remarkably like one another, and Bergman's cinematographer, Sven Nykvist, emphasizes the similarity between them, filming them from the same angles and in the same light. The nurse herself is troubled. She pours out her problems to the actress, who by default assumes the role of her confessor. The nurse's anger at the actress's continuing silence only prompts her to speak more. This was as much a case-study as a movie.

HANNAH AND HER SISTERS

Woody Allen's debt to Bergman is well charted. His 1982 comedy, *A Midsummer Night's Sex Comedy*, reworked Bergman's *Smiles of a Summer Night*, and when he tried to escape his comic roots and make a 'straight' film,

Interiors, in 1978, he was accused of aping Bergman. Like the Swedish director, he was a magnet for the press and they constantly searched for overlaps between his private life and his movies.

Many critics considered Allen's 1986 film *Hannah and her Sisters* to be his most successful attempt at reconciling European-style art-house cinema and his own brand of New York-based comedy. It earned him some of the best reviews of his career. 'Virtually non-stop exhilaration,' Vincent Canby exulted in the *New York Times*. 'The great American film of the 80s,' Andrew Sarris wrote in the *Village Voice*. The film opens with Elliot (Michael Caine) contemplating cheating on his loyal and affectionate wife, Hannah (Mia Farrow). Lee (Barbara Hershey) is the focus of his lust. 'God she's beautiful,' he muses in a voice-over as he ogles her. 'Stop it, you idiot, she's your wife's sister.' There are moments in the film which reflect and even anticipate events in his life in an uncanny way. Allen was to leave his real-life partner Mia Farrow and marry her daughter Soon-Yi a few years later.

Hannah and her Sisters was Allen's 14th feature as writer and director. It was one of his most ambitious – and one of his longest. He tackled big subjects – death, disease, lust, betrayal – with levity and wit, and interwove the stories of Hannah, Lee, and her other, even more ditzy sister, Holly (Dianne Wiest) with exemplary skill. His cinematographer Carlo di Palma followed the example set by cameraman Gordon Willis in *Manhattan* in making everyday New York buildings and streets look magical. The actors are all excellent – and the presence of Max von Sydow as Lee's gloomy artist boyfriend cannot help but evoke memories of Bergman films.

Nevertheless, in Allen's cocooned corner of Manhattan, infidelity remains a lifestyle choice, even caterers know about art and architecture, and accountants read modernist poems. It is a never-never land in which no one really suffers and nothing much seems to be at stake. That is why all those grand comparisons the critics drew with Bergman do not ring true.

PERFECTIONISM AND STOMACH ACHES – BERGMAN RETIRES

His bowels were giving him trouble, he was tortured by insomnia and he was scared of getting old. 'I had seen far too many of my colleagues falling in the ring like tired clowns, bored by their own dullness, booed off or killed by polite silence and dragged out of the lights by kindly and contemptuous circus hands,' he wrote. Not long after completing *Fanny and Alexander* (1983), Bergman retired from directing films. 'He can't stand the pressure because he's a perfectionist. He wants everything to be just the way he asked for it. Too often there are unpleasant surprises, and he just can't take it,' Max von Sydow commented of the decision. Bergman continued to write screenplays and work in the theatre, but with his withdrawal, European art-house cinema lost its most influential figure.

Fanny and Alexander was a kind of summing up of his career. Set in a Swedish town in 1907 – just over a decade before he was born – it tells the story of two children growing up in a strict Lutheran background not unlike his own. The children seem to lead a happy, pampered existence with relatives who dote on them, but once their widowed mother (Ewa Froeling) marries an uptight priest, their lives change dramatically. Their new stepfather beats, bullies and tortures them – all in God's name.

At once a magical evocation of childhood and a chronicle of unhappiness and abuse, *Fanny and Alexander* seemed to herald a new beginning in Bergman's career. It was not as ponderous or as self-conscious as some of his earlier studies of suffering artists. In the event, it was a final word.

BERGMAN'S VOICE LINGERS ON

After his retirement, Bergman began to be seen as a Prospero figure. Film culture had changed by the 1990s, the age of Tarantino, and his brand of meditative art-house cinema seemed very old-fashioned. When he was awarded the 'Palme des Palmes' at the 50th Cannes Festival in 1997 there was a dispiriting sense that he was the last of a dying breed.

Nobody could prise him out of retirement, but Bergman's voice is still heard. His former wife Liv Ullmann has directed two films with scripts by him, *Private Confessions* (1996) and *Trolosa* (2000), and both reveal that Bergman's preoccupations have changed little over the years. The former deals with a mother (Pernilla August) in her mid-30s, married to a vicar, who begins an affair with a younger man, also a theologian. In a series of conversations, she talks to the old priest (Max von Sydow) who confirmed her many years before about her adulterous relationship. *Trolosa* records in lightly veiled form an adulterous affair that Bergman had in the late 1940s. 'Our love tore our hearts apart and from the very beginning carried its own seeds of destruction,' he wrote of his relationship with journalist, Gun Hagberg.

It is too simplistic to view Bergman's films as *romans à clef* but the autobiographical elements in his work are always apparent. *Trolosa* even features a character called 'Bergman' (Erland Josephson), an old man living by the sea, who listens, rapt, as a 'voice' tells him a story. The voice takes the form of Marianne (Lena Endre), a beautiful actress and mother married to Markus (Thomas Hanzon), a successful composer. Almost as a dare, without any thoughts of the consequences, she begins an affair with Markus's best

friend David (Krister Henriksson), a crumpled, charming, curmudgeonly, twice-divorced writer. Is David supposed to be Bergman? That is what the screenplay suggests.

BERGMAN'S SUCCESSOR

'A young master's first masterpiece,' Bergman commented of young Swedish director Lukas Moodysson's first feature, *Fucking Amal*, a story about the friendship of two teenage girls growing up in a dead-end town. Bergman predicted that Moodysson was to be the new face of Swedish cinema: 'We place unreasonable expectations which hopefully won't be overbearing.' Moodysson's second feature, *Together* (2000), confirmed his promise. It broached many of the same themes as Bergman's work – squabbling spouses, unhappy kids, infidelity and betrayal – but in a new setting: a Swedish hippy commune in the mid-1970s. The hippies believe in free love, death to all fascists, and the right not to wear underwear in the kitchen while suffering from yeast infections. Moodysson is satirical at his characters' expense, showing up their pretensions, selfishness and eccentricities, but he does not patronize them. Their suffering is every bit as acute as that endured by the ill-matched couples and neglected children in Bergman's own movies. What is missing is Bergman's trademark solemnity.

Together has had greater international exposure than any Swedish film since *Fanny and Alexander*. There is hardly a hint of gloom or introspection about it. Perhaps, then, the old clichés about doom-ridden, navel-gazing Scandinavian cinema are finally crumbling.

above Fanny and Alexander Ekdahl (Pernilla Allwin and Bertil Guve), the eponymous protagonists of Ingmar Bergman's last film before his retirement from the movie business.

opposite Woody Allen, one of Bergman's most faithful devotees, paid his own wry tribute to the master in his 1986 film, *Hannah and Her Sisters*, in which the married Michael Caine begins an adulterous affair with Barbara Hershey.

La Nouvelle Vague

In the late 1950s, a group of like-minded young French filmmakers and critics led by François Truffaut, Claude Chabrol, Jean-Luc Godard, Jacques Rivette and Eric Rohmer turned their back on what they witheringly called *'le cinéma du papa'*. The films they objected to were ossified literary adaptations, full of picture-postcard scenery and overdressed actors and actresses. Their brand of cinema was characterized by an enthusiasm for real locations, an emphasis on hand-held camerawork and the use of natural light, and abrasive, iconoclastic storylines. Their great influences were not European writers or painters or art-house directors, but Hollywood mavericks. They saw genius in the work of such figures as Howard Hawks, Raoul Walsh, Alfred Hitchcock, Vincente Minnelli, Jerry Lewis (the comedian they nicknamed 'le roi du crazy'), and B-Western directors like Alan Dwan, Budd Boetticher and Anthony Mann.

François Truffaut's article, 'A Certain Tendency of French Cinema', published in the magazine *Cahiers du Cinéma* in 1954, was their unofficial manifesto. Truffaut argued passionately for a more personal style of filmmaking: one in which directors would take risks and leave their thumbprints on their work. This was the creed known as *'La Politique des Auteurs'*. He, in turn, was influenced by critic and writer Alexandre Astruc, who originated the idea of the 'camera pen' in the 1940s. Astruc called for directors to devise a language for film – not simply to ape the traditions of the novel or the theatre.

Although they dismissed the hoary old traditions of French 'quality' cinema, these young directors were not knee-jerk populists. Like the critics on *Cahiers*, with which they were intimately associated, they were very particular in their enthusiasms and aversions. As a group, they became known as the New Wave (*la Nouvelle Vague*). They loved coining irreverent slogans: 'All you need to make a movie is a girl and a gun,' 'The cinema is truth 24 times a second' and 'A film should have a beginning, a middle and an end, but not necessarily in that order,' were three of Godard's most famous maxims.

AGNES BLAZES A TRAIL

The New Wave had its roots in the early 1950s, in the work of young director Agnès Varda. Her first feature, *La Pointe Courte*, which she described as 'a bomb of nonconformity', was made in 1954, several years before the debuts of Truffaut and Godard. The 25-year-old director, drawing her inspiration from Brecht and from William Faulkner's modernist novel, *Wild Palms*, told two entirely separate stories side by side – one about a couple with marital difficulties, the other about fishermen fighting for their rights. Unconventionally funded – the technicians and

above Jean-Claude Brialy and
Bernadette Lafonte in Claude
Chabrol's *Le Beau Serge* (1958),
one of the films which heralded
the birth of the French New Wave.

actors formed a co-op – and shot on a tiny budget, *La Pointe Courte* failed to make much impact at the box-office. Nevertheless, its influence was immense and it earned Varda the nickname: 'the grandmother of the New Wave'.

LE BEAU SERGE

Fiery principles are all very well, but making full-length movies needed money. Claude Chabrol, a critic on *Cahiers du Cinéma*, subsidized his first feature, *Le Beau Serge* (1958) with money that his wife had inherited. It is a gripping but dour tale with little of the flashiness of later New Wave films. Jean-Claude Brialy stars as François, an urbane, young professional who has left his rural roots far behind him. The film follows him back to the little village where he grew up. He is distressed to discover that his best friend Serge (Gérard Blain), who never left the village, has turned into a self-pitying, boorish drunk. Whereas more traditional French films depicted the countryside in an idyllic light, Chabrol showed its ugliest aspects: the deadening monotony, the drinking, the lack of facilities or social life or opportunity.

Les Cousins, the film Chabrol shot the next year with the same two actors, is like *Le Beau Serge* in reverse. This time, Blain plays the provincial student, all at sea in the big city. He is staying in Paris with his cynical, urbane cousin (Brialy). He struggles with his exams and lacks the sophistication to impress the young women who troop in and out of the cousin's apartment. In Chabrol's universe, nothing is clear-cut. Brialy steals Blain's girlfriend, but he is hardly the conventional villain. Nor is Blain any kind of hero. One is the poor country cousin, the other the rich city boy. Their differences in temperament and upbringing spark the tragedy which ends the movie.

The box-office success of *Les Cousins* enabled Chabrol to set up his own production company and to back the films of various other young French directors. By then, an entire new generation of young filmmakers had embraced the New Wave's proclamations: it is estimated that between 1958 and 1963, over 150 French directors also made debut features. Ironically, given their iconoclastic approach to the establishment, many relied on state subsidies to make their first films.

THE 400 BLOWS

Truffaut's 1959 debut feature, *The 400 Blows* (*Les Quatre Cents Coups*), owed much to Rossellini's *Germany, Year Zero*. The hero was again a disaffected adolescent, and although Antoine Doinel (Jean-Pierre Léaud) was not growing up in a bomb-strewn city, his plight seemed almost as bleak. He was unhappy at school; his family neglected him; he played truant, and told lies to cover his tracks. He was a truculent, stubborn kid, always in trouble with the authorities. The film captures perfectly the confusion and rebelliousness of its young protagonist, but Truffaut, who refused to moralize about Antoine, showed more than the brutality of his existence. There is also humour and lyricism in the film, which was poetically shot in black and white by cinematographer Henri Decae.

A BOUT DE SOUFFLE

Michel Poiccard (Jean-Paul Belmondo), an ex-airline steward turned petty criminal, steals a car in Marseilles and heads to Paris. En route, he shoots and kills a cop on a motorbike with a gun he finds in the glove compartment. His

plan now is to flee to Italy with his American girlfriend Patricia (Jean Seberg), but the police are on his trail and he is too careless to escape them.

Plot-wise, Jean-Luc Godard's 1960 feature *A Bout de Souffle* (*Breathless*) does not amount to much, but this was easily the most influential New Wave film. The studied arrogance and impishness of its director is matched by that of its antihero, the effortlessly cool and sardonic Belmondo. With his cigarette hanging from his bottom lip, his felt hat and jacket, and white socks, Belmondo looks like a cross between a left-bank intellectual and an American gangster (he reveres Bogart). With her close-cropped hair and *New York Herald Tribune* T-shirt, his girlfriend (Seberg) is equally stylish. Cameraman Raoul Coutard used natural light for the film, which abounds in jump cuts, whip pans and improvised tracking shots. *A Bout de Souffle* was anarchic and liberating – 'the best film around now', as its trailer proclaimed – and it made Godard, almost overnight, into 'the world's most discussed, interviewed and quoted filmmaker'.

GODARD THE JOKER

Godard's films of the 1960s were playful, polemical, melancholic, and exuberant by turns. His second film, *Le Petit Soldat* (1960), was temporarily banned by the French authorities because of its barbed critique of French colonialist behaviour in Algeria. *Vivre sa Vie* (1962), starring his wife Anna Karina as a young woman forced into prostitution, seemed inspired in equal measure by Brechtian theatre and the kind of doomed romanticism you find in Baudelaire's poetry or 19th-century novels about fallen women – it was indeed loosely based on Zola's 1966 work *Nana*. *Two or three things I know about her* (*2 ou 3 choses que je sais d'elle*), which charts the life of a housewife who works one day a week as a prostitute, and was less a piece of storytelling than a polemical essay attacking consumerism, the exploitation of women and American cultural imperialism.

With magnificent perversity, Godard sent up the whole idea of glossy, big-budget international filmmaking in *Le Mépris* (1963), an American-financed adaptation of an Alberto Moravia novel. In one famous shot near the start of

left Jean-Pierre Léaud as the rebellious young urchin Antoine Doinel in François Truffaut's *400 Blows* (1959). Over the following two decades, Truffaut would continue to chart Doinel's adventures in a series of further films.

below Anna Karina as the tragic heroine in Jean-Luc Godard's *Vivre sa Vie* (1962), loosely adapted from Zola's novel, *Nana*.

the film, he parodies the way actresses' bodies are fetishized on the big screen. The shot seems to go on forever, the camera panning slowly across Brigitte Bardot's body. Godard is using wide screen to mock the prurience and voyeurism of the audience. They have come to see the actress – and he is showing her to them in 70mm.

AUTUMNAL TALES

Eric Rohmer is the most elusive of the New Wave directors. It used to be claimed that not even his wife knew he was a filmmaker. 'Rohmer' itself is an alias – his real name is Jean-Marie Maurice Scherer. An ex-*Cahiers du Cinéma* critic, he directed his first feature, *La Signe du Lion* (1960) in the same year that Godard made *A Bout de Souffle*, but whereas Godard's early movies were full of jump cuts and startling camerawork, Rohmer's approach was more stately. He made films in collections: firstly, the six *Moral Tales*, from 1962 to 1972; in the 1980s *Comedies and Proverbs*; and then *The Four Seasons*. Shot on small budgets with skeleton crews, the films probed away at the thoughts and feelings of an array of different characters.

Rohmer is a deceptively good storyteller, spinning out his narratives with such subtlety that we hardly notice the developments. *A Summer's Tale* (1996) – one of the *Four Seasons* series – illustrates this low-key approach perfectly. Gaspard (Melvil Poupard), a young graduate with a couple of weeks to kill before beginning a new job, decides to spend them in a little seaside town in the vague hope that his girlfriend (who's on holiday in Spain) will turn up to

MAY '68 AND ALL THAT

The student uprisings of May 1968 had a profound effect on French film culture – and on Godard in particular. He embraced revolutionary left-wing politics with typical fervour and retired from the mainstream – some would argue that he had never really been part of it – and his work became more obscure. He remained prolific, but as his work became less accessible, audiences gradually lost interest.

After Godard fell under the spell of Brecht, Mao and radical student politics, the careers of the other New Wave directors also underwent some surprising transformations. Truffaut's films became venerated in exactly the same way as those of the traditional French directors he had so vociferously opposed in the 1950s. Chabrol continued to churn out films, making countless well-crafted murder mysteries and occasional literary adaptations as well, for example his *Madame Bovary* in 1991. Rivette, the most rarefied of the New Wave directors, enjoyed an unlikely Indian summer in the 1990s with his four-hour film about a painter and his model, *La Belle Noiseuse* (1991), his version of *Joan of Arc* (1994) and his austere thriller, *Secret Defence* (1997).

above Thandie Newton in Bernardo Bertolucci's *Besieged* (1998), a low-budget film which invoked the memory of the New Wave.

opposite Eric Rohmer's masterly *An Autumn's Tale* (1998), which rounded off his *Four Seasons* series.

meet him. While there, his love life becomes ever more confused. A waitress falls for him, but when he goes with her to a local disco, he is attracted to the voluptuous Solene. When the girlfriend finally does arrive, Gaspard is suddenly forced to choose between three women. Somehow, without either him or the audience realizing, he has manoeuvred himself into an almighty tangle.

The paradox about Rohmer's shooting style is that his films seem spontaneous but at the same time highly contrived. He uses very long takes, giving the impression that the actors, not the director, are shaping the scene. 'He doesn't give direction at all,' Alexia Portal, the star of *An Autumn's Tale* (1998), claimed. 'He doesn't like to talk about the psychology of the characters... he doesn't want the actors to think too much about what they're going to do and say.' Indeed, at times they even seem to be improvising, but every word they deliver is exactly as written. Like Hitchcock, about whom he once wrote a book with Claude Chabrol, he prepares each new film meticulously. His quiet and reflective brand of filmmaking, 'a cinema of thoughts rather than actions' as he once characterized it, is poles apart from that of his old colleague, Godard. The contrast between the two filmmakers suggests that the New Wave was never quite as homogeneous as critics like to suggest.

NEW WAVE ACOLYTES

Italian director Bernardo Bertolucci once claimed that he was prepared 'to die' for the cause of New Wave cinema. His debut feature *The Grim Reaper* (1962) was scripted by Pier Paolo Pasolini, but its evocation of Rome's low-life thieves and prostitutes, its freewheeling narrative style, and edgy black and white cinematography also suggested a strong debt to his French contemporaries. The story concerns an investigation into the killing of a prostitute. As a faceless interrogator quizzes the various suspects, Bertolucci uses flashbacks to show what they were doing at the time of her death. He was only 22 when he made the film. His next feature, *Before the Revolution* (1964), about a young middle-class student trying to embrace radical politics, won him an international reputation. His early films shared many of the same preoccupations – sex, politics, delinquency – as those of Godard. However, his filmmaking style was much more baroque than that of the New Wave directors he so admired, and he put more emphasis on visual elegance than they usually did.

Relatively late in his career, after epics like *The Last Emperor* (1987), *The Sheltering Sky* (1990) and *Little Buddha* (1994), Bertolucci returned to his New Wave roots with the chamber piece, *Besieged* (1998). A story about a relationship between a reclusive English composer and an African refugee, it used the same tricks – jump cuts, handheld camera work – that Godard had 'patented' 30 years before in *A Bout de Souffle*.

THE SACRED MONSTER

German *Wunderkind* Rainer Werner Fassbinder demands comparison with Godard if only because he was as prolific, provocative and headstrong as the French director. Like Godard, he could switch in an instant between melodrama and social polemic. He, too, was obsessed with Hollywood. Between 1966 and 1982, he made dozens of films which questioned the reality of life in Adenauer's brave new post-war West Germany. His movies remorselessly exposed the racism lurking beneath the surface of an ostensibly tolerant society, highlighted the homophobia and probed away at the country's ambivalent attitude towards its not very distant Nazi past.

The typical Fassbinder hero was a German everyman – not a good-looking, plain Joe like the types played by Gary Cooper and James Stewart in American movies, but a stumbling, unkempt, mixed-up, small-timer who struggles to distinguish between good and evil. His favourite character in fiction was Franz Biberkopf in Alfred Döblin's novel, *Berlin Alexanderplatz*, which he adapted for TV in 1979/80. Franz is a simple man just released from prison into the maelstrom of 1930s German society. He tries to earn an honest living, but is sucked into the criminal underworld and seduced by Nazi propaganda.

Some of Fassbinder's movies are shabbily lit and designed, and look as if they were made in a matter of days (which they probably were). Others, like *The Marriage of Maria Braun* (1978), *Lili Marleen* (1980), *Lola* (1981) and *Veronika Voss* (1982) were made on bigger budgets, and are as well crafted as the Hollywood melodramas they draw on so heavily. Fassbinder was a mess of contradictions: a misogynist who provided tremendous roles for women – and turned a handful of actresses, including Hanna Schygulla, Barbara Sukowa and Ingrid Caven into international stars; and a relentlessly honest social satirist, whose films occasionally descended into a sentimentality that even Disney might have blanched at. Fassbinder stood up for society's losers, but often showed them behaving far more cruelly to one another than those ostensibly exploiting them. He was the galvanizing force in the New German Cinema of the 1970s, but whereas the films made by other German directors of the period, like Volker Schlondorff and Margarethe von Trotta, now seem dated, his work remains as vital as ever.

WENDERS – THE THOUGHTFUL FACE OF THE NEW WAVE

Wim Wenders was both obsessed with American culture and deeply distrustful of it. He shared the same ambivalence towards Hollywood as his French New Wave contemporaries a generation before. 'Hollywood has colonized our subconscious,' he once remarked.

Born in Düsseldorf in 1945, Wenders grew up in an era when Germany – striving to rebuild after the war – seemed a grey and austere country in comparison to the US. The young Wenders loved rock and roll, Chuck Berry in particular, and American comics. His awestruck affection for the country's wide-open spaces and dynamic consumer culture is evident in such movies as *Paris, Texas* (1984), *Hammett* (1982) and *The American Friend* (1977), his tribute to US gangster movies. But his affection for America has not stopped him making barbed and satirical observations about the violence, alienation and exploitation in the land of the free. Think of the suicidal Jeremy Davies and his fellow misfits in *The Million Dollar Hotel* (1999), or Travis (Harry Dean Stanton) wandering, catatonic, through the Mojave desert in *Paris, Texas*, and you realize that his relationship with the US is tinged with suspicion as well as affection.

Wenders is a colder and more cerebral director than was Rainer Werner Fassbinder. His first feature, *Summer in the City* (1971), his diploma film, was not especially highly regarded, but its follow-up, *The Goalkeeper's Fear of the Penalty* (1972), whose protagonist murders a woman for no apparent reason, established him as an important new voice in New German Cinema.

above A dusty, battered-looking Harry Dean Stanton adrift in the desert at the start of Wim Wenders' *Paris, Texas* (1984).

opposite Bruno Ganz and Dennis Hopper in *The American Friend* (1977), Wim Wenders' tribute to American gangster movies.

DRAGGING A SHIP OVER A MOUNTAIN

All New Wave directors shared one essential trait – their belief that anything was possible; their ambition often seemed close to hubris. Werner Herzog, a key figure in New German Cinema, is renowned for the single-minded ruthlessness with which he pursues each new project, whether feature or documentary. This ruthlessness is shared by many of the characters in his films. In *Aguirre, Wrath of God* (1972), he charted the journey downriver through the Peruvian jungle, in search of El Dorado, undertaken by a demented Spanish conquistador, Aguirre (Klaus Kinski). By the end of the film, Aguirre has proclaimed himself emperor and is yelling orders at birds and monkeys. Herzog intended the film as a critique of colonialism, but there is the creeping sense that he admires the vaunting ambition of the film's deranged antihero.

Herzog was reunited with Klaus Kinski on the 1982 epic, *Fitzcarraldo*, again set deep in the South American jungle. This time, Kinski plays an opera lover who wants to bring Caruso to the jungle. To do so, he will have to drag a ship over a mountain. As if in sympathy with the film's hero, this is precisely what Herzog did. Coproducer George Sluizer had to co-ordinate the sequence. 'There was no question of asking myself if the boat should go up the mountain. That was a given fact. It was only how the bloody hell we got the bloody thing up there,' Sluizer later commented. 'There was madness, arrogance and danger; Werner goes to the absolute limit.'

*White Trash
Heroes*

22

Easy Rider
1969

Depression-era gangsters Bonnie Parker and Clyde Barrow first met in Texas in early 1930. Bonnie was a 19-year-old delinquent, the wife of an imprisoned murderer; Clyde was a 21-year-old petty thief and vagabond with a record of misdemeanours that stretched back right into his teen years. They were not an attractive couple – Arthur Penn, director of *Bonnie and Clyde* (1967), later called them 'scrawny white trash'. Together, Parker and Barrow embarked on a four-year crime spree, stealing from rich and poor alike. They were kidnappers, and were believed to have committed 13 murders.

In the 1930s, there was an indulgence toward such criminals. Gangsters like John Dillinger and Baby Face Nelson were regarded as folk heroes for standing up to the banks. As the American economy went into freefall, many farmers were forced off their land and robbing those responsible was seen as a way of righting the injustice of it all – a form of social protest. Parker and Barrow were hardly conventional folk heroes, but they had a mystique about them. There are famous old newspaper photographs of Bonnie Parker leaning on a fender of a car and of Barrow sitting, holding a machine gun. In those pictures, at least, they looked stylish and defiant. They also died spectacular deaths, ambushed by police on a lonely road in Louisiana and shot to pieces, an incident re-created in graphic fashion in Penn's film.

It is easy to see why Penn, and screenwriters David Newman and Robert Benton, were so fascinated with the couple. They had seen Godard's *A Bout de Souffle* with its apotheosis of the gangster, the girl and the gun. Penn was friendly with the *Nouvelle Vague* directors. 'We were exchanging ideas at the time, and each of us in his own vocabulary was talking about a new kind of film narrative,' he later commented. 'It was a very lively period, fresh, free and open to invention.'

After initially mediocre box-office returns, *Bonnie and Clyde* eventually became an enormous hit and ushered in a new era in Hollywood filmmaking: an era of director-led, actor-driven movies in which the studios tackled subjects that they would not have gone near only a few years before.

CAPTAIN AMERICA

The stories behind the making of *Easy Rider* (1969) tend to overshadow the film itself. Peter Biskind's influential book, *Easy Riders, Raging Bulls*, chronicles the hazardous production history: actor-director Dennis Hopper's erratic behaviour, the fight for credit, the drug-taking, the struggle to raise the budget. In the end, Columbia put up money for the film. The film's depiction of two hippy motorcyclists, Billy the Kid (Dennis Hopper) and Captain America (Peter

Fonda) travelling cross-country on some apocalyptic, drug-fuelled journey to New Orleans struck a chord with young audiences, made the studio a fortune, and provoked a mini-revolution in the way Hollywood worked.

Easy Rider was produced by BBS, the company run by Bob Rafelson, Bert Schneider and Steve Blauner. Everything about BBS – and about *Easy Rider* – alarmed the old guard at the studios. These were young, freewheeling mavericks who smoked dope and did not try to hide their disdain for the studio system. There was enormous tension between the young filmmakers and executives who still remembered the days when studio bosses were able to treat directors and actors like chattels. In Hollywood, as in US society as a whole, the new generation pitted itself against the establishment. The studio bosses were disdainful of the hippy filmmakers who had suddenly landed in their midst – what mattered most to them, though, was the bottom line. The studios realized that Hopper and Fonda had tapped into a new, mass audience that their own more mainstream movies had failed to find. They were therefore prepared to back the new filmmakers, regardless of what they felt about their politics or personal behaviour. It was a fraught relationship on both sides. Each understood that the new-found freedom would last only as long as the films continued to make money.

HEAD

Released a year before *Easy Rider*, Bob Rafelson's *Head* (1968) was equally groundbreaking – in its own confused way. This was a film spin-off from the popular TV series starring The Monkees, the group Rafelson and his associates had put together in imitation of the Beatles.

Head was a deeply schizophrenic film. It showcased the band – four squeaky clean youngsters with dubious musical ability – and also allowed its director to emulate the movies made by his European New Wave idols. The film has a peculiarly warped logic which suggests the filmmakers were not entirely clear-headed when they made it. There are images of a giant Victor Mature bestriding the studio lot; of ex-heavyweight champ Sonny Liston boxing against one of the band members; of female impersonators and topless models; scenes parodying Westerns and war movies, and satirical asides about the evils of mass consumption.

The film was shown in the Directors' Fortnight at the Cannes Festival. 'I remember the French flipping out over this movie but not having a clue what it was about. They didn't know who the Monkees were. For them, there were just these hallucinogenic images up there on the screen and this non-narrative film,' Rafelson remarked. He admitted that the film was strongly influenced by the French New Wave. 'I liked that complete disrespect for the film itself, that violation of the celluloid – the idea of handling it roughly and of not aiming for perfect lighting.'

Acid also played its part. Rafelson and Jack Nicholson co-wrote the screenplay under its influence. At the time, Nicholson was an out-of-work actor and aspiring writer, living in Harry Dean Stanton's basement. 'That's where we wrote – in an odd, dark little room with just a small bed and a desk. It was more like a prison cell than anything else.' *Head* was not so much a movie ahead of its time as a movie out of time, and, 30 years on, it seems as bizarre and baffling as ever.

DESIGNER TRASH
In the 1930s, the enemies had been the banks; in 1967, at the height of the Vietnam war, the government was the enemy. Middle-class students were as fearful and resentful of the Vietnam draft as Depression-era farmers had been of the financiers who evicted them from their properties. *Bonnie and Clyde* may have been set in the 1930s, but its themes were instantly recognizable to 1960s audiences, who embraced the couple as symbols of a counter-culture. The film was shot in Texas, away from the interfering hand of the studio. Penn and his cameraman Bernie Guffey tried to emulate the free-flowing style of the New Wave films. The director refused to be censorious about *Bonnie and Clyde*, and his actors, Warren Beatty and Faye Dunaway, were infinitely better looking than the real-life Barrow and Parker. This was a time of new sexual freedom and they were an emblematic couple. Beatty's Clyde is hardly a stud – it is hinted that he is impotent – but he treats Bonnie with old-world gallantry. Well-dressed, witty and defiant, they certainly were not 'scrawny white trash'.

THE BLUE-COLLAR PIANIST

There is gridlock on a long Californian road. The traffic has slowed down to less than walking pace. Two dusty, hung-over oil workers, on their way to work, are getting restive. One, Robert (Jack Nicholson), clambers out of the car, makes abusive signs at some of the other drivers, and walks towards the truck in front of him. It is carrying an upright piano. He jumps up, throws off the dust sheet and starts hitting the keyboard. Eventually, he sits down and begins to play a concerto. The sound is drowned out by the engines and horns, but it is obvious he is a virtuoso.

It is a key moment in Bob Rafelson's *Five Easy Pieces* (1970). Suddenly, we realize that the womanizing, hard-drinking, blue-collar Jack-the-Lad with the slow-witted waitress girlfriend Rayette (Karen Black) is not what he seems. He is a mixed-up former musician who has dropped out of his previous, pampered, middle-class existence. He learns from his sister that his father is ill and heads cross-country to visit the old man before he dies.

There are countless other films of the period which depict young outsiders at loggerheads with their parents' generation. Unlike most, *Five Easy Pieces* avoids glib references to drugs, counter-culture, hippydom, Vietnam etc. It shows its protagonist as deeply confused, restive and angry, but not sure what he is chafing against. The film hints at the divide in US society between the affluent middle classes and the blue-collar workers. They seem to live in different worlds. Whereas *Head* was flashy and eccentric, *Five Easy Pieces* is a thoughtful, complex character study. Nicholson's role – as the rebel with the nagging conscience – anticipates the many similar characters he would play in the 1970s, most notably R.P. McMurphy in *One Flew Over the Cuckoo's Nest* (1975). Only the film's sexual politics grate: the working-class

opposite The real-life Bonnie and Clyde were white trash criminals, but as played by Warren Beatty and Faye Dunaway, they could not help but take on a patina of glamour.

below left Bob Rafelson's *Head* (1968) was one of the more schizophrenic films of the late 1960s: it both served as a showcase for squeaky clean pop band The Monkees and allowed Rafelson to emulate the work of the European New Wave.

below right Fannie Flagg, Karen Black and Jack Nicholson enjoy a night out at the bowling alley in Bob Rafelson's *Five Easy Pieces* (1970).

women whom Robert meets in the course of the movie are caricatured as dim-witted, sexually voracious slatterns. Rafelson does not allow them the dignity of the other characters, whether Robert himself or his brother's graceful musician wife (Susan Anspach), with whom he starts an affair.

In 1972, Rafelson and Nicholson made an even more oblique and low-key character study, *The King of Marvin Gardens*, in which Nicholson played a reclusive DJ with a renegade, Atlantic City-based brother Jason (Bruce Dern), whom he calls the 'king of Marvin Gardens'. Both brothers are out of touch with reality. The DJ is obsessed with his childhood memories, while Jason is planning to rip off a gangster boss and run away to Hawaii on the proceeds. Eccentric, rambling, understated, the film was not a major box-office success, and it was a miracle that the studios agreed to finance it in the first place. For once it seemed actors and directors really were calling the shots. 'We wanted to make great films, honest, realistic, behavioural pictures – now the emphasis is on guns, gadgets and explosions,' Dern observed in an interview in the late 1990s. 'For us, the quality of involvement of the actor was paramount – the most important thing that went on.'

LAST MOVIES

The Young Turks who dominated the Hollywood of the early 1970s were not as homogeneous a group as popular myth suggests; nor were they always iconoclastic. Peter Bogdanovich's *The Last Picture Show* (1971), one of the greatest movies of the era, had little in common with the world of *Easy Rider*. Set in a small, windswept Texas town in the late 1950s, it was the first mainstream Hollywood feature to be shot in black and white since the early 1960s. Instead of hippy anthems, Bogdanovich fills the soundtrack with eerie old country-and-western standards. The mood is melancholic and downbeat.

Bogdanovich adapted *The Last Picture Show* from Larry McMurtry's novel. His protagonists, teenagers coming to grips with adult life, are instantly recognizable from other rites-of-passage movies. There is the high-school jock (Jeff Bridges), his quiet, studious friend (Timothy Bottoms), the school idiot (Sam Bottoms), and the Lolita-like teen temptress (Cybill Shepherd), but Bogdanovich – a critic as well as a filmmaker – brings an unexpected pathos and depth to stock situations. The town is dying. Its one cinema is about to close. The older folk are trading on their memories, the younger ones want to get away. The film captures the heartache and yearning of characters like Sam the Lion (Ben Johnson), a handsome old-timer fallen on hard times, and Lois Farrow (Ellen Burstyn), the once beautiful woman with the alcohol problem. The most poignant scenes of all are those involving Ruth (Cloris Leachman), the neglected, middle-aged wife of the school's basketball coach. She begins an affair with Sonny (Timothy Bottoms), but is devastated when he breaks off the relationship. These are all vulnerable, unhappy people. The life seems to have gone out of the town they love.

The Last Picture Show is a quiet, beautifully crafted film, steeped in nostalgia. Dennis Hopper's similarly titled *The Last Movie*, also made in 1971, was in a completely different style. Rambling, self-indulgent, the director's follow-up to *Easy Rider* explores what happens when a hedonistic Hollywood film crew pitches up in a small Peruvian town to make a Western. The locals are bemused and fascinated by the antics of the Americans. Hopper makes many

opposite Dennis Hopper alienated the Hollywood studio bosses with his rambling, self-indulgent *The Last Movie* (1971). Here, he is pictured with Stella Garcia.

below Jack Nicholson and Bruce Dern as brothers in Rafelson's haunting, downbeat *The King of Marvin Gardens* (1972).

telling points about the self-destructive behaviour of the crew and its shoddy treatment of the townsfolk. They are like latter-day conquistadors, wreaking havoc in the lives of their colonial subjects. Unfortunately, the film itself was dangerously close to what it was trying to satirize.

THE MAD CHILEAN

One of Hopper's advisers on *The Last Movie* was the Chilean maverick, Alexandro Jodorowsky, a filmmaker of staggering eccentricity who would never have caught Hollywood's attention in any other era. A magician, a musician, a therapist, a clown, a cartoonist, journalist and counter-culture guru, as well as a filmmaker, he played the role of Holy Fool to America's New Wave.

His background was as bizarre as the storyline of his films. Born in Chile in 1930, the son of a Russian lingerie salesman, he spent his childhood in a backwater town on the border with Bolivia. Ignored by his parents, Jodorowsky spent every spare moment reading novels and watching movies. He went to France in the early 1950s to study mime with Marcel Marceau, produced musicals for Maurice Chevalier, and in the mid-1960s set up home in Mexico, where he ran his own theatre company. Swept along in the hedonistic euphoria of the era, he began experimenting with drugs and making films, apparently regarding the two activities as intimately related.

His breakthrough film, one which won him notoriety on every campus in America and attracted the attention of John Lennon, was *El Topo* (1971). It is an impossible film to classify. It might best be described as a cross between a spaghetti Western and a religious allegory, with large dashes of surreal humour and mime thrown in. Jodorowsky stars as El Topo ('the mole'), a bearded avenger who rides out of the desert into a small town where a massacre has taken place, and the streets are dripping with blood. El Topo goes on to castrate the bandit leader responsible for the slaughter. In between the bloodletting, there are scenes of monks waltzing with outlaws and of El Topo worshipping at a water-gushing rock in the shape of a penis. Jodorowsky's enemies compared him to Charles Manson, and the religious authorities in Mexico, where he made the film, accused him of holding naked black masses in Mexico City's main cathedral.

Jodorowsky's next feature, *The Holy Mountain* (1975), financed by John Lennon, was even odder than *El Topo*. It started with a bloody re-creation of the Spanish conquest of Mexico (featuring a cast of thousands of trained toads in paper costumes), went on to re-create the Crucifixion, and also featured imagery of legless dwarves, innumerable references to Tarot, and some political satire. 'I was trying to broaden the mind. I always used to say that I asked of movies what hippies asked of drugs – I tried to make a film which would blow the mind,' Jodorowsky said in his defence. He borrowed animals from Mexico City's largest zoo for the movie, paying a small fee – but he was only allowed to use them at night.

As his struggles to make further films suggest, Jodorowsky was a talent who could only ever have flourished in the late 1960s and early 1970s. International financiers would not have gone near him a few years later.

THE LONG GOODBYE

In the auteur-driven Hollywood of the 1970s, the old rules about tidy plotting and conforming to genre conventions no longer applied. Most of the key films of the era were structured in a looser, more free-flowing way than old-style studio pictures. Typical were John Milius's 1978 effort, *Big Wednesday*, about draft-dodging beach bums, Coppola's sprawling Vietnam epic *Apocalypse Now* (1979), Scorsese's boxing melodrama *Raging Bull* (1980) and teen dramas like George Lucas's *American Graffiti* (1973). They improvised around genre conventions in the same way that a jazz musician might.

In *The Long Goodbye* (1973), Robert Altman reinvented Raymond Chandler's private-eye hero Philip Marlowe for 1970s audiences. In doing so, he exposed some of the liberties that earlier directors had taken with the character. He was accused of tarnishing a myth, but, in its own perverse way, his version made perfect sense: when you are a struggling detective on $25-a-day expenses, it is difficult to look as dapper and hard-boiled as Humphrey Bogart or Dick Powell. Altman's Marlowe (memorably played by Elliot Gould) is therefore presented as a ramshackle bum. His apartment is a mess. His neighbours are generally to be found sunbathing outside it, topless. He may be an accomplished detective, but he faces a constant struggle to find his cat. He dresses in roughly the same uniform as Powell or Bogart – namely a dark suit – but with his shock of hair and rambling gait, he looks nothing like them.

Altman claimed to have been baffled by Chandler's novel, and he was not happy with Leigh Brackett's screenplay, despite Brackett having written *The Big Sleep* for Howard Hawks way back in 1946. He therefore encouraged his cast to

above Robert Altman's *The Long Goodbye* (1974). After Dick Powell and Humphrey Bogart, Elliot Gould couldn't help but seem a very slovenly Philip Marlow.

improvise, and to work around the script rather than directly from it. The result is a laid-back, loose-ended, but fascinating variation on the classical gumshoe drama. Marlowe is trying to get a friend off a murder rap, but his investigations lead him down endless blind alleys and force him to tangle with vicious mobsters, a roaring, drunken, Hemingway-like novelist (Sterling Hayden), and the inevitable, untrustworthy *femme fatale*. Whereas Bogart always at least gave the illusion that he knew what was going on, Gould seems utterly bewildered right from the outset. Altman's Marlowe is as far removed from the stereotype of the handsome, wisecracking private dick as his two hard-drinking, golf-playing, womanizing soldier-surgeon jokers Hawkeye (Donald Sutherland) and Trapper John (Gould) in *M*A*S*H* (1969) are from conventional war heroes.

It was now acceptable to make films in which the protagonists were mixed-up, sexually confused, neurotic and unhappy. It was not only the characters who were changing but also the relationships between them. Mike Nichols paved the way for Altman's gallery of bums (and arguably for Woody Allen's neurotic outsiders too) in *The Graduate* (1967). Instead of the clean-cut, WASP American youth, his hero is a dweebish Jewish boy (Dustin Hoffman), fresh out of college and uncertain how to spend the rest of his life. What he does know is that he has a crush on his next-door neighbour, the glamorous, middle-aged Mrs Robinson (Anne Bancroft). In Hal Ashby's brilliant, barbed romantic comedy, *Harold and Maude* (1971) the adolescent hero, Bud Cort, starts an affair with the 80-year-old woman. This was the kind of coupling that would have horrified a studio boss like Louis B. Mayer who was famous for espousing family values.

opposite Here's to you, Mrs Robinson! Dustin Hoffman stares transfixed at Anne Bancroft's outstretched leg in Mike Nichols' *The Graduate* (1967).

23

Rashomon
1950

The Bandit under the Tree

A bandit (Toshiro Mifune) resting under a tree catches sight of a beautiful woman. She is riding through the forest alongside her nobleman husband. The bandit pursues the couple, rapes the woman and, after a fight, kills the husband. This, in a nutshell, is the basis of Akira Kurosawa's *Rashomon* (1950). The story unfolds in a complex series of flashbacks. Three men take shelter from a storm. One, a priest, discusses the trial of the bandit that he has just attended. There were four witnesses – the bandit, the woman, the murdered nobleman (who testifies via a medium from beyond the grave) and a woodcutter who stumbled on the scene. Each offers a different version of the same events. The main facts are not in dispute, but the characters' motivations are. Why did they behave as they did? Who is really guilty? The more evidence the court hears, the less clear-cut the answers to the questions become.

Why do people lie to one another? What causes them to see the same events in such different ways? Kurosawa was fascinated by that strange human tendency to twist the truth. 'They (human beings) are unable to be honest with themselves about themselves. They cannot talk about themselves without embellishing. The script portrays such human beings – the kind who cannot survive without lies to make them feel they are better people than they really are,' he wrote of the film in his autobiography.

Rashomon was a box-office hit in Japan, but its real significance lay in the enthusiasm it stirred up abroad. The film was screened at the 1951 Venice Festival, where it won the Grand Prix. Many Western critics had not seen a Japanese film and to them *Rashomon* was a revelation. With its imagery of bandits, samurai and unusual, geisha-like beauties, and its picturesque 11th-century Japanese settings, the film seemed wondrously exotic. At the same time, its self-reflexive, multilayered storyline was perfectly in keeping with Western modernist fiction. European and American reviewers proclaimed the film a masterpiece. They were consumed with curiosity about its director and about Japanese cinema in general. They were also fascinated by the dynamic performance of Toshiro Mifune, whose bandit was at once graceful and aggressive, sympathetic and barbarous. 'He said in a single action what took ordinary actors three moments to express,' Kurosawa remarked of Mifune. 'He put forth everything directly and boldly, and his sense of timing was the keenest I had ever seen in a Japanese actor. And yet, with all his quickness, he also had surprisingly fine sensibilities.'

Thanks to *Rashomon*, Japanese cinema became a cult in the West. Kurosawa's success enabled such other giants of the Japanese industry as Ozu and Mizoguchi to establish international reputations. Hollywood remade

**CONTEMPORARY
FILMS
presents**

AKIRA KUROSAWA'S YOJIMBO

above Akira Kurosawa's *Yojimbo* (1961) was a huge success in the west. Sergio Leone liked it so much that he borrowed the plot for *A Fistful of Dollars*.

opposite Akira Kurosawa's masterpiece, *The Seven Samurai* (1954), made an international star out of actor Toshiro Mifune.

the film as a Western in 1964, with Paul Newman as the bandit and Claire Bloom as the woman he rapes. Many American and European courtroom dramas also borrowed its ingenious plot structure.

The best of Kurosawa's subsequent films, among them *The Seven Samurai* (1954), *Throne of Blood* (1957), *Yojimbo* (1961) and *Ran* (1985), combined lyricism and action in a breathtaking way. While he drew on Western sources – *Throne of Blood* was loosely based on *Macbeth* and *Ran* on *King Lear* – successive generations of American filmmakers looked to him for inspiration. John Sturges turned the warriors of *The Seven Samurai* into cowboys in his Western, *The Magnificent Seven*. George Lucas took Kurosawa's stock characters and sent them into space in the *Star Wars* films.

It was Kurosawa's misfortune to become so closely associated in Western eyes with samurai films. Many of his greatest works were set in modern times. In *High and Low* (1962), adapted from Ed McBain's *King's Ransom*, he tells the story of a businessman (Mifune) who is blackmailed by a kidnapper after his child goes missing. What starts as a hostage crisis thriller gradually turns into something more subtle and provocative. Kurosawa touches on issues such as inequality and snobbery. The businessman lives high up in the hills, removed from the squalor of everyday life in the crammed township below. He has to work out whether his son's life is worth more than that of his servant's child. Equally striking was *Ikiru* (1952), about a clerk who learns he has cancer. In despair at how he has wasted his life, he resolves to find a project he can fight for and – in doing so – redeem himself at the last. This was not a story about a hero lashing out with his sword. The cause he fights for is nothing grander than helping a mothers' group build a park on some abandoned property.

THE ABANDONED PROSTITUTE

The year after *Rashomon* won the main prize at the Venice Festival, another Japanese film repeated the feat. Kenji Mizoguchi's *The Life of Oharu* (1952) was very different in tone. Instead of sword-wielding samurai and bandits, the heroine here is an abandoned woman, forced into prostitution. Instead of Kurosawa's dynamic action sequences, Mizoguchi offered a series of slow, complex tracking shots. Mizoguchi (1898–1956) was preoccupied with the plight of women in a patriarchal society, in contemporary and medieval Japan. 'Comparing today with the Nara (710–794) and Genroku (1688–1703) periods,' he reflected, 'women (in Japan) have always been treated like slaves.'

Oharu is the quintessential Mizoguchi heroine. The film opens in heart-rending fashion. Well into her 50s, and having lost her looks, she is still trying to eke out an existence through prostitution. Close to despair, she visits a Buddhist temple. One of the statues reminds her of the first man she loved. There is a flashback to when she was a young woman with a respected position in court as a lady-in-waiting. Her crime was to start an affair with a man too far below her in social standing. Once the relationship was discovered, she was banished from court – as were her parents. Her lover was executed. Then began her downward spiral. She became concubine to a wealthy lord. She had a child, a son, who was taken away from her. She turned to prostitution, and years later, when she caught sight of her son, he rejected her. Finally, Oharu is reduced to begging, mocked, humiliated, and held up as an example of a fallen woman. Her suffering serves to expose the hypocrisy and brutality of the society that has reduced her to such a wretched state.

Mizoguchi's empathy with downtrodden women had its roots in his own childhood experiences. Growing up in a poor area of Tokyo, he saw his father abuse and bully his mother and his sister. He had a natural affinity with all other victims of injustice too – not that this stopped him browbeating colleagues: he was a ruthless perfectionist who would regularly drive actors, writers and crew members to exhaustion.

Following in *Oharu*'s wake, his next two features, *Ugetsu* (1953) and *Sansho the Bailiff* (1954), also won prestigious awards at the Venice Festival. With three films made in three successive years, Mizoguchi established himself as a giant of world cinema. This was ironic given that his first film was completed in 1921. He had already spent more than 30 years working in the Japanese industry before he came to international attention.

In *Sansho the Bailiff*, a brother and sister are captured by slave traders and thrown into captivity in a labour camp run by the cruel and ruthless Sansho. Like Oharu, they are from a privileged family, but their father, a former governor, has been forced into exile and they have tumbled down the social scale as a consequence. Sansho treats them like animals, but the son refuses to become embittered. In his lowest moments, he forces himself to remember his father's maxim: 'Remember to be sympathetic. Without mercy man is like a beast. Every man is entitled to happiness.'

Ugetsu (1953) is likewise a tale of broken families. In this case, the protagonists are humble village potters in 16th-century Japan who dream of

above Mizoguchi's last complete film, *Street of Shame* (1956), offered a stark insight into the lives of present-day geishas.

opposite Oshima's *In the Realm of the Senses* (1976) reconstructed the story of illicit lovers Abe Sada and Kichizo in 1930s Japan.

making their fortune in the big city. They are caught up in the maelstrom of war, and one is so concerned with looking after his money that he fails to protect his wife and children, who are massacred by rampaging mercenaries. The other fulfils his ambition of becoming a powerful samurai, but only by deceit, and his notion of himself as a courageous, hard-living warrior takes a battering when he learns that his wife has become a prostitute.

OZU

Yasujiro Ozu (1903–1963) was the third of the great Japanese auteurs recognized in the West in the 1950s – and the most idiosyncratic. His shooting style obeyed few of the recognized rules of filmmaking. He thought nothing of breaking the 180-degree rule: that in filming any scene the camera should stay within a 180-degree space to one side of the action. Crossing the line meant distorting spatial relationships, and a character who was on the left side of the screen would suddenly seem to be on the right. John Ford broke the 180-degree rule several times on *Stagecoach* (with the result that audiences never quite knew in which direction the Indians were heading), but most Hollywood directors considered the rule to be sacred.

Ozu rarely used zooms or dissolves; he would place the camera at a low level and allow it to observe what was happening. He refused to indulge in directorial flourishes or flashy editing. In his masterpiece, *Tokyo Story* (1953), he tells the story of an elderly couple from a small town visiting their children in the big city. Although the mother is ill, few of the children are sympathetic towards them. Ozu's camera is there to bear witness and nothing more.

STREET OF SHAME

Mizoguchi's last complete film, *Street of Shame* (1956), is set in a Tokyo brothel in the 1950s as the Japanese parliament debates whether or not to ban prostitution. Again, the filmmaker's sympathies are with the women. They are in a paradoxical position: society is set against them precisely because they are victims. They all have different reasons for having become prostitutes: one wants to raise money to start a business, one needs the cash to look after her ailing husband, one is estranged from her son (who despises her), another is new to the city. Many of Mizoguchi's earlier films dealt with characters in an equally bleak predicament, but whereas *Ugetsu* and *The Life of Oharu* were period pieces, with exquisite costume and production design, *Street of Shame* is all the harsher for being set in the present day.

IN THE REALM OF THE SENSES

In 1936, in a case which scandalized Japan, Abe Sada strangled and then castrated her lover Kichizo. She was arrested with his genitals in her pocket. This true-life story provided the backcloth for the most controversial Japanese film of the post-war era, Nagisa Oshima's *In the Realm of the Senses* (1976).

It is the high point of Japanese militarism. As the soldiers tramp the streets, Kichizo (Tatsuya Fuji) and Abe Sada (Eiko Matsuda) begin a destructive and obsessive relationship. Sada is a new recruit in the brothel run by Kichizo's wife. Kichizo seduces her. Their affair becomes all-consuming.

Despite its well-chronicled problems with British and American censors (both of whom banned it), *In the Realm of the Senses* is not titillating or voyeuristic. Obsessive sex is its subject-matter, and Oshima deals with the couple's lovemaking frankly and without prurience. Given the repressive nature of the society that they live in, Abe Sada and Kichizo's retreat into the 'realm of the senses' seems courageous. While the soldiers prepare for war, they ensconce themselves in the brothel and try desperately to keep the outside world at bay. In their quest for sensual pleasure, their lovemaking grows ever more intense and destructive.

CRUEL STORIES OF YOUTH

Oshima was a leading light in the Japanese New Wave of the late 1950s. Like many young radicals, he was deeply disillusioned with post-war Japan. The country had struck a security pact with its former enemy, the US, and had fallen prey to American consumer culture. With one party continually in power and the country experiencing its 'economic miracle', there was little political dissent.

His superb 1960 film *Death by Hanging* stands alongside Polish director Krzysztof Kieslowski's *A Short Film about Killing* as the most powerful indictment of capital punishment ever brought to the screen. Based on a true story of a young Korean man condemned to death for raping and killing a Japanese schoolgirl, it works on a variety of different levels. It exposes Japanese anti-Korean prejudice, something Oshima touched on in several other films. It mocks the cruel, mindless bureacracy of the Japanese courts. At

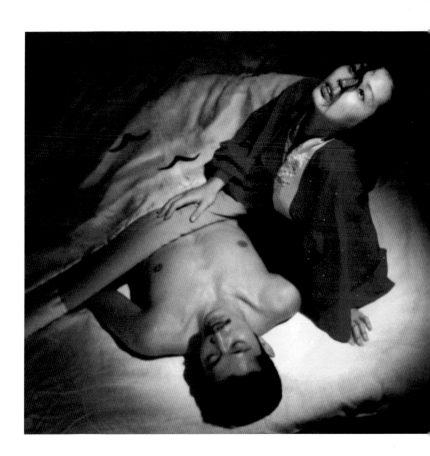

times, it also seems like an absurdist drama: when the young Korean fails to die the first time he is hanged, he is nursed back to health so that the process can be repeated. By then, he has forgotten all about his crime and so the court officials re-enact it to remind him of his guilt. They are oblivious to the fact that they are repeating the crime by killing him.

'BEAT' TAKESHI

In 1998, emulating Kurosawa and Mizoguchi, a new Japanese director won the main prize at the Venice Festival with his film, *Hana-Bi*. Takeshi Kitano was from a very different tradition to the old masters. A comedian, writer and artist, he was a huge celebrity in Japan, where he appeared on TV several times a week and wrote countless newspaper columns. Born in 1947, he had been brought up in a poor part of Tokyo. After abandoning early ideas of becoming an engineer, he began to flourish as a comedian in the city's *yakuza*-controlled comedy clubs. His brand of humour was often very cruel: he once featured a man with the shakes in his show and gave him a fan 'to make him useful'. He knew little of classical Japanese cinema, often telling journalists that he had not watched many movies.

Western audiences first saw him as an actor as the prison camp Sgt-Major in Oshima's *Merry Christmas, Mr Lawrence* (1983). His character was a Japanese everyman: brutal, heavy-drinking, big-hearted, and with a sly sense of humour. His early movies were slick, existential gangster thrillers. *Violent Cop* (1990) and *Sonatine* (1993) were full of superbly choreographed shoot-outs in which Kitano himself – looking as impassive as Buster Keaton – was

RAGE AGAINST THE MACHINE
Oshima's movies railed against the conformity of Japanese society and the old Left's failure to mount a meaningful challenge to the status quo. With other Japanese New Wave filmmakers like Shohei Imamura and Yoshishige Yoshida, he turned against the thoughtful, humanistic cinema of the West's three favourite Japanese directors, Yasujiro Ozu, Kenji Mizoguchi and Akira Kurosawa. His rebellion paralleled that of the French New Wave against *'le cinéma du papa'*. Taking his cue from American teen pictures, he celebrated delinquency and insubordination: his 1960 film was actually called *Cruel Story Of Youth*. He also attacked the racism and brutality of Japanese society.

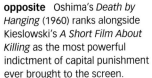

opposite Oshima's *Death by Hanging* (1960) ranks alongside Kieslowski's *A Short Film About Killing* as the most powerful indictment of capital punishment ever brought to the screen.

above Kitano followed in the footsteps of Mizoguchi and Kurosawa by winning The Golden Lion at the Venice Festival with his 1998 film, *Hana-Bi*.

above right Actor-director Takeshi Kitano as the gangster in *Sonatine* (1993).

invariably in the middle of the carnage. In between the fights, he would often include playful, slapstick sequences reminiscent of old Mack Sennett movies.

Bloody action sequences were his trademark. 'Frankly, violence in my films is like smoking to me. It's something I can create any time,' he once remarked. Whenever he strayed from type, for example when he made *Kids Return* (1996), his rites-of-passage yarn about two school dropouts who become involved in petty crime, or *Kikujiro* (1999), a Chaplin-style road movie about a boy and a small-time gangster on a journey across Japan, critics and audiences complained.

Hana-Bi (1997) was the film in which he most successfully reconciled the opposing sides of his star persona. A combination of terminal-illness melodrama, crime thriller, and story about the redeeming powers of art, it brought together stomach-churning violence with slapstick humour and moments of breathtaking lyricism. The movie was partly autobiographical. Like Horubi, the wheelchair-bound police officer who turns to art, Kitano began to paint while he was recovering from a horrific motorbike accident which nearly killed him in the mid-1990s. Kitano used many of his own drawings and paintings in *Hana-Bi* as a way of avoiding the clichés that blight so many cop movies. His own character, Nishi, was a tough-as-nails police

officer who one moment would be beating up loan sharks or robbing a bank and then the next, treating his dying wife with tenderness and romanticism.

Japanese magazines proclaimed that Kitano's 'sense of danger' was his greatest asset. He was rebellious and irreverent – an individualist in a conformist society. As Western film festivals began to fête him, there were grumblings back home that he was losing his edge. As if to disprove them, he took a leading role in the most controversial Japanese film since *In the Realm of the Senses*, Kinji Fukasaku's *Battle Royale* (2000). The subject-matter must have seemed familiar to anyone who remembered Oshima's early features. This was another tale of cruel youth, a story of high-school students who are left on an uninhabited island, given various lethal weapons (sickles, bombs and guns among them), and told to fight to the death.

The media blamed the film for exacerbating the problem of teenage violence but the director claimed he was reflecting the violence that existed in Japanese society. Teenage audiences queued to see the film in their thousands. More than 40 years since the days of the Japanese New Wave, the same arguments were heard over again. Just as in Oshima's heyday, a new generation of filmmakers was using the ingredients of exploitation cinema, namely sex and violence, to attack an establishment they found stifling and complacent.

Sequels

24

Keystone Cops

'Anything that is a prototype – and every film is a prototype – is extremely inefficient.' **(Sir Anthony Havelock-Allan)**

Most industries take a painstaking approach to research and development. Once a company has perfected a new product – whether an aeroplane or a special brand of vacuum cleaner – it is able to mass-manufacture it and sell it again and again. The secret is getting the design or the formula right from the very start. Such business principles do not apply to the film industry. All movies are prototypes, and there is no guarantee that they are going to succeed at the box-office. Nor is there any sure-fire formula for repeating success. Producers have various well-worn strategies for minimizing the risk of failure – they can spend a fortune on marketing a film, on the basis of its stars, its state-of-the-art special effects or its genre.

They can ensure continuity of production by setting up studios along industrial lines. Before the anti-Trust legislation of the late 1940s, the major Hollywood studios were vertically integrated, and controlled production, distribution and exhibition. This enabled them to give their movies the best possible chance of reaching an audience.

NOBODY KNOWS ANYTHING

In his insider's guide to Hollywood, *Adventures in The Screen Trade*, scriptwriter William Goldman coined a famous phrase: 'nobody knows anything'. Neither the most powerful studio boss nor the most lowly film director had a clear idea of which movies would make money, or even why. Often, films which seemed like sure-fire commercial successes on paper flopped disastrously.

The 1990s yielded several prime examples: *Hudson Hawk* (1991), a big-budget Bruce Willis vehicle; *Last Action Hero* (1993), starring Arnold Schwarzenegger (then at the height of his popularity); and *Waterworld* (1995), a futuristic epic with Oscar-winning actor Kevin Costner, all failed at the US box-office despite having massive production budgets and hugely elaborate distribution campaigns behind them. Films were becoming ever more expensive to make. In 1998, the Hollywood studios were spending an average of $70 million per feature – $50 million on production and $20 million on marketing and distribution – and few made a profit. The only consolation were the extra markets Hollywood could sell its products to: foreign sales sometimes redeemed a wretched domestic performance (this was the case with *Waterworld*), the video market had become increasingly lucrative, and the growth of satellite and cable TV provided profitable new outlets. Nevertheless, for every box-office success, there were always several other films that had disappeared without trace. Filmmaking remained the same risky business at the end of the 20th century that it had been a hundred years before.

SAME FILM, DIFFERENT TITLE

Box-office hits are so elusive that when one comes along, the temptation is to try to clone it as quickly as possible. That is why film history is littered with so many remakes and sequels.

British filmmaker Hugh Stewart recalls meeting Peter Rogers, producer of the *Carry On* films, and asking him what he was working on. 'Same story, different title,' Rogers replied. Between *Carry On Sergeant* (1959) and *Carry On Columbus* (1992), Rogers and director Gerald Thomas mass-produced *Carry On* movies, each with the same repertory of stars (Kenneth Williams, Charles Hawtrey, Joan Sims and Sid James among them), each with the same bawdy, end-of-the-pier humour, and each with a very similar storyline. The *Carry On* series was hugely popular in the UK. It did not matter that foreign audiences were baffled by the jokes — which were recycled again and again. The films were budgeted modestly enough to make a tidy profit in the British market without having to rely on overseas sales.

The 'same story, different title' philosophy stretches right back to the silent era. The Nick Carter action-adventures and Max Linder comedies in France, Mack Sennett's Keystone Cops comedies and Fatty Arbuckle vehicles in the

opposite Pam Grier, the high priestess of blaxploitation movies, in her 1974 vehicle, *Foxy Brown*.

below Ursula Andress and Sean Connery in *Dr No* (1962), the first in the long-running James Bond series.

US, the *Pimple* comedies and Betty Balfour *Squibs* films in the UK all thrived on repeating themselves ad nauseam. In the 1930s, the so-called Poverty Row studios in Hollywood turned out low-budget cowboy and detective serials in huge quantities. Meanwhile, the bigger studios made more prestigious serials – *The Thin Man*, starring William Powell and Myrna Loy, and the *Andy Hardy* series, starring Mickey Rooney, among them.

Certain genres, in particular detective films, slapstick farces and family comedies, lent themselves to the serial format and offered endless scope for sequels. The Hollywood series was an ideal training ground for untried talent and a way of earning audience loyalty over a long period. Occasionally, these films boasted big-name stars and opulent production values. With its familiar mix of songs and risqué wisecracks, the *Road to* series, starring Bob Hope, Bing Crosby, and Dorothy Lamour, became hugely popular with audiences in the 1940s. The Abbott and Costello comedies are credited with saving Universal studios from bankruptcy around the same time. Nevertheless, serial films rarely had the same prestige as the big budget 'A' vehicles, which they were shown alongside.

As exhibition patterns changed after the war, and double bills became more popular, there was no longer the same enthusiasm for serial films in US cinemas. Their natural home was now TV. Their blend of cosy familiarity and repetition worked best now, it was believed, on the small screen. The situation in the UK was different, largely because TV ownership was far less widespread, and the most popular British films of the 1950s remained serial films. The Rank Organization enjoyed enormous success with its Norman Wisdom comedies. In such films as *Trouble in Store* (1954) and *Just my Luck* (1957), Wisdom, dressed in his trademark cloth cap and ill-fitting, second-hand suit, was always cast as the loveable little outsider. These films were released every year just in time for Christmas, and audiences flocked to see them in a spirit of such festive good cheer that they were able to stomach the films' treacly mawkishness. Rank did almost as well with the *Doctor* series, adapted from Richard Gordon's novels about the misadventures of a feckless young doctor on the wards and in the bedrooms. Popular though these films were in the UK, few believed that serials could become international blockbusters. That was to change in 1962, when Cubby Broccoli and Harry Saltzman made *Dr No*, the first of their James Bond movies.

007 – A LICENCE FOR SEQUELS

Broccoli and Saltzman carried out exhaustive auditions to cast James Bond. Trevor Howard, Cary Grant, David Niven and Patrick McGoohan were among the stars they considered for the part. In the end, largely because of the impression he had made on Broccoli's wife, Scottish actor Sean Connery won the role. Despite all the brouhaha around the search for the perfect actor to play Bond, expectations among the crew about the new film were not especially high. Chris Blackwell, who later formed Island Records, helped coordinate the location shooting in the West Indies. 'I don't think anybody in Jamaica thought it was that great. They thought it was a bit of a B-movie to tell the truth,' Blackwell remembers. Only when the crew saw the magnificent sets created by production designer, Ken Adam, back at Pinewood Studios in England, did they realize the scope of the film they were making. Adam's

BLAXPLOITATION

Depending on your point of view, the emergence of 'blaxploitation' films in the early 1970s was either an expression of African America's anger at the white establishment, or yet another Hollywood marketing wheeze to make money from a new genre. Gordon Parks's *Shaft* (1971) kick-started blaxploitation cinema. It spawned two sequels, *Shaft's Big Score* (1972) and *Shaft in Africa* (1973), and a TV series.

Shaft may have seemed a routine assignment, but Parks was not an anonymous hack director. A former photojournalist with *Life* magazine, he made his first movie, *The Learning Tree*, in 1969. A lyrical, largely autobiographical account of a boy's experiences growing up black in 1920s Kansas, the film failed to find an audience. *Shaft*, by contrast, was overtly commercial. Parks took the old private-eye clichés and remoulded them in an abrasive and entertaining fashion. John Shaft (Richard Roundtree) was the hero – a handsome, hard-bitten gumshoe tussling with the mafia in downtown Harlem. As Isaac Hayes' Oscar-winning theme song proclaimed, Shaft was 'a black private dick who's a sex machine to all the chicks'.

Some critics, who failed to notice that *Shaft* was at least partly tongue-in-cheek, complained about the film's sexual politics. There was a double standard at work. Whereas James Bond was allowed to be as promiscuous as he wanted, Shaft was attacked for behaving in exactly

the same way. This was evidence of how uncomfortable white Hollywood was with blaxploitation cinema right from the outset.

Whereas *Shaft* could be enjoyed as a stylish, self-mocking thriller, Melvin Van Peebles' *Sweet Sweetback's Baadassssss Song* (1971) was openly confrontational. Its hero Sweetback (played by Van Peebles himself) was designed to unsettle and upset white America. A pimp raised in a whorehouse who goes on the run after killing a cop, he was both violent and sexually voracious. He was also a very engaging antihero. Van Peebles undercut the social comment in the movie with knockabout, picaresque humour.

The later blaxploitation films of the 1970s were strictly formulaic. Both *Coffy* (1973) and *Foxy Brown* (1974), for example, were revenge stories in which the resilient but effortlessly stylish heroine (Pam Grier) hunted down the drug dealers who had killed or maimed her nearest and dearest. The stories may have been hackneyed, but Grier was too imposing an actress to seem merely a stock type or white producer's fantasy figure. Her career was resurrected in spectacular fashion in 1998 when Quentin Tarantino cast her as the lead in *Jackie Brown*. Two years later, as if to confirm the renaissance in blaxploitation cinema, her co-star in that film, Samuel L. Jackson, took the lead in the remake of *Shaft* (2000).

above Al Pacino in *The Godfather II* (1974), which many critics described as the best sequel ever.

production design along with the mesmeric theme music (composed by Monty Norman), the shadowy, voyeuristic credits (designed by Maurice Bender) and John Barry's soundtrack music were key factors in establishing Bond as a worldwide phenomenon.

To begin with, the Bond films were uncompromising thrillers in which the Cold War loomed large. Connery played Bond as a wry but very tough spy who mixed charm and sadism in equal measure. As the series progressed, gadgetry, special effects and tongue-in-cheek humour became more and more prominent. By the time Roger Moore took over the role in the 1970s, Bond's missions had become ever more outlandish – he was even sent into space in *Moonraker* in 1979 – and the villains he pitted himself against had become more and more like pantomime baddies. Not that audiences seemed to mind. By some strange alchemy, the secret agent created by novelist Ian Fleming was transformed into one of cinema's biggest global brands – as recognizable to audiences as Disney's Mickey Mouse or Charlie Chaplin.

After 30 years and more than 20 movies, Bond remains as popular as ever. *The World is not Enough* (1999), directed by Michael Apted and starring Pierce Brosnan, made more than $300 million at the box-office worldwide.

BOND'S IMITATORS

The Bond movies may have steered ever closer towards self-parody as the 1960s progressed, but that did not stop a host of imitators from trying to emulate their success. *Our Man Flint* (1966) and *In Like Flint* (1967) starred James Coburn as an American variation on Bond. Rat-pack member Dean Martin had a stab at being a secret agent in the 'Matt Helm' series. Robert Vaughn and David McCallum, wearing their natty 1960s suits, pitted their wits against the sinister secret force SMERSH in *The Man From U.N.C.L.E* films made for NBC between 1964 and 1968. The only credible rival to Bond, however, was Harry Palmer (Michael Caine) in three thrillers adapted from Len Deighton's espionage novels: *The Ipcress File* (1965), *A Funeral in Berlin* (1966) and *The Billion Dollar Brain* (1967). Palmer was bespectacled and unkempt, a wiseacre Cockney bohemian who knew how to cook a bit, had an eye for the women, and could face anything – torture included – with deadpan equanimity. The contrast between Harry Palmer and James Bond is perfectly illustrated by the music that John Barry wrote for each. Whereas the Bond soundtrack is brassy and hard-driving, the score for *The Ipcress File* is wonderfully sleazy and laid-back. When the character of Palmer was resurrected in the mid-1990s for two further adventures, Caine was then much older and Harry Palmer seemed like a spy from another era. Neither of the new films was given a theatrical release in the UK.

HORROR FRANCHISES

Shot on a minuscule budget, John Carpenter's *Halloween* (1978) sparked a mini horror boom, spawning countless sequels and imitators. It is a deceptively simple tale: an escaped lunatic wreaks havoc in a small midwestern town on Hallowe'en, terrorizing babysitters and kids alike. Carpenter packs the film with references to directors he admires – Hitchcock and Howard Hawks in particular – and uses every device he can think of to crank up the tension. The mask-wearing, knife-wielding killer Michael Myers became a household name and there were half-a-dozen sequels of varying quality, all of them popular at the box-office.

Other filmmakers attempted to emulate *Halloween*'s success. The *Friday the 13th* series used well-nigh identical storylines, and Wes Craven's *Nightmare On Elm Street* series, which began in 1984, introduced the flamboyant new villain Freddie Krueger (Robert Englund), a scrofulous, salivating bogeyman with razors for fingers who haunts the dreams of various clean-living American teenagers. Horror movies remained popular throughout the 1990s. The success of Wes Craven's *Scream* and its various sequels suggested that teen audiences still had an unquenchable thirst for such fare.

THE KEYSTONE COPS REVISITED

European filmmakers are often reticent about sequels. They see it as undignified to serve up the same characters and storylines all over again just because one film has been a hit. Hollywood has no such qualms and if there is a chance of making extra money, sequels are immediately given the green light. The *Airplane!* and *National Lampoon* movies of the 1980s and 1990s were only intermittently funny, but these farces seemed like gilt-edged classics by comparison with the *Police Academy* movies, turned out at regular intervals between 1984 and 1996. The plots, featuring a bunch of goofy, lecherous cops, harked back in their own cheerfully crass way to the world of Mack Sennett's Keystone Cops. The films were celebrating incompetence. Audiences should not therefore have been surprised that they were so incompetently made themselves.

THE BEST SEQUEL EVER

The Indiana Jones and *Star Wars* films were partly inspired by action-adventure serials. Once *Raiders of the Lost Ark* (1981) and the original *Star Wars* (1977) succeeded at the box-office, it was inevitable that the visionaries behind them, Steven Spielberg and George Lucas, would make further movies in the same vein. Without the sequels, the merchandising and ancillary sales would eventually have ground to a halt. As a rule of thumb, however, no sequel is as good as the original. Few major filmmakers who have enjoyed a critical success are prepared to risk their reputations by tackling the same subject all over again.

There was a world of difference between Spielberg making a new Indiana Jones film and Francis Ford Coppola trying to trump the critical success that he had enjoyed with his adaptation of Mario Puzo's epic gangster novel, *The Godfather* (1972), winner of a Best Picture Oscar. On *The Godfather Part II*, Coppola was working with the same crew (including ace cinematographer Gordon Willis) and many of the same actors. Marlon Brando may have died at the end of *The Godfather*, but now Coppola had enlisted Robert De Niro to play Brando's character, Vito Corleone, as a young man. To the sceptics' amazement, the new film turned out better (and won more Oscars) than its predecessor. It was dubbed the best sequel ever made. Sadly, Coppola could not repeat the magic on *The Godfather Part III* (1990), but at least he had the chutzpah to keep on trying. Shortly before the death of Mario Puzo in 1999, Coppola even announced that he intended making a fourth *Godfather* film.

right Given that the Indiana Jones films were inspired by action-adventure serials, it was only to be expected that Steven Spielberg would make several. Here, Jones (Harrison Ford) runs for his life in *Raiders of the Lost Ark* (1981), the first in the series.

25

Breaking the Waves
1996

Dogme95

LARS AND HIS LITTLE BROTHER

In May 1998, Lars von Trier set out in his van on the drive from Denmark to France for the Cannes Film Festival. He hated flying – hence the long, bumpy journey by road and ferry. Von Trier was the ageing *enfant terrible* of European cinema. In a period when Hollywood films dominated box-office charts worldwide as never before, the Danish director had become a totemistic figure, the leader of the resistance. Two years before, he had won the critics' prize in Cannes with his melodrama, *Breaking the Waves* (1996), one of the key films of the 1990s. Starring Emily Watson as Bess, a young Scottish woman from a remote Presbyterian community who marries an oil-rig worker Jan (Stellan Skarsgård), it combined the emotional sweep of big Hollywood weepies of the 1950s with a perversity and humour that was all von Trier's own.

'I employ a style that on the face of it may seem a bit weird for broad audiences, but which is nevertheless acceptable because the story is 100% undismissable,' von Trier claimed of a film which might best be described as a highbrow tearjerker. 'At the same time, the intellectuals will be able to permit themselves to cry because the style is so refined.' With its unusual shooting style (jerky, hand-held widescreen) and scenes of Bess talking, squeaky-voiced, to God, *Breaking the Waves* could easily have seemed trite, but

Watson's searing performance and the sheer dynamism of von Trier's shooting style defied anyone to laugh. By the end of the film, director and star have transformed a naive, diffident Highland woman into a full-blown martyr – a latterday Joan of Arc.

By the time he arrived back on the Riviera in 1998, there was huge curiosity about his new movie. Critics already knew the storyline: *The Idiots* was a satire following a group of idealistic young Danes who set up a commune in which they all behave as if they are mentally retarded. As generally happened with von Trier films, *The Idiots* divided audiences. Some felt it was morally reprehensible, a slick, glib but shallow fable in which von Trier wantonly made fun of retards. Others believed that beneath the apparently tasteless slapstick and anti-bourgeois jokes, this was a passionate and idealistic film about a utopia gone wrong. The 'idiots' were trying to set up their own innocent, nonmaterialistic ideal world, but, for all their high-minded intentions, jealousies and prejudices soon undermined the grand project.

The controversy over the film itself was soon forgotten. What obsessed audiences and critics far more were the constraints under which it had been shot. This was the first of the feature films made by the Danish New Wave group, Dogme95, which had issued its manifesto, 'The Vow of Chastity', three

THE VOW

I swear to submit to the following set of rules drawn up and confirmed by Dogme95:

1. Shooting must be done on location. Props and sets must not be brought in (if a particular prop is necessary for the story, a location must be chosen where this prop is to be found).

2. The sound must never be produced separate from the images, or vice versa. (Music must not be used unless it occurs where the scene is being shot.)

3. The camera must be hand-held. Any movement or immobility attainable in the hand is permitted. (The film must not take place where the camera is standing; shooting must take place where the film takes place.)

4. The film must be in colour. Special lighting is not acceptable. (If there is too little light for exposure the scene must be cut or a single lamp be attached to the camera.)

5. Optical work and filters are forbidden.

6. The film must not contain superficial action. (Murders, weapons, etc. must not occur.)

7. Temporal and geographical alienation are forbidden. (That is to say that the film takes place here and now.)

8. Genre movies are not acceptable.

9. The film format must be Academy Ratio.

10. The director must not be credited.

Furthermore, I swear as a director to refrain from personal taste! I am no longer an artist. I swear to refrain from creating a 'work', as I regard the instant as more important than the whole. My supreme goal is to force the truth out of my characters and settings. I swear to do so by all means available and at the cost of any good taste and any aesthetic considerations.

Thus I make my VOW OF CHASTITY.

years before, in March 1995. This 'Vow', drawn up by von Trier and a younger director, Thomas Vinterberg, provided an 'indisputable set of rules' that all Dogme directors were obliged to follow.

THE VOW DECIPHERED

For some, the Vow was a wearisome retreading of a path already covered by the French New Wave 40 years before. Sceptics regarded it as a provocation – yet another of von Trier's polemical stunts. Others saw it as a practical guide to low-budget filmmaking. There was much resentful talk of the 'emperor's new clothes': older directors complained that they had been making Dogme-style films for years, but had not needed to draw up manifestos to justify themselves.

Dogme95 was both playful and serious. Vinterberg referred to the challenge of observing the Vow as a 'sport', and freely admitted that the movement was an excellent international marketing tool for Danish cinema. He denied that he and von Trier were trying to set up an exclusive club. 'People have seen it as elite and snobbish and I'm very sad about that,' he commented. 'It's not meant to be. It's without copyright. I actually hope people can see through that and realize that Dogme is democratic. It makes it easier for everyone to make films. When you watch the film, you forget about the Dogme concepts within the two first minutes of the film. That's how it is supposed to be... This is not a commercial idea. The fundamental idea is to break free, to stay alive as a filmmaker. Repetition strangles you.'

Dogme sparked a mini-renaissance in innovative, low-budget cinema at a time when mainstream Hollywood films were becoming especially bloated. It was no coincidence that Dogme emerged internationally at the same time that James Cameron was making his soggy $100-million extravaganza, *Titanic*, the most expensive movie ever.

As if to underline that the Vow was not written in stone, von Trier, Vinterberg, Søren Kragh-Jacobsen and Kristian Levring, the first four Dogme directors, regularly broke some of its rules. Making a Dogme movie was akin to taking a driving test: a few lapses were allowed – as long as you did not actually drive up onto the kerb or run down a senior citizen. Any director who made a Dogme film had to have it passed. As long as it conformed to most of the rules, it would be issued with a certificate signed by the founding fathers of Dogme.

Vinterberg's Dogme film, *Festen*, which was unveiled alongside *The Idiots* in the main competition at Cannes in 1998, deviated from Dogme rules in several key ways. It was shot on video and then transferred to 35mm – thereby stretching the rule about Academy Ratio to the limits. Dogme directors were enjoined not to make 'genre movies', but *Festen* – about a family reunion at which a son (Ulrich Thomsen) accuses his father of child abuse and of driving one of his daughters to suicide – could easily be classified alongside country-house dramas like Renoir's *The Rules of the Game* or Bergman's *Smiles of a Summer Night*. There were also suspicions that Vinterberg had taken liberties with props and lighting. In the end, though, the quibbles become immaterial. *Festen* works well because it is beautifully written and acted – not because it is a Dogme movie. The same might be observed of Søren Kragh-Jacobsen's *Mifune's Last Song* (1999), a lyrical comedy about a recently married city slicker heading back to the countryside to look after his retarded brother, and of Kristian Levring's *The King is Alive* (2000), about tourists stranded in the Namibian desert performing *King Lear*.

DOGME'S ANTECEDENTS

Von Trier and Vinterberg freely acknowledged their debt to the French New Wave of Godard and Truffaut. 'In 1960 enough was enough! The movie had been cosmeticized to death, they said; yet since then the use of cosmetics has exploded,' reads one fiery paragraph of the Dogme95 Manifesto. However, neither they nor Godard had a monopoly on provocative, low-budget filmmaking. Dogme had many antecedents.

The movies shot by Andy Warhol and his acolytes in the 1960s and early 1970s now seem like Dogme movies before their time. Paul Morrissey's sleazy, New York low-life comedy, *Trash* (1970), is a prime example. Fuzzily shot, full of hand-held camerawork, it is a cautionary tale about an impotent junkie (Joe Dallesandro) roaming through seedy New York looking for kicks. It obeys nearly all of the rules drawn up later in von Trier and Vinterberg's Vow. As if to emphasize that he was a kindred spirit, Morrissey attempted to make a Dogme movie himself in the late 1990s. Ironically, given that Dogme films were supposed to be cheap to finance, he could not find the necessary backing.

The cinema of John Cassavetes (1929–1989) shared many of Dogme's hallmarks. Cassavetes was an established mainstream Hollywood actor who raised finance from his well-paid acting jobs in films like *Rosemary's Baby* and *The Dirty Dozen* to direct a series of groundbreaking independent films. This was precisely the same strategy that Orson Welles used to pay for movies like his *Othello* and *Chimes at Midnight*, made long after he had fallen out of favour with the Hollywood studios. Such Cassavetes efforts as *Husbands* (1970), a rambling yarn about three American men who embark on a drunken binge

following the death of a friend, and *The Killing of a Chinese Bookie* (1976), about a nightclub owner pitted against the mob and dying a very slow death, had the same roughness and improvisatory quality as the later Dogme features.

Underground American filmmaker Kenneth Anger is too exotic a figure to be labelled alongside von Trier and Vinterberg, but his work showed how it was possible to make movies without paying the slightest attention to the mainstream. He had grown up in Hollywood and was even to be seen briefly as a child actor in Max Reinhardt's film of *A Midsummer Night's Dream* (1935). He chronicled the seamy side of Tinseltown history in his two best-selling books, *Hollywood Babylon* and *Hollywood Babylon 2*. His own movies, films like *Lucifer Rising*, *Fireworks* and *Scorpio Rising*, owed as much to magician Aleister Crowley, to Egyptian myth, and to his homo-erotic fascination with leather-clad bikers and sailors as to Hollywood norms.

Vinterberg turned a country hotel into a living hell in *Festen*. Donald Cammell and Nicolas Roeg did something similar 30 years before with a West London house in *Performance* (1968). It is here that a gangster (James Fox) flees only to be caught up in the mind games and gender-twisting conspiracies of his androgynous rock-star host (Mick Jagger). Warner Brothers were utterly baffled by the film, which they refused to release unless it was extensively re-edited. Cammell and Jagger wrote to them, telling them to leave it alone. 'This film is about the perverted love affair between Homo Sapiens and Lady Violence,' they informed the baffled studio executives. 'In common with its subject, it's necessarily horrifying, paradoxical and absurd... you want to emasculate the most savage and affectionate scenes in our

opposite Lars Von Trier's *The Idiots* (1998), was the first of the Dogme95 movies.

right A family celebration gets very badly out of hand as old wounds are re-opened in Thomas Vinterberg's *Festen* (1998).

movie. If *Performance* doesn't upset audiences, it's nothing.' This was precisely the kind of extravagant and provocative language that von Trier later used to justify his projects to sceptical financiers.

The films made by British painter and director Derek Jarman (1942–1994) were stylized in a way Dogme movies were not, but Jarman too was aiming at a 'poor cinema' which encouraged directors to escape from the constraints and expense of conventional narrative features. A former production designer who had worked on Ken Russell's *The Devils*, he was a curious hybrid: a quintessentially English director who revered Powell and Pressburger and British documentary-maker Humphrey Jennings, but also part of the gay avant-garde. His films had as much in common with the experimental work of French poet/aesthete Jean Cocteau and of Kenneth Anger as with anything made by earlier British directors. His best work was shot for tiny budgets on 8mm – a format generally associated with home movies. Thus, long before digital cameras became available, Jarman was proving that filmmaking was open to anyone. He made pop promos, notably for the Smiths, the anarchic punk satire *Jubilee* (1977), a version of Shakespeare's *The Tempest* (1979) and one of Christopher Marlowe's *Edward II* (1991).

US independent cinema reacted against the Hollywood mainstream in the 1980s in the same way that the Danish directors did 10 years later. The success of Jim Jarmusch's superb, low-budget feature, *Stranger than Paradise* (1984), pitched somewhere between a road movie, a beatnik comedy and a study of street-level America as seen by a Hungarian outsider, inspired a whole generation of US indie directors, many of whose work was showcased at the Sundance Festival. Even as big a commercial hit as Quentin Tarantino's *Reservoir Dogs* had a certain kinship with Dogme95. Packed full of filmic references and in-jokes about US popular culture, it was a genre piece – about a heist gone wrong – but had a dynamism and freshness about it that was seldom found in Hollywood mainstream thrillers. In the wake of Tarantino's success, Hollywood embraced US indie cinema with the same enthusiasm that it had shown for the work of Dennis Hopper in the late 1960s. All the

studios set up specialist art-house divisions (Sony Pictures Classics and Fox World Cinema among them) to distribute and produce non-mainstream products. Disney bought Miramax, the company behind Tarantino's films. This led to a bizarre situation in which the same multinational companies responsible for releasing anodyne mainstream fare also handled the edgiest, most provocative independent work.

One Miramax film which Disney could not stomach was Larry Clark's *Kids* (1995), about an AIDS-infected teenage Jack the Lad whose pet hobby is seducing virgins. Rather than abandon the film, Miramax set up a new company to release it. The film was made in the same freewheeling, provocative way as the Dogme films. Scripted by a teenager (Harmony Korine), it caught perfectly the hedonistic, self-destructive lifestyles of a group of young skateboarding, drug-taking New Yorkers. The hand-held camerawork, idiosyncratic dialogue – Korine's version of street patois – and jumpy editing gave the film a freshness at odds with its grim subject-matter.

Korine's debut feature, *Gummo* (1997), seemed like a cross between a Dogme film and an ethnographic documentary about small-town America. It is full of hand-held camerawork, although this had less to do with von Trier and Vinterberg than with Korine's admiration for British TV-drama director Alan Clarke, one of the great pioneers of Steadicam, in-your-face filmmaking. Korine brought a Surrealist edge to downbeat, blue-collar America. *Gummo*'s impressionistic imagery of delinquents shooting cats, a little girl lost wandering above the subway with pink bunny ears on her head, and of lonely, bored teenagers sniffing glue provoked revulsion in some critics, but others recognized Korine's lyricism, his deadpan humour – and the honest way in which he debunked the myth of the all-American teenager.

In 1999, Korine made his own Dogme film, *Julien Donkey-Boy*. It was shot by British cameraman Anthony Dod Mantle, who had also worked on *Festen* and *Mifune*. The main character, loosely based on Korine's uncle, was a sweet-natured but mentally unstable New Yorker. As if to reflect his tenuous grasp of reality, Korine shot the film in jerky, improvisatory fashion. The narrative does

not make much immediate sense, but the imagery – of a grumpy old patriarch (played by German director Werner Herzog) drinking cough mixture out of a slipper, or of a disabled man wandering up and down a set of stairs on his arms, or of the uncle (played as a young man by Ewen Bremner) roaming the city in a beatific daze – is startling and often ingenious.

BRITISH AMATEUR NIGHT

'It's my version of Dogme – British amateur night,' British director Mike Figgis quipped about his decision to embrace low-budget filmmaking in the late 1990s. His 1998 feature, *The Loss of Sexual Innocence*, took Ernest Hemingway's *Nick Adams Stories* as inspiration. It offered a version of the Adam and Eve myth while also charting key events in the life of Nick (played as a teenager by Johnny Rhys Meyers and as an adult by Julian Sands), a character clearly based on Figgis himself. The film is disjointed and episodic. It was more akin, Figgis claimed, to a series of short stories than to the three-act narrative structure favoured by Hollywood. Locations ranged from a very grey-looking Newcastle-upon-Tyne to sun-drenched Africa. The links between the various episodes are not immediately apparent, but the characters' motivations are: they are driven by the same emotions – love, lust, jealousy, habit, superstition and anger – as the protagonists in most other movies. The point was clear: Figgis's filmmaking style may have changed, but human behaviour had not.

Figgis followed up *The Loss of Sexual Innocence* with a Dogme-style adaptation of Strindberg's *Miss Julie* (1999), shot over a fortnight on a small set at Elstree Studios with a lightweight camera. He then made his most adventurous film yet, *Timecode* (2000), shot with several cameras at once, and without conventional editing. The screen was divided into four, allowing audiences the chance of choosing which strand of the narrative to follow. Rather than use montage or showy effects, Figgis relied on nothing more than sound editing to emphasize one scene over another. Radical on a formal level, *Timecode* offered a storyline which could have come straight out of an afternoon soap opera. Its characters were the Hollywood in-crowd: actors, producers and directors, cheating husbands, bickering lesbian lovers and lecherous masseurs, all with oversized egos.

Figgis was an example of an established director inspired by Dogme to embrace low-budget filmmaking. What was an aesthetic decision for him was a matter of necessity for a new generation of directors working with digital cameras. The success of *The Blair Witch Project* (1999) proved that tiny-budget films could outperform blockbusters – with the help of astute marketing. The new technology now enabled just about anyone to make a movie. Unfortunately, the technology could not guarantee quality or ensure that the new films would be seen anywhere. 'It was obvious that the filmmakers hadn't developed their work, they hadn't developed the scripts. I saw work done on digital that I never would have seen on film. You get people making films that shouldn't be making them,' Geoffrey Gilmore, director of the Sundance Festival, the main testing ground for new talent in the US, told trade paper *Variety* on the eve of the 2001 Festival. His sentiments were echoed by critics and festival directors in Europe exposed to a new wave of Dogme-inspired low-budget movies. Most, sadly, turned out to be unwatchable.

above Four for the price of one: (going clockwise) Salma Hayek, Jeanne Tripplehorn, Stellan Skarsgård, Saffron Burrows and Kyle McLachlan in Mike Figgis' mischievous splitscreen digital satire, *Timecode* (2000).

opposite left Derek Jarman's anarchic punk satire, *Jubilee* (1977).

opposite right Larry Clark's *Kids* (1995) was made in the same freewheeling, provocative style as the later Dogme films.

General Index

Index of Films

Photograph Acknowledgements

AKG, London 6–7, 8, 13 right, 62 top

British Film Institute 61 left, 86, 108 left

Raymond Cauchetier 150–151

Courtesy of Everett Collection 11, 13 left, 18, 26, 33 bottom right, 36–37, 38, 39, 46 top, 51, 64–65, 66 right, 68, 80–81, 83 left, 90, 91, 92 bottom, 118, 134, 140 left, 140 right, 141, 142, 153 top, 153 bottom, 170, /ABC 70 left, /American International 177, /Argos 171, /Avco Embassy 165, /Columbia 35 top, 83 right, 110, 120 right, 121, 160–161, 162, /Compass International 85 left, /Eagle–Lion 103 left, 103 right, /Fox 94, /Hollywood Pictures 20, /Janus Films 146 top, 147, /MGM 17, 24, 53, 55, 56, 74 right, 75 left, 75 right, 108 right, 115, 117, 127, /Miramax 173 right, /New Line Cinema 78, /October Films 180–181, /Paramount 25, 48, 120 left, 128 right, 129, 135 left, 179, /RKO Radio Pictures 42, 74 left, 116, 138–139, /Rank 98–99, /20th Century Fox 22–23, 122 right, Unifilm/ Embrafilme 143, /United Artists 57, 69 top, 82, 92 top, 93, 114 left, 164, /Universal 41 top, 41 bottom, 67, 163, /Universal–International 101 left, /Dreamworks 137, /Warner Bros 111 top, 136

Kobal Collection 14–15, 16 bottom, 27, 52, 66 left, 149/Bandai Visual 173 left, /Columbia 124–125, /Edison 10, /Epoch 12, /Fox 95, /Gainsborough 100, /Hammer 33 top left, /Les Films du Losange, /La Sept Cinéma 154, / /Melies 4–5, 28–29 top, /MGM 34, /Mosfilm 49, 62 bottom, /Paramount 76, 111 bottom, 178/Producers' Releasing Corp 131 right, /Rank 77/RKO 32, 72–73, 131 left, /Sennett 174–175, /Sozo/ SHA 172, /20th Century Fox 122 left, 128 left, /UFA 30, 31, /United Artists 88–89, /Jean Vigo 61 right, /Warner Bros/DC Comics 21, /Zentropa 182

The Moviestore Collection 9, 16 top, 40, 44–45, 47, 54, 71, 101 right, 114 right, 155/Anglo Amalgamated 63, /Columbia 158–159, 161, /Ealing Studios 106–107, /GFD 102, /MGM 135 right, /PEA 96, /Screen Gems 184 right, /UIP/ Dreamworks 123, /Universal 130, /Warner Bros 70 right, 126, 160

The Ronald Grant Archive 43 left, 46 top, /AJYM Films 152, /Blue Light 184 left, /Buñuel/Dali 58–59, /Cineguild 104, /Cinematorgraph 146 bottom, /Constatin Film 97, /Daiei 166–167, /Maya Deren 60, /Ealing Studios 105 top, 105 bottom, /Eon Productions 176, /Independent Pics 185, /Lucas Films 85 right, /MGM 112–113, /Orion Pictures 148, /Paramount 84, /Pathé 87, /Roadmovies 156, 157, /Svensk Filmindustri 144–145, /Toho 168, 169/Trinacre Films 69 bottom, /20th Century Fox 35 bottom, 132–133, /Universal 19, /Vestron 79, /Vortex 43 right, /Warner Bros 109, /Whaley–Malen Prods 183

Executive Editor **Julian Brown**
Editor **Tarda Davison-Aitkins**
Executive Art Editor **Geoff Fennell**
Designer **Lou Griffiths**
Picture Researcher **Zoë Holtermann**
Senior Production Controller **Louise Hall**

First published in -2001 by Hamlyn, a division of Octopus Publishing Group Limited
2–4 Heron Quays, London E14 4JP

ISBN 0 600 60084 X

A catalogue record for this book is available from the British Library

Printed in China

02-1280-58

B £20.00